George Washington Julian

Political Recollections

1840 to 1872

George Washington Julian

Political Recollections
1840 to 1872

ISBN/EAN: 9783337070649

Printed in Europe, USA, Canada, Australia, Japan

Cover: Foto ©Suzi / pixelio.de

More available books at **www.hansebooks.com**

POLITICAL RECOLLECTIONS

1840 to 1872.

BY

GEORGE W. JULIAN.

CHICAGO:
JANSEN, McCLURG & COMPANY.
1884.

PREFACE.

The following chapters are devoted mainly to facts and incidents connected with the development of anti-slavery politics from the year 1840 to the close of the work of Reconstruction which followed the late civil war. Other topics, however, are occasionally noticed, while I have deemed it proper to state my own attitude and course of action respecting various public questions, and to refer more particularly to the political strifes of my own State. In doing this, I have spoken freely of conspicuous personalities in connection with their public action, or their peculiar relations to myself; but my aim has been to deal fairly and state only the truth, while striving to weave into my story some reminiscences of the men and events of by-gone times, which may interest the reader. In the endeavor to elucidate the orderly progress of anti-slavery opinions and their translation into organized action, I have summarized

(3)

and re-stated many of the familiar facts of current
Américan politics during the period embraced;
but I hope I have also made a slight contribution
to the sources of history bearing upon a world-
famous movement, touching which we should
"gather up the fragments that nothing be lost."

G. W. J.

CONTENTS.

CHAPTER I.

THE HARRISON CAMPAIGN—THE BEGINNING OF ANTI-SLAVERY POLITICS.

CHAPTER II.

CAMPAIGN OF 1844—ANNEXATION AND SLAVERY.

CHAPTER III.

CAMPAIGN OF 1848—ITS INCIDENTS AND RESULTS.

CHAPTER IV.

REMINISCENCES OF THE THIRTY-FIRST CONGRESS.

CHAPTER V.

THE THIRTY-FIRST CONGRESS (CONTINUED).

CHAPTER VI.

THE EVOLUTION OF THE REPUBLICAN PARTY.

CHAPTER VII.

THE REPUBLICAN PARTY (CONTINUED).

CHAPTER VIII.

PROGRESS OF REPUBLICANISM.

CHAPTER IX.

THE NEW ADMINISTRATION AND THE WAR.

CHAPTER X.

THE NEW ADMINISTRATION AND THE WAR (CONTINUED).

CHAPTER XI.

INCIDENTS AND END OF THE WAR.

CHAPTER XII.

RECONSTRUCTION AND SUFFRAGE—THE LAND QUESTION.

CHAPTER XIII.

MINERAL LANDS AND THE RIGHT OF PRE-EMPTION.

CHAPTER XIV.

RECONSTRUCTION AND IMPEACHMENT.

CHAPTER XV.

GRANT AND GREELEY.

CHATER XVI.

CONCLUDING NOTES.

POLITICAL RECOLLECTIONS.

CHAPTER I.

THE HARRISON CAMPAIGN—THE BEGINNING OF ANTI-SLAVERY POLITICS.

The "hard-cider" frolic of 1840—The issues—Swartwout and political corruption—The demand for a change—Character of Gen. Harrison—Personal defamation—Mass-meetings and songs—Crushing defeat of the Democrats—First appearance of the slavery issue in politics—Pro-slavery attitude of Harrison and Van Buren—Events favoring the growth of anti-slavery opinion—Clay and Mendenhall—Texas annexation and John Tyler.

THROUGH the influence of early associations, I began my political life a Whig, casting my first presidential ballot for General Harrison, in 1840. I knew next to nothing of our party politics; but in the matter of attending mass-meetings, singing Whig songs and drinking hard cider, I played a considerable part in the memorable campaign of that year. So far as ideas entered into my support of the Whig candidate, I simply regarded him as a poor man, whose home was a log cabin,

(11)

and who would in some way help the people
through their scuffle with poverty and the " hard
times"; while I was fully persuaded that Van
Buren was not only a graceless aristocrat and a
dandy, but a cunning conspirator, seeking the
overthrow of his country's liberties by uniting the
sword and the purse in his own clutches, as he
was often painted on the party banners. In these
impressions I was by no means singular. They
filled the air, and seemed to be wafted on every
breeze. Horace Greeley's famous campaign organ, "The Log Cabin," only gave them voice and
fitting pictorial effect, and he frankly admitted in
later years that his Whig appeals, with his music
and wood engravings of General Harrison's battle
scenes, were more "vivid" than "sedately argu-
mentative." No one will now seriously pretend
that this was a campaign of ideas, or a struggle
for political reform in any sense. It was a grand
national frolic, in which the imprisoned mirth and
fun of the people found such jubilant and uproar-
ious expression that anything like calmness of
judgment or real seriousness of purpose was out
of the question in the Whig camp.

As regards party issues, General Harrison, singularly enough, was not a Whig, but an old fashioned State-Rights Democrat of the Jeffersonian
school. His letters to Harmar Denny and Sherrod
Williams committed him to none of the dogmas
which defined a Whig. No authentic utterance of

his could be produced in which he had ever expressed his agreement with the Whig party on the questions of a protective tariff, internal improvements, or a national bank. There was very high Whig authority for saying that the bank question was not an issue of the canvass, while Van Buren's great measure for separating the currency from the banks became a law pending the Presidential struggle. In fact, it was because no proof of General Harrison's party orthodoxy could be found, that he was nominated; and the Whig managers of the Harrisburg Convention felt obliged to sacrifice Henry Clay, which they did through the basest double-dealing and treachery, for the reason that his right angled character as a party leader would make him unavailable as a candidate. As to John Tyler, he was not a Whig in any sense. It is true that he had opposed the removal of the deposits, and voted against Benton's expunging resolutions, but on all the regular and recognized party issues he was fully committed as a Democrat, and was, moreover, a nullifier. The sole proof of his Whiggery was the apocryphal statement that he wept when Clay failed to receive the nomination, while his political position was perfectly understood by the men who nominated him. There was one policy only on which they were perfectly agreed, and that was the policy of avowing no principles whatever; and they tendered but one issue, and that was a change of the national administration. On

this issue they were perfectly united and thoroughly in earnest, and it was idle to deny that on their
own showing the spoils alone divided them from
the Democrats and inspired their zeal.

The demand of the Whigs for a change was
well-founded. Samuel Swartwout, the New York
Collector of Customs, had disgraced the Government by his defalcations; and, although he was a
legacy of Mr. Van Buren's "illustrious predecessor," and had been "vindicated" by a Senate committee composed chiefly of his political opponents,
he was unquestionably a public swindler, and had
found shelter under Mr. Van Buren's administration. He was the most conspicuous public rascal
of his time, but was far from being alone in his
odious notoriety. The system of public plunder
inaugurated by Jackson was in full blast, and an
organized effort to reform it was the real need of
the hour; but here was the weak point of the Whigs.
They proceeded upon the perfectly gratuitous assumption that the shameless abuses against which
they clamored would be thoroughly reformed
should they come into power. They took it for
granted that a change would be equivalent to a
cure, and that the people would follow them in
thus begging the very question on which some
satisfactory assurance was reasonably required.
They seemed totally unconscious of the fact that
human nature is essentially the same in all parties,
and that a mere change of men without any change

of system would be fruitless. They laid down no programme looking to the reform of the civil service. They did not condemn it, and their sole panacea for the startling frauds and defalcations of Van Buren's administration was the imagined superior virtue and patriotism of the Whigs. In the light of this fact alone, it is impossible to account for the perfectly unbounded and irrepressible enthusiasm which swept over the land during the campaign, and so signally routed the forces of Democracy. Something more than empty promises and windy declamation was necessary, and that something, in an evil hour, was supplied by the Democrats themselves.

General Harrison was a man of Revolutionary blood. He commanded the confidence of the chief Fathers of the Republic. He was a man of undoubted bravery, and had made a most honorable record, both as a soldier and a civilian, upon ample trial in both capacities. He was unquestionably honest and patriotic, and the fact that he was a poor man, and a plain farmer of the West, could properly form no objection to his character or his fitness for the Presidency. But the Democratic orators and newspapers assailed him as an " imbecile." They called him a " dotard " and a "granny." They said he had distinguished himself in war by running from the enemy. One Democratic journalist spoke of him, contemptuously, as a man who should be content with a log cabin and a

barrel of hard cider, without aspiring to the Presidency.   The efforts to belittle his merits and
defile his good name became systematic, and
degenerated into the most unpardonable personal abuse and political defamation.   This
was exactly what the Whigs needed to supplement
their lack of principles.   It worked like a charm.
It rallied the Whig masses like a grand battle-cry.
Mass-meetings of the people, such as had never
been dreamed of before, became the order of the
day.   The people took the work of politics into
their own keeping, and the leaders became followers.   The first monster meeting I attended was
held on the Tippecanoe battle-ground, on the 29th
and 30th of May.   In order to attend it I rode on
horseback through the mud and swamps one hundred and fifty miles; but I considered myself amply
compensated for the journey in what I saw and enjoyed.   The gathering was simply immense; and
I remember that James Brooks, since conspicuous
in our national politics, tried to address the multitude from the top of a huge log cabin.   Large
shipments of hard cider had been sent up the Wa-
bash by steamer, and it was liberally dealt out to
the people in gourds, as more appropriate and old-
fashioned than glasses.   The people seemed to be
supremely happy, and their faces were so uniformly
radiant with smiles that a man who was detected
with a serious countenance was at once suspected
as an unrepentant " Loco-foco."   But by far

the largest meeting of the campaign was that
held at Dayton, on the 12th day of September,
where General Harrison spoke at length. He was
the first " great man" I had seen, and I succeeded in
getting quite near him; and, while gazing into his
face with an awe which I have never since felt for
any mortal, I was suddenly recalled from my rapt
condition by the exit of my pocket-book. The
number in attendance at this meeting was estimated at two hundred thousand, and I think it
could not have been far out of the way. I am sure
I have never seen it equaled, although I have witnessed many great meetings within the past forty
years. The marked peculiarity of all the gatherings 'of this campaign was a certain grotesque
pomp and extravagance of representation suggest-
ive of a grand carnival. The banners, devices and
pictures were innumerable, while huge wagons
were mounted with log cabins, cider barrels, canoes,
miniature ships, and raccoons.

But the most distinguishing feature of the campaign was its music. The spirit of song was
everywhere, and made the whole land vocal. The
campaign was set to music, and the song seriously
threatened to drown the stump speech. Whiggery was translated into a tune, and poured itself
forth in doggerel rhymes which seemed to be born
of the hour, and exactly suited to the crisis. I
give a few specimens, partly from memory, and

2

partly from " The Harrison and Log Cabin Song
Book" of 1840, a copy of which is before me :

> What has caused the great commotion, motion, motion,
>   Our country through?
>   It is the ball a-rolling on, on,
> For Tippecanoe and Tyler too—Tippecanoe and Tyler too;
> And with them we'll beat little Van, Van, Van;
>   Van is a used up man;
>   And with them we'll beat little Van.
>
> Like the rushing of mighty waters, waters, waters,
>   On it will go,
>   And in its course will clear the way
> For Tippecanoe and Tyler too—Tippecanoe and Tyler too;
> And with them we'll beat little Van, Van, Van;
>   Van is a used up man;
>   And with them we'll beat little Van.

The famous " ball" alluded to in this song origi-
nated with the Whigs of Allegheny County, Pennsylvania, and was sent by them to a Mass Convention held at Baltimore.   It was ten or twelve feet
in diameter, and upon the ends of it, on blue
ground, were stars corresponding in number with
the States of the Union.   On its wide spaces of red
and white stripes various inscriptions were made,
including the following, which belongs to the
poetry and music of the campaign :

> With heart and soul
> This ball we roll;
> May times improve
> As on we move.
>
> This Democratic ball
> Set rolling first by Benton,

Is on another track
From that it first was sent on.

Farewell, dear Van,
You're not our man;
To guide the ship,
We'll try old Tip.

The following, sung to the tune of "Old Rosin the Bow," was quite as popular:

Come ye who, whatever betide her,
　To Freedom have sworn to be true,
Prime up with a cup of hard cider,
　And drink to old Tippecanoe.

On top I've a cask of as good, sir,
　As man from the tap ever drew;
No poison to cut up your blood, sir,
　But liquor as pure as the dew.

Parched corn men can't stand it much longer,
　Enough is as much as we'll bear;
With Tip at our head, in October,
　We'll tumble Van out of the chair.

Then ho! for March fourth, forty-one, boys,
　We'll shout till the heavens' arched blue
Shall echo hard cider and fun, boys,
　Drink, drink to old Tippecanoe.

The following kindred verses will be familiar to everybody who remembers the year 1840:

Ye jolly young lads of Ohio,
　And all ye sick Vanocrats, too,
Come out from among the foul party,
　And vote for old Tippecanoe.

Good men from the Van jacks are flying,
　Which makes them look kinder askew,

For they see they are joining the standard
With the hero of Tippecanoe.

They say that he lived in a cabin,
And lived on old cider, too;
Well, what if he did? I'm certain
He's the hero of Tippecanoe.

I give the following verses of one of the best,
which used to be sung with tremendous effect:

The times are bad, and want curing;
They are getting past all enduring;
Let us turn out Martin Van Buren,
And put in old Tippecanoe.
The best thing we can do,
Is to put in old Tippecanoe.

It's a business we all can take part in,
So let us give notice to Martin
That he must get ready for sartin',
For we'll put in old Tippecanoe.
The best thing we can do
Is to put in old Tippecanoe.

We've had of their humbugs a plenty;
For now all our pockets are empty;
We've a dollar now where we had twenty,
So we'll put in old Tippecanoe.
The best thing we can do,
Is to put in old Tippecanoe.

The following verses are perfectly characteristic:

See the farmer to his meal
Joyfully repair;
Crackers, cheese and cider, too,
A hard but homely fare.

> Martin to his breakfast comes
> At the hour of noon ;
> Sipping from a china cup,
> With a golden spoon.
>
> Martin's steeds impatient wait
> At the palace door;
> Outriders behind the coach
> And lackeys on before.

After the State election in Maine, a new song appeared, which at once became a favorite, and from which I quote the following :

> And have you heard the news from Maine,
> And what old Maine can do?
> She went hell-bent for Governor Kent,
> And Tippecanoe and Tyler too,
> And Tippecanoe and Tyler too.

Such was this most remarkable Whig campaign, with its monster meetings and music, its infinite drolleries, its rollicking fun, and its strong flavor of political lunacy. As to the canvass of the Democrats, the story is soon told. In all points it was the reverse of a success. The attempt to manufacture enthusiasm failed signally. They had neither fun nor music in their service, and the attempt to secure them would have been completely overwhelmed by the flood on the other side. It was a melancholy struggle, and constantly made more so by the provoking enthusiasm and unbounded good humor of the Whigs. It ended as a campaign of despair, while its humiliating catastrophe must have awakened inexpressible disappointment and disgust both among the leaders and masses of the party.

This picture of party politics, forty-three years ago, is not very flattering to our American pride, but it simply shows the working of Democratic institutions in dealing with the "raw material" of society and life at that time. The movement of 1840 was necessarily transient and provisional, while underneath its clatter and nonsense was a real issue. It was unrecognized by both parties, but it made its advent, and the men who pointed its way quietly served notice upon the country of their ulterior purposes.

As long ago as the year 1817, Charles Osborn had established an anti-slavery newspaper in Ohio, entitled "The Philanthropist," which was followed in 1821 by the publication of Benjamin Lundy's "Genius of Universal Emancipation." In 1831 the uprising of slaves in Southampton County, Virginia, under the lead of Nat. Turner, had startled the country and invited attention to the question of slavery. In the same year Garrison had established "The Liberator," and in 1835 was mobbed in Boston, and dragged through its streets with a rope about his neck. In 1837 Lovejoy had been murdered in Alton, Illinois, and his assassins compared by the Mayor of Boston to the patriots of the Revolution. In 1838 a pro-slavery mob had set fire to Pennsylvania Hall, in Philadelphia, and defied the city authorities in this service of slavery. Presi-

dent Jackson and Amos Kendall, his Postmaster
General, had openly set the Constitution at defiance by justifying the rifling of the mails and the
suppression of the circulation of anti-slavery newspapers in the South. The "gag" resolutions had
been introduced in the House of Representatives in
1836, which provoked the splendid fight of Adams,
Giddings and Slade for the right of petition and
the freedom of speech. Dr. Channing had published his prophetic letter to Henry Clay, on the
annexation of Texas, in 1837, and awakened a profound interest in the slavery question on both
sides of the Atlantic. We had been disgraced by
two Florida wars, caused by the unconstitutional
espousal of slavery by the General Government.
President Van Buren had dishonored his administration and defied the moral sense of the civilized
world by his efforts to prostitute our foreign policy
to the service of slavery and the slave trade. In
February, 1839, Henry Clay had made his famous
speech on "Abolitionism," and thus recognized the
bearing of the slavery question upon the presidential election of the following year. The Abolitionists had laid siege to the conscience and humanity
of the people, and their moral appeals were to be a
well-spring of life to the nation in its final struggle
for self-preservation ; but as yet they had agreed
upon no organized plan of action against the aggressions of an institution which threatened the
overthrow of the Union and the end of Republican

government. But now they were divided into two
camps, the larger of which favored political action,
organized as a party, and nominated, as its candidate for President, James G. Birney, who received
nearly seven thousand votes.

This was a small beginning, but it was the beginning of the end. That slavery was to be put down
without political action in a government carried
on by the ballot was never a tenable proposition,
and the inevitable work was at last inaugurated.
It was done opportunely. Harrison and Van Buren
were alike objectionable to anti-slavery men who
understood their record. To choose between them
was to betray the cause. Van Buren had attempted to shelter the slave trade under the national
flag. He had allied himself to the enemies of the
right of petition and the freedom of debate, as the
means of conciliating the South. He had taken
sides with Jackson in his lawless interference
with the mails at the bidding of slave-holders. In
a word, he had fairly earned the description of "a
Northern man with Southern principles." General
Harrison, on the other hand, was a pro-slavery Vir-
ginian. While Governor of Indiana Territory he
had repeatedly sought the introduction of slavery
into that region through the suspension of the ordinance of 1787, which had forever dedicated it to
freedom. He had taken sides with the South in
1820 on the Missouri question. He had no sympathy with the struggle of Adams and his asso-

ciates, against the gag and in favor of the right of
petition, and regarded the discussion of the slavery
question as unconstitutional. The first draft of
his inaugural was so wantonly offensive to the anti-
slavery Whigs who had aided in his election, that
even Mr. Clay condemned it, and prevailed on the
General to modify it. He had declared that "the
schemes of the Abolitionists were fraught with horrors, upon which an incarnate devil only could
look with approbation." With such candidates the
hour had fairly struck for anti-slavery men, who believed in the use of the ballot, to launch the grand
movement which was finally to triumph over all
opposition; while to oppose this movement, however honestly, was to encourage men to choose
between parties equally untrustworthy, and by thus
prolonging their rule to defeat all practical anti-
slavery work. It was the singular mistake of the
non-voting Abolitionists at this time, that, while
they looked forward to political action as the ultimate result of their moral agitation, they vehemently opposed the formation of an anti-slavery political
party, and either withheld their votes or divided
them between these pro-slavery chieftains, though
giving by far the larger proportion to the Whig
candidate.

From this time forward anti-slavery progress was
more marked. The struggle over the right of
petition in Congress continued, and was characterized by a constantly increasing measure of fierceness on the part of the South. This is vividly

depicted in a passage from the diary of Mr. Adams, in March, 1841, in which he declares that "The world, the flesh, and all the devils in hell are arrayed against any man who now, in this North American Union, shall dare to join the standard of Almighty God to put down the African slave trade; and what can I, upon the verge of my seventy-fourth birthday, with a shaking hand, a darkening eye, a drowsy brain, and with all my faculties dropping from me one by one as the teeth are dropping from my head, what can I do for the cause of God and man, for the progress of human emancipation, for the suppression of the African slave-trade? Yet my conscience presses me on; let me but die upon the breach."

The celebrated trial of Mr. Adams the following year, for presenting a petition from the citizens of Haverhill, requesting Congress to take steps toward a peaceable dissolution of the Union, was a great national event, and his triumph gave a new impulse to the cause of freedom. The censure of Mr. Giddings which followed, for offering resolutions in the House embodying the simplest truisms respecting the relations of the General Government to slavery, and the elaborate State paper of Mr. Webster, which provoked these resolutions, in which he attempted to commit the Government to the protection of slavery on the high seas, in accordance with the theories of Mr. Calhoun, still further kept alive the anti-slavery agitation, and

awakened the interest of Northern men. A kindred
aid, unwittingly rendered the anti-slavery cause,
was the infamous diplomacy of General Cass, our
Ambassador to France in 1842, in connection with
the Quintuple Treaty for the suppression of the
African slave trade. His monstrous effort to shield
that trade under the flag of the United States was
characterized by Mr. Adams as " a compound of
Yankee cunning, of Italian perfidy, and of French
légéreté, cemented by shameless profligacy un-
paralleled in American diplomacy." In October,
1842, Henry Clay himself became an anti-slavery
agitator through his famous " Mendenhall Speech,"
at Richmond, Indiana. In response to a petition
asking him to emancipate his slaves, he told the
people " that whatever the law secures as property
is property," and described his slaves as " being well
fed and clad," and as looking " sleek and hearty."
" Go home, Mr. Mendenhall," said he, " and mind
your own business, and leave other people to take
care of theirs." Mr. Mendenhall was an anti-slavery Quaker; but Mr. Clay, while rebuking him
severely, took pains to compliment the society itself on its practically pro-slavery attitude, and thus
stung into redoubled earnestness and zeal the men
who had recently been driven out of it on account
of their " abolitionism." On the day following this
speech, which was the Sabbath, he was escorted to
the yearly meeting by Elijah Coffin, its clerk, seated
in a very conspicuous place, honored by every

mark of the most obsequious deference, and thus made the instrument of widening the breach already formed in the society, while feeding the antislavery fires which he was so anxious to assuage.

The work of agitation was still further kept alive by conflicts between the Northern and Southern States respecting the reclamation of fugitives from crime. Virginia had demanded of New York the surrender of three colored sailors who were charged with having aided a slave to escape. Governor Seward refused to deliver them up, for the reason that the Constitutional provision on the subject must be so understood as that the States would only be required to surrender fugitives accused of an offense considered a crime in the State called upon to make the surrender as well as in the State asking for it. Similar controversies occurred between other States, in all of which the South failed in her purpose. The anti-slavery spirit found further expression in 1843 in Massachusetts, whose Legislature resolved to move, through the Representatives of the State in Congress, an Amendment to the Constitution, basing representation on the free population only of the States; which proposition gave rise to a most memorable debate in the national House of Representatives. It was in August of the same year that the voting Abolitionists held a National Convention in Buffalo, in which all the free States, except New Hampshire, were represented; while in the following year the Methodist Episcopal Church was rent in twain by the same unmanageable question, which had previously divided other ecclesiastical communions.

In the meanwhile, the question of Texan annexation had been steadily advancing to the political front, and stirring the blood of the people both North and South. This " robbery of a realm," as Dr. Channing had styled it, was the unalterable purpose and unquenchable desire of the slaveholding interest, and its accomplishment was to be secured by openly espousing the principle that the end justifies the means, and setting all consequences at defiance. This is exactly what the Government did. The diplomacy through which the plot was prosecuted was marked by a cunning, audacity, and perfidy, which, in these particulars, leave the administration of John Tyler unrivalled in its ugly pre-eminence, and form one of the blackest pages in the history of the Republic. The momentous question was now upon us; and on the dawning of the year 1844, all parties saw that it was destined to be the overshadowing issue in the ensuing presidential campaign.

CHAPTER II.

THE CAMPAIGN OF 1844—ANNEXATION AND SLAVERY.

The nomination of Clay—His position on the slavery question and annexation—Van Buren's letter to Hammet, and its effect upon the South—His repudiation, and the nomination of Polk—The surprise of the country—Unbounded confidence of the Whigs—The course of the New York Democrats—The "Kane Letter"—Trouble among the Whigs on the annexation question—Fierceness of the contest, and singular ability of the leaders—The effect of Clay's defeat upon the Whigs—Causes of the defeat—The Abolitionists, and the abuse heaped upon them—Cassius M. Clay—Mr. Hoar's mission to South Carolina—Election of John P. Hale—Annexation and war with Mexico—Polk's message, and the Wilmot proviso—The Oregon question, and Alex. H. Stephens.

THE times were serious. The fun and frolic of 1840 had borne no fruit, and that part of our history could not be repeated. The campaign of 1844 promised to be a struggle for principle; and among the Whigs all eyes were turned for a standard bearer to Mr. Clay, who had been so shabbily treated four years before. He was unanimously nominated on the first of May, with Theodore Frelinghuysen as the candidate for Vice President. The party issues were not very sharply defined, but this was scarcely necessary with a candidate who was proverbially regarded as himself "the embodiment of Whig principles." On the subject of annexation, he clearly defined his position in his letter of the 17th of April to the "National Intelligencer." He declared that annexation and war with Mexico were identical, and placed himself squarely against it, except upon conditions specified, which would make the project of immediate annexation impossible. On the slavery question, he had not yet seriously offended the anti-slavery element in his own party, and was even trusted by some of the voting anti-slavery men. In a speech at Raleigh, in April of this year, he declared it to be "the duty of each State to sustain its own domestic institutions." He had publicly said that the General Government had nothing to do with slavery, save in the matters of taxation, representation, and the return of fugitive slaves. He had condemned the censure of Mr. Giddings in 1842 as an outrage, and indorsed the principles laid down in his tract, signed "Pacificus," on the relations of the Federal Government to slavery, and the rights and duties of the people of the free States. In his earlier years, he had been an outspoken emancipationist, and had always frankly expressed his opinion that slavery was a great evil. These considerations, and especially his unequivocal utterances against the annexation scheme, were regarded as hopeful auguries of a thoroughly united party, and its triumph at the polls; while

Mr. Webster, always on the presidential anxious-
seat, and carefully watching the signs of the political zodiac, now cordially lent his efforts to the
Whig cause.

With the Democracy, Mr. Van Buren was still a
general favorite. His friends felt that the wrong
done him in 1840 should now be righted, and a
large majority of his party undoubtedly favored
his renomination. But his famous letter to Mr.
Hammet, of Mississippi, dated March 27th, on the
annexation of Texas, placed a lion in his path. In
this lengthy and elaborate document he committed
himself against the project of immediate annexation, and the effect was at once seen in the decidedly unfriendly tone of Democratic opinion in the
South. He had been faithful to the Slave oligarchy in many things, but his failure in one was
counted a breach of the whole law. By many acts
of patient and dutiful service he had earned the
gratitude of his Southern task-masters; but now,
when driven to the wall, he mustered the courage
to say, " Thus far, no farther "; and for this there
was no forgiveness. General Jackson came to his
rescue, but it was in vain. The Southern heart
was set upon immediate annexation as the golden
opportunity for rebuilding the endangered edifice
of slavery, and Mr. Van Buren's talk about national
obligations and the danger of a foreign war was
treated as the idle wind. The Southern Democrats
were bent upon his overthrow, and they went

about it in the Baltimore Convention of the 27th of May as if perfectly conscious of their power over the Northern wing of the party. They moved and carried the "two-thirds rule," which had been acted on in the National Convention of 1832, and afterward in that of 1835, although this could not have been done without the votes of a majority of the convention, which was itself strongly for Van Buren. The rule was adopted by a considerable majority, the South being nearly unanimous in its favor, while the North largely " supplied the men who handed Van Buren over to his enemies with a kiss." Even General Cass, the most gifted and accomplished dough-face in the Northern States, failed to receive a majority of the votes of the Convention on any ballot, and James K. Polk was finally nominated as the champion of immediate annexation, with George M. Dallas as the candidate for Vice President.

The nomination was a perfect surprise to the country, because Mr. Polk was wholly unknown to the people as a statesman. Like Governor Hayes, when nominated in 1876, he belonged to the " illustrious obscure." The astonished native who, on hearing the news, suddenly inquired of a bystander, " Who the devil is Polk ? " simply echoed the common feeling, while his question provoked the general laughter of the Whigs. For a time the nomination was somewhat disappointing to the Democrats themselves ; but they soon rallied, and

3

finally went into the canvass very earnestly, and
with a united front. The Whigs began the campaign in high hopes, and in fact with unbounded
confidence in their success. Their great captain
was in command, and they took comfort in his
favorite utterance that "truth is omnipotent, and
public justice certain." To pit against him such
a pigmy as Polk seemed to them a miserable
burlesque, and they counted their triumph as
already perfectly assured. They claimed the advantage on the question of annexation, and still
more as to the tariff, since the act of 1842 was
popular, and Polk was known to be a free-trader of
the Calhoun school. As the canvass proceeded,
however, it became evident that the fight was to
be fierce and bitter to the last degree, and that the
issue, after all, was not so certain. Mr. Polk,
notwithstanding his obscurity, was able to rouse
the enthusiasm of the party, North and South, to a
very remarkable degree. The annexation pill was
swallowed by many Democrats whose support of
him had been deemed morally impossible. In New
York, where the opposition was strongest, leading
Democrats, with William Cullen Bryant at their
head, denounced the annexation scheme and repudiated the paragraph of the National platform
which favored it, and yet voted for Polk, who owed
his nomination solely to the fact that he had committed himself to the policy of immediate and un-
conditional annexation, thus anticipating the sickly

political morality of 1852, when so many men of re-
pute tried in vain to save both their consciences and
their party orthodoxy by "spitting upon the platform and swallowing the candidate who stood upon
it." History will have to record that the action of
these New York Democrats saved the ticket in that
State, and justly attaches to them the responsibility
for the very evils to the country against which they
so eloquently warned their brethren. The power of
the spoils came in as a tremendous make-weight,
while the party lash was vigorously flourished, and
the "independent voter" was as hateful to the party
managers on both sides as we find him to-day. Those
who refused to wear the party collar were branded
by the "organs" as a "pestiferous and demoralizing brood," who deserved "extermination." Discipline was rigorously enforced, and made to take
the place of argument. As regards the tariff question, Mr. Polk's letter to Judge Kane, of Philadelphia, of the 19th of June, enabled his friends completely to turn the tables on the Whigs of Pennsylvania, where "Polk, Dallas, and the tariff of
1842," was blazoned on the Democratic banners, and
thousands of Democrats were actually made to believe that Polk was even a better tariff man than
Clay. This letter, committing its free-trade author
to the principle of a revenue tariff, with "reasonable incidental protection to our home industries,"
was translated into German and printed in all the
party papers; and as a triumphant effort to make

the people believe a lie, and a masterpiece of political duplicity employed by a great party as a means of success, it had no precedent in American politics.   In later times, however, it has been completely eclipsed by the scheme of "tissue ballots," and other wholesale methods of balking the popular will in the South, by the successful effort to cheat the nation out of the right to choose its Chief Magistrate in 1876, and by the startling bribery of a great commonwealth four years later, now unblushingly confessed by the party leaders who accomplished it.

In the meantime the spirit of discontent began to manifest itself among the Whigs of the South respecting Mr. Clay's attitude on the question of annexation, and in a moment of weakness he wrote his unfortunate "Alabama letter," of the 27th of July.   In that letter he said: "I do not think that the subject of slavery ought to affect the question one way or the other.   Whether Texas be independent or incorporated into the United States, I do not believe it will prolong or shorten the duration of that institution."   He also declared that he would be "glad to see it, without dishonor, without war, with the common consent of the Union, and upon just and fair terms."   These words were perfectly chilling to his anti-slavery supporters, who were utterly opposed to annexation on *any* terms, because the power of slavery would thus inevitably be extended and strengthened in the United States. The letter was an irreparable mistake. It was a fresh example of his besetting tendency to mediate between opposing policies, and undoubtedly drove from his support many who would otherwise have followed the Whig banner to the end.

But the Whigs kept up the fight. The issues were joined, and it was too late to change front. The real question in dispute was that of annexation, and the election of Polk was certain to secure it, and to involve the nation in war. Clay was unquestionably right in saying that annexation and war were indentical; and, although on the slavery question he might be feared as a compromiser, there was no reason to doubt that, if elected, he would vigorously resist the annexation scheme, except upon conditions already stated, which could not fail to defeat it as a present measure and avoid the calamities of war. I was inexpressibly disappointed and grieved by his letter; but I agreed with Cassius M. Clay, that opposition to annexation except "with the common consent of the Union" was practically absolute opposition, and I therefore kept up the fight in which I had enlisted in the beginning and made my first venture as a stump speaker. I cared little about the old party issues. I had outgrown the teaching of the Whigs on the subject of protection, and especially their pet dogma of "the higher the duty the lower the price of the protected article." As to a na-

tional bank, I followed Webster, who had pronounced it "an obsolete idea"; and I totally repudiated the land policy of the Whigs, having at that
early day espoused the principle that the public
lands should cease to be a source of revenue, and
be granted in small homesteads to the landless
poor for actual settlement and tillage.   But on the
subject of slavery, though it had escaped my attention in the hurrah of 1840, I was thoroughly
aroused.   This came of my Quaker training, the
speeches of Adams and Giddings, the anti-slavery
newspapers, and the writings of Dr. Channing, all
of which I had been reading with profound interest since the Harrison Campaign.   Being perfectly
sure that annexation would lead to slavery-exten-
sion and war, I thought it my clear and unhesitating duty to resist the election of Polk with all my
might.   This I did to the end, and in doing it I
employed substantially the same arguments on
which I justified my separation from the Whigs
four years later.

The contest proceeded with its variety of charges
and counter-charges, and was prosecuted on both
sides with extraordinary vigor and zeal in every
part of the Union.   I think it was everywhere and
pre-eminently a struggle between the men of brains
on either side.   I am quite sure this was true in
my own State.   Indiana was remarkable at that
time, not only for her gifted stump orators, but for
her men of real calibre and power of argument.

On the side of the Whigs were such men as Oli-
ver H. Smith, Joseph G. Marshall, George G.
Dunn, Joseph L. White, Richard W. Thompson,
Caleb B Smith, George H. Proffit, Henry S. Lane,
Samuel W. Parker, and James H. Cravens. The
Democrats could boast of Tilghman A. Howard,
James Whitcomb, Edward A. Hannegan, William
W. Wick, John Law, Joseph A. Wright, Jesse D.
Bright, John W. Davis, Thómas J. Henly, and
John L. Robinson. The best talking talent of the
nation was called into service, including such
Democratic giants as Thomas H. Benton, William
Allen, Silas Wright, Robert J. Walker, James
Buchanan, and Daniel S. Dickenson; and such
Whigs to match them as Daniel Webster, Rufus
Choate, Thomas F. Marshall, Thomas Corwin, S.
S. Prentiss, Thomas Ewing, and W. C. Preston.
The fight was more ably if not more hotly con-
tested than any preceding national struggle,
raging and blazing everywhere, while the forces
marshaled against each other were more evenly
balanced than in any contest since the year
1800. The race was so close that the result
hung in agonizing doubt and suspense up to the
evening following the election. Party feeling rose
to a frenzy, and the consuming desire of the Whigs
to crown their great Chief with the laurels of
victory was only equaled by that of the Democrats
for the triumph of the unknown Tennessean whose

nomination had provoked the aggravating laughter of the enemy in the beginning.

It is not possible to describe the effect of Mr. Clay's defeat upon the Whigs. It was wholly unexpected, and Mr. Clay especially remained sanguine as to his triumph up to the last moment. When the result became known, it was accepted by his friends as a great national calamity and humiliation. It shocked and paralyzed them like a great tragedy. I remember very vividly one zealous Whig, afterward a prominent Free Soiler and Republican leader, who was so utterly overwhelmed that for a week he lost the power of sleep, and gave himself up to political sorrow and despair. Letters of the most heart-felt condolence poured in upon Mr. Clay from all quarters, and the Whigs everywhere seemed to feel that no statesman of real eminence could ever be made President. They insisted that an overwhelming preponderance of the virtue, intelligence and respectability of the country had supported their candidate, while the larger element of ignorance and " unwashed " humanity, including our foreign-born population, gave the victory to Mr. Polk. Their faith in republican government was fearfully shaken, while the causes of the great disaster were of course sought out, and made the text of hasty but copious moralizings. One of these causes was the Kane letter, which undoubtedly gave Mr. Polk the State of Pennsylvania. Another was the

baneful influence of "nativism," which had just
broken out in the great cities, and been made the
occasion of such frightful riot and bloodshed in
Philadelphia as to alarm our foreign-born citizens,
and throw them almost unanimously against the
Whigs. The Abolitionists declared that Mr.
Clay's defeat was caused by his trimming on the
annexation question, which drew from him a
sufficient number of conscientious anti-slavery men
to have turned the tide in his favor. The famous
Plaquemine frauds in Louisiana unquestionably
lost that State to Mr. Clay. This infamous conspiracy to strangle the voice of a sovereign State
was engineered by John Slidell, and it consisted
of the shipment from New Orleans to Plaquemine
of two steamboats loaded with roughs and villains,
whose illegal votes were sufficient to turn the
State over to the Democrats.

But the cause of Mr. Clay's defeat which was
dwelt upon with most emphasis and feeling was
the action of the Liberty party. Birney, its candidate for President, received 66,304 votes, and these,
it was alleged, came chiefly from the Whig party.
The vote of these men in New York and Michigan
was greater than the Democratic majority, so that
if they had united with the Whigs, Clay would
have been elected in spite of all other opposition.
Mr. Polk's plurality over Clay in New York was
only 5,106, while Birney received in that State
15,812; and Horace Greeley insisted that if only

one third of this vote had been cast for Mr. Clay,
he would have been President. The feeling of the
Whigs against these anti-slavery men was bitter
and damnatory to the last degree. The Plaquemine frauds, the Kane letter, and everything else,
were forgotten in the general and abounding wrath
against these "fanatics," who were denounced as
the betrayers of their country and of the cause
which a very great and critical opportunity had
placed it in their power to save. "The Abolitionists deserve to be damned, and they will be," said
a zealous Whig to an anti-slavery Quaker; and
this was simply the expression of the prevailing
feeling at the time, at least in the West.

But this treatment of the Abolitionists was man-
ifestly unjust. Their organization four years before was neither untimely nor unnecessary, but belonged to the inevitable logic of a great and domi-
nating idea. A party was absolutely necessary
which should make this idea paramount, and utterly
refuse to be drawn away from it by any party divisions upon subsidiary questions. It should be
remembered, too, that the Liberty party was made
up of Democratic as well as Whig deserters, and
that if it had disbanded, or had not been formed,
the result of this election would have been the
same. The statement of Mr. Greeley, that one
third of Birney's vote in New York would have
elected Clay, was unwarranted, unless he was able
to show what would have been the action of the

other two thirds. In justice to these Abolitionists
it should also be remembered and recorded, to say
the very least, that Mr. Clay himself divided with
them the responsibility of his defeat by his Alabama letter, and that now, in the clear perspective
of history, they stand vindicated against their
Whig assailants, whose fevered brains and party
intolerance blinded their eyes to the truth. Doubtless there were honest differences of opinion as
to the best method of serving the anti-slavery cause
in this exasperating campaign, and these differences may still survive as an inheritance; but abolitionism, as a working force in our politics, had to
have a beginning, and no man who cherishes the
memory of the old Free Soil party, and of the
larger one to which it gave birth, will withhold
the meed of his praise from the heroic little band
of sappers and miners who blazed the way for the
armies which were to follow, and whose voices,
though but faintly heard in the whirlwind of 1840,
were made significantly audible in 1844. Although
they were everywhere totally misunderstood and
grossly misrepresented, they clearly comprehended
their work and courageously entered upon its performance. Their political creed was substantially
identical with that of the Free Soilers of 1848
and the Republicans of 1856 and 1860. They
were anything but political fanatics, and history
will record that their sole offense was the espousal
of the truth in advance of the multitude, which
slowly and finally followed in their footsteps.

But the war against slavery was not at all intermitted by the victory of the Democrats.   Events
are schoolmasters, and this triumph only quickened
their march toward the final catastrophe.   Cassius
M. Clay, who had espoused the Whig cause in this
canvass with great vigor and zeal, and on anti-
slavery grounds, re-enlisted in the battle against
slavery, and resolved to prosecute it by new
methods.   He had been sorely tried by Mr. Clay's
Alabama letter and the Whig defeat, but he was
now armed with fresh courage, and resolved to
" carry the war into Africa " by the establishment of
his newspaper, the " True American," in Lexington,
in his own State.   His arraignment of slavery was
so eloquent and masterly that a large meeting of
slave-holders appointed a committee to wait on
him, and request the discontinuance of his paper.
His reply was :   " Go, tell your secret conclave of
cowardly assassins that Cassius M. Clay knows
his rights, and how to defend them."   These words
thrilled all lovers of liberty, and sounded to them
like a trumpet call to battle.   Another fruitful
event was the effort of Massachusetts, in the fall of
this year, to protect her colored seamen in the
ports of Charleston and New Orleans, where they
were seized on merchant ships and sold into
slavery under local police regulations.   When Mr.
Hoar visited Charleston as the accredited agent of
his State for the purpose of taking measures to
test the constitutionality of these regulations, the

Legislature of South Carolina, by a vote of one hundred and nineteen against one, passed a series of outrageous resolutions culminating in a request to the Governor to expel him from the State as a confessed disturber of the peace. He was obliged summarily to depart, as the only means of escaping the vengeance of the mob. This open and insolent defiance of the national authority could not fail to strengthen anti-slavery opinion in the Northern States. The same end was served by an unexpected movement in New Hampshire. This State, like Massachusetts and Vermont, had taken ground against annexation, but it wheeled into line after Polk was nominated. John P. Hale, however, then a Democratic member of Congress from that State, refused to follow his party, and for this reason, after he had been formally declared its choice for re-election, he was thrown overboard, and another candidate nominated. No election, however, was effected, and his seat remained vacant during the 29th Congress, but he obtained a seat in the Legislature in 1846, and the following year was chosen United States Senator, while Amos Tuck, afterward a prominent Free Soiler, was elected to the Lower House of Congress. These were pregnant events, and especially the triumph of Hale, who became a very formidable champion of freedom, and a thorn in the side of slavery till it perished.

In the meantime the hunger for immediate annexation had been whetted by the election of Mr.

Polk, and its champions hurried up their work, and
pushed it by methods in open disregard of the Constitution and of our treaty obligations with Mexico.
In the last hours of the administration of John
Tyler the atrocious plot received its finishing
touch and the Executive approval, and, in the apt
words of the ablest and fairest historian of the
transaction, "the bridal dress in which Calhoun had
led the beloved of the slaveocracy to the Union was
the torn and tattered Constitution of the United
States." War with Mexico, as prophesied by the
Whigs, speedily followed. As early as August,
1845, General Taylor was ordered by President
Polk to advance to a position on the Nueces. In
March of the following year, in pursuance of further
orders, his army again advanced, taking its position
on the east bank of the Rio Grande, and, of course,
on the soil of Mexico. Hostilities naturally followed, and after two battles the President, in his
message to Congress, declared that " American
blood has been shed on American soil." This
robust Executive falsehood, with which the slave
power compelled him to face the civilized world,
must always hold a very high rank in the annals of
public audacity and crime. It is what Thomas
Carlyle might have styled "the second power of a
lie," and is only rivaled by the parallel falsehood of
Congress in declaring that " by the act of the Republic of Mexico a state of war exists between that
Government and the United States." In the mes-

sage of the President referred to, he recommended that a considerable sum of money be placed at his disposal for the purpose of negotiating a peace, and it was on the consideration of this message that David Wilmot fortunately obtained the floor, and moved his memorable proviso for the interdiction of slavery in any territory which might be wrested from Mexico by our arms. This was the session of Congress for 1846-47, and the proposition passed the House with great unanimity as to Northern members. At the following session of Congress, on the 28th of February, 1848, the proviso again came before the House, and the motion to lay it on the table failed, all the Whigs and a large majority of the Democrats from the free States voting in the negative. It passed the House on the 13th of December following, on a similar division of parties and sections, but the Senate refused to concur, and the Thirtieth Congress adjourned without making any provision whatever for the organization or government of our recently acquired Territories.

It is worth while to notice in passing that on the first introduction of the Wilmot proviso, in August, 1846, General Cass was decidedly in its favor, and regretted that it had been talked to death by the long speech of John Davis; but on the 24th of December, 1847, he wrote his famous "Nicholson letter," proclaiming his gospel of "popular sovereignty." in the Territories, which proved the seed-plot of

immeasurable national trouble and disaster. " I
am strongly impressed with the opinion," said he,
" that a great change is going on in the public
mind on this subject—in my own mind as well as
others "; and he had before declared, on the
19th of February, that the passage of the Wilmot
proviso " would be death to the war, death to all
hope of getting an acre of territory, death to the
administration, and death to the Democratic party."
This was thoroughly characteristic, and in perfect
harmony with his action, already referred to, respecting the Quintuple treaty; but it showed how
the political waters were being troubled by the
slavery question, and how impossible it was to ac-
commodate the growing anti-slavery feeling of the
country by any shallow expedients.

But another conspiracy against freedom was now
hatched; and if the Senate had strangled the Wilmot proviso, it was gratifying to find the House
ready to strangle this monster of senatorial birth.
I allude to the now almost forgotten " Clayton
Compromise," which passed the Senate by a decided majority on the 26th of July. By submitting. the whole question of slavery in all our Territories to the Supreme Court of the United States,
as then constituted, it would almost certainly have
spawned the curse in all of them, including Oregon,
which had long been exposed to peril and massa-
cre by the reckless opposition of our slave-masters
to a government there without the recognition of

slavery.   The defeat of this nefarious proposition,
which was happily followed by the passage of a
bill giving Oregon a territorial government, is
largely due to Alexander H. Stephens, whose motion to lay it on the table in the House prevailed
by a small majority.   In this action he had the
courage to separate himself from the great body
of the leading men of his own section ; but in doing
so he was prompted by his supreme devotion to
slavery.   This he has since denied and labored to
explain in his private correspondence and published
works, but the record is fatally against him.   He
was unwilling to trust the interests of the South in
the hands of the Supreme Court, and his speech of
August 7th, in the House of Representatives, in
defense of his motion, gave very plausible reasons for his apprehensions ; but the Dred Scott
decision of a few years later showed how completely he misjudged that tribunal, and how opportunely his blindness came to the rescue of freedom.
It seems now to have been providential ; for in this
Continental plot against liberty the superior sagacity of Calhoun and his associates was demonstrated by subsequent events, while Mr. Stephens,
with his great influence in the South, could almost
certainly have secured its triumph if he had become
its champion instead of its enemy.

4

CHAPTER III.

THE CAMPAIGN OF 1848—ITS INCIDENTS AND RESULTS.

The approach of another presidential campaign—Party divisions
threatened by the Wilmot proviso—Nomination of Gen. Cass
—The "Nicholson Letter"—Democratic division in New
York—The nomination of Gen. Taylor—Whig divisions—
Birth of the Free Soil party—The Buffalo Convention—
Nomination of Van Buren and Adams—Difficulty of uniting
on Van Buren—Incidents—Rev. Joshua Leavitt—The work
of the campaign—Mr. Webster and Free Soil—Greeley and
Seward—Abuse of Whig bolters—Remarkable results of the
canvass.

THE approach of another presidential year was
thus marked by a steadily growing interest in the
question of slavery. The conflict with it seemed
far more irrepressible than ever before. The
Liberty party had nominated John P. Hale as its
candidate in 1847. The Whigs in Massachusetts
were threatened with an incurable division into
"Conscience Whigs" and "Cotton Whigs," grow
ing out of the question of annexation and the
government of our new Territories. The same
causes were dividing the Democrats of New York,
and the feud was seriously aggravated by remembering the defeat of Mr. Van Buren in 1844, for

the one sin of opposing the immediate annexation of Texas, while a large majority of the party favored his nomination. The Van Buren element in the Democratic party threatened revolt in other States, while both Whigs and Democrats in the North were committed to the policy of the Wilmot proviso. This was to be the great question of the ensuing national canvass, and the roused spirit of the people of the free States seemed clearly to foreshadow the triumph of freedom in the organization and government of our Mexican acquisitions.

But the virtue and courage of our politicians were now to be severely tried. The power of party discipline and the tempting bait of the spoils were to be employed as never before in swerving men from their convictions. The South, of course, was a perfect unit, and fully resolved upon the spread of slavery over our Territories. It had always been the absolute master of the Northern Democracy, and had no dream of anything less than the supremacy of its own will. Its favorite candidate was now Gen. Cass, and he was nominated by the Baltimore National Convention on the 22d day of May. It was a fit nomination for the party of slavery. He had been thirsting for it many years, and had earned it by multiplied acts of the most obsequious and crouching servility to his southern overseers. Again and again he had crawled in the dust at their feet, and, if they could not now reward him with the presidency, it seemed utterly useless for any Northern man to hope for their favor. The "Nicholson letter" was not all that the South wanted, but it was a very important concession, and with Gen. Cass as its interpreter it meant the nearest thing possible to a complete surrender. In this National Convention the State of New York had two sets of delegates, both of which were formally admitted, as a compromise; but the members of the Van Buren or Free Soil wing refused to take their seats, and thus held themselves in reserve for such revolutionary work as should afterward seem to them advisable.

The Whig National Convention met in Philadelphia on the 7th of June. The party seemed completely demoralized by the defeat of Mr. Clay in the previous canvass, and was now in search of "an available candidate," and inspired by the same miserable policy of expediency which had been so barren of results in 1840. The Northern Whigs appeared to be unanimously and zealously committed to the prohibition of slavery in our Territories, but equally unanimous and zealous in the determination to succeed in the canvass. For more than a year Gen. Taylor had been growing into favor with the party as a candidate, and he had now become decidedly formidable. The spectacle was a melancholy one, since it demonstrated the readiness of this once respectable old party to make complete shipwreck of everything wearing the semblance of principle, for the sake of success.

General Taylor had never identified himself in any way with the Whig party. He had spent his life as a mere soldier on the frontier, and had never given a vote. He had frankly said he had not made up his mind upon the questions which divided the parties. He not only refused to be the exponent of Whig principles, but accepted the nomination of bodies of men not known as Whigs, who scouted the idea of being bound by the acts of any national convention. He was a very large slave-owner, and thus identified in interest, and presumably in sympathy, with the South; but he could not be induced to define his position. His active supporters were chiefly from the slave-holding States and those free States which had generally given Democratic majorities, while the men most violent in their opposition to the Wilmot proviso were his most conspicuous followers; but the Whigs from the free States vouched for his soundness on the slavery issue. His letters contained nothing but vague generalities, and he utterly declined to commit himself on the question that was stirring the nation to its depths. To the different sections of the Union he wore a different face, and each section seemed confident that the other would be duped, while cordially joining in a common struggle for the spoils of office which constituted the sole bond of union. His early letters, before he fell into the hands of the politicians, were frank and unstudied, reflecting his character as a plain old soldier without any political training; but his later letters were diplomatic, not wanting in style and finish, and obviously written by others. His second letter to Allison, on which the campaign was finally fought, was written in the room of Alexander H. Stephens, in Washington, after consulting with Toombs and Crittenden, and afterward forwarded to Taylor, who gave it to the world as his own. He had constantly about him a sort of political body-guard, or "committee of safety," to direct his way during the canvass, and no one could reasonably pretend that any principle whatever would be settled by the election. He had whipped the Mexicans, and the Whig platform was "Rough and Ready," "A little more Grape, Captain Bragg," and political success.

The nomination, moreover, was accomplished by methods which made it exceedingly exasperating to Mr. Clay and his friends. The treachery of the Whig managers to their great leader exceeded that which had sacrificed him at the Harrisburg Convention of 1839. The Whigs of Virginia nominated Taylor on the credit of a forged despatch, to the effect that Kentucky had decided in his favor, and thus abandoned her favorite son. General Scott had expressed his willingness to run for Vice President if Clay should be nominated for President, but the member of Congress who had been authorized to make this known kept it a secret. Clay allowed his name to go be-

fore the Convention on the assurance of Governor
Bebb that Ohio would stand by him, but the delegation voted for Scott. On the first ballot, even
seven delegates from Kentucky voted for Taylor,
and he was nominated by 171 votes, with 63 for
Scott, and only 32 for Clay. Of the votes for
Taylor, on the first ballot, 97 were cast by
States that had voted for Polk in 1844; and of
the 94 Whig delegates from the Free States he received the votes of only four. He was nominated
as the candidate of the Whigs who believed in the
extension of slavery, by a Convention which repeatedly and contemptuously voted down the Wilmot proviso, already endorsed by all the Whig
Legislatures of the Free States, while no platform
of principles was adopted; and Horace Greeley
was thus perfectly justified in branding it as " the
slaughter-house of Whig principles." Such an
exhibition of shameless political prostitution has
rarely been witnessed, and three of the leading
Whigs of Massachusetts—Charles Allen, Henry
Wilson, and Stephen C. Phillips—left the Convention in disgust, and severed their connection with
the party forever.

In this state of the country, and of the old parties, a new organization and another nomination became inevitable. The followers of Mr. Van Buren,
in New York and other States, were aching
for the opportunity to make themselves felt in
avenging the wrong done to their chief in 1844,

and were quite ready to strike hands with the members of the Liberty party. The members of that party were generally ready to withdraw their candidate for President and unite with the anti-slavery Whigs and Democrats of the Northern States, if an honorable basis of action could be agreed upon. The "Conscience Whigs" of Massachusetts, and thousands of Whigs in other States, who regarded the freedom of our Territories as a vital issue, and were thoroughly soured by the nomination of General Taylor, were equally anxious to fuse with the other elements of political discontent, and make their voices heard in a new and independent organization. There was little time for delay, and as soon as the troubled political elements would permit, a call was issued for a National Free Soil Convention, at Buffalo, on the 9th of August.

The Convention was historic. It marked a new and significant departure in party politics, and was a conspicuous milestone in the anti-slavery journey. It met in a spacious pavilion, and was one of the largest political gatherings ever assembled in the country, and animated by unbounded earnestness and enthusiasm. Its leading spirits were men of character and undisputed ability. The "Barnburners" of New York were largely in attendance, including such veteran leaders as Preston King, Benjamin F. Butler, David Dudley Field, Samuel J. Tilden, and James W. Nye. Ohio sent a formidable force headed by Joshua R. Giddings, Salmon P. Chase, and Samuel Lewis. The "Conscience Whigs" of Massachusetts were well represented, with Charles Francis Adams, Stephen C. Phillips, and Francis W. Bird, in the front. The Liberty party sent its delegates, including such men as the Rev. Joshua Leavitt, Samuel Lewis, and Henry B. Stanton. The disappointed Clay Whigs were there, led by such representative men as Joseph L. White, who were eager to lay hold of any weapon by which they could hope to strike down the betrayers of the Whig cause. The "Land Reformers" and "Workingmen" of New York were represented, as also the special advocates of "Cheap postage for the people," who longed to be rid of the tariff of twenty-five cents on the privilege of sending a single letter through the mails, and whose wishes afterward found expression in the platform.

Could these elements be harmonized? Could the bolters from the Whig party overcome their traditional hatred of Martin Van Buren? If so, could the Liberty party men be prevailed upon to give up their chosen candidate, and labor for the election of the "foxy old politician" whose reputation for tricky and ambidextrous political methods had become proverbial? If not, could the Barnburners, with their large following, be united on the candidate of the Liberty party, or some new man? These questions had to be met; but preliminary to the nomination was the construction of a platform. This was accomplished without serious difficulty, and, considering the circumstances of the country, it was perhaps the most admirable declaration of principles ever promulgated by any party. It was chiefly the work of Mr. Chase, assisted by Charles Francis Adams, Benjamin F. Butler, and others, and it declared, among its pregnant and telling sentences, that " Congress has no more power to make a slave than to make a king," and that " it is the duty of the Federal Government to relieve itself from all responsibility for the existence or continuance of slavery wherever that Government possesses authority to legislate and is thus responsible for its existence." The reading of these declarations called forth thunders of applause, while the last plank in the platform " resolved, that we inscribe on our banner free soil, free speech, free labor, and free men, and under it we will fight on and fight ever, until a triumphant victory shall reward our exertions."

The nominating Convention assembled in the large Universalist Church in Buffalo. Mr. Van Buren was not understood as desiring the nomination, but it was now authoritatively stated that he would accept it if tendered, and that he would, without hesitation or evasion, accept the platform of the Convention. The different elements of this movement had been in conference, and the time for action was at hand. In common with my Whig

associates, I had all along felt that I could not support Mr. Van Buren under any circumstances;
but the pervading tone of earnestness in the Convention, and the growing spirit of political fraternity, had modified our views. We saw that several
of the great leaders of the Liberty party were quite
ready to meet the " Barnburners" on common
ground. It seemed very desirable to combine with
so large a body of helpers, and to profit by their
experience and training in the school of practical
politics. Mr. Van Buren had certainly gone great
lengths as the servant of the slave power, but there
was *one* great and vital issue to freedom on which
he had taken the right side, and maintained it without flinching in the presence of a great temptation ;
and for this he had been anathematized by the
South, and driven into retirement. If nominated by
the anti-slavery men of the free States, and squarely
committed to their principles, it was altogether im-
probable, if not morally impossible, that he would
again lend himself to the service of slavery. Besides, the whole country had been so demoralized
by this evil that it was not easy to find any public
man of eminence whose record had been spotless;
and it was a part of the work of earnest anti-slavery
men to forget party memories and prejudices for the
sake of the cause, and to cultivate the virtues of
hope and trust, rather than the spirit of doubt and
suspicion, in dealing with a man who was now
ready to unfurl the flag of freedom, and had been

stricken down by her foes. The nomination of Mr. Van Buren would undoubtedly mean the freedom of our Territories and the denationalization of slavery, and this was the great point. In this movement there was no element of compromise. It was wholly unhampered by a Southern wing; and even should the nominee betray the men who now trusted him, their choice of him, as their standard bearer, would be vindicated by the circumstances of the hour.

Mr. Chase, then in the prime of his manhood, and a splendid figure, was the president of this nominating Convention, and its work proceeded. There was a feeling of intense anxiety about the result, and an earnestness and real seriousness which I have never witnessed in any other Convention. There were leading Whigs and Liberty party men, whose action in respect to Mr. Van Buren was not yet generally known. Several delegates remarked, " I want to know what Samuel Lewis will do before I decide," or, " I want to hear from Joshua Leavitt." After the nomination of Mr. Van Buren had been moved, Mr. Leavitt rose from his seat, and all eyes were instantly turned upon him. He was then in middle life, and his tall and erect form and fine physiognomy were singularly striking. He was full of emotion, and seemed at first to lack the power of utterance, while the stillness of death prevailed in the Convention. He began by saying: " Mr. Chairman, this is the most solemn experience of my life. I feel as if in the immediate presence of the Divine Spirit." He paused here for a few moments, while there did not seem to be a dry eye in the Convention ; but he proceeded grandly with his speech, defined his position, and seconded the motion for Mr. Van Buren's nomination, upon which the mingled political enthusiasm and religious fervor of the Convention broke over all bounds, and utterly defied description. Men laughed and cried at the same time, and gave themselves up to the perfect abandon of their feelings. All divisions had completely died away, and the nomination of Mr. Van Buren by acclamation became a matter of course. Charles Francis Adams was then nominated for Vice President, when the Convention adjourned, and its members returned to their homes to prepare for the coming canvass under the banner of " Van Buren and Free Soil—Adams and Liberty."

The new national party was now launched, and the work of this presidential canvass began in earnest. John A. Dix, then one of the United States Senators from New York, was nominated for Governor, with Seth M. Gates, the anti-slavery colleague of Adams and Giddings in Congress, for Lieutenant-Governor. The Free Soil State Convention of Ohio set the ball in motion in that State, and the new party, by securing the balance of power in the Legislature, was able to place Mr. Chase in the Senate of the United States. Stephen

C. Phillips was nominated for Governor in Massachusetts, where the movement was very formidable, and exceedingly annoying to the " Cotton Whigs." Like conventions were held in Indiana and other free States, organizations effected, and candidates nominated, while the movement extended to the border slave States, in which it afterward did excellent service. The canvass of the Democrats was not remarkably enthusiastic. The division of the party and the probable loss of the State of New York had a very depressing influence. The Whig canvass was perhaps marked by still less earnestness and spirit. It was hollow and false, and the best men in the party felt it. The only enthusiasm of the campaign was in the new party, and it was perfectly spontaneous and fervid. The most remarkable feature of this contest was the bitterness of the Whigs toward the Free Soilers, and especially those who had deserted from the Whig ranks. They seemed to be maddened by the imputation that they were not perfectly sound on the Free Soil issue. This was particularly true of Mr. Webster, who had been branded by Mr. Adams as a " Traitor to freedom," as far back as the year 1843, and who afterward justified these strong words in his " Seventh of March Speech." In the Whig State Convention of Massachusetts, held at Springfield, in 1847, Mr. Webster, speaking of the Wilmot proviso, had said : " Did I not commit myself to that in the year 1838, fully, entirely ? I do

not consent that more recent discoverers shall take
out a patent for the discovery. Allow me to say,
sir, it is not their thunder." He then claimed Free
Soil as a distinctive Whig doctrine, and in a speech
at Abingdon, he now said: "The gentlemen who
have joined this new party, from among the Whigs,
pretend that they are greater lovers of liberty and
greater haters of slavery than those they leave behind them. I do not admit it. I do not admit any
such thing. I think we are as good Free Soil men
as they are." The same ground was urged by
Washington Hunt, James Brooks, and other leading
Whigs; and Mr. Greeley declared that "at no time
previously had Whig inculcations throughout the
free States been so decidedly and strongly hostile to
the extension of slavery, and so determined in re-
quiring its inhibition by Congress, as during the
canvass of 1848." These statements appear very
remarkable, when it is remembered that the Whig
nominee was a Louisiana planter, and the owner
of three hundred negroes, and that he was nominated at the bidding of the slave-holding wing of the
party, and by a convention which not only contemptuously voted down the Wilmot proviso, but
treated its advocates as "fanatics." But even Governor Seward strangely clung to the old party after
the death and burial of its conscience, and seriously
brought his personal integrity into question by
urging the support of General Taylor upon those
who favored the abolition of slavery. In a speech

at Cleveland, Ohio, in October of that year, he said: "Freedom insists on the emancipation and development of labor; slavery demands a soil moistened with tears and blood—freedom a soil that exults under the elastic tread of man in his native majesty. These elements divide and classify the American people into two parties," and he proceeded to argue as if the Whigs and Democrats were thus divided, when he knew that both were in the absolute control of the slave power.

The Free Soilers, of course, did not particularly relish these moral lectures on slavery by men who had sold their principles at public auction for the chance of office and plunder through the elevation of a mere military chieftain to the Presidency. But the Whigs were not content with claiming the complete monopoly of anti-slavery virtue, and parading it before the country; they became abusive and insulting to the full measure of their insincerity. Their talk about "renegades" and "apostates" anticipated the abuse heaped upon the Greeley men of 1872, when the Republican party had so completely triumphed over the integrity of its earlier life. The course of the Whigs in Indiana supplies a striking illustration. After the presidential election of 1844, I resolved that I would never vote for another slaveholder, and the course of events and my own reflections had constantly strengthened this purpose. I saw no honorable way of escape, and my position was well known to

my Whig brethren; but, as soon as General Taylor
was nominated, the policy of brow-beating and
threats was invoked. I had no taste for politics,
and had determined to devote myself entirely to
my profession. I was especially anxious to avoid
any strife with the Whigs, who were overwhelmingly in the ascendant in Eastern Indiana, and in
whose ranks were most of my clients and best
friends. But the party leaders talked to me in the
imperative mood. They saw my embarrassment,
and seemed determined to coerce me into submission by the supposed extremity of my situation;
and I was obliged to offer them open defiance. I
was made an elector for Van Buren and Adams in
the Fourth Indiana District, and entered upon the
contest with a will; and from that time forth I was
subjected to a torrent of billingsgate which rivalled
the fish market. Words were neither minced nor
mollified, but made the vehicles of political wrath
and the explosions of personal malice. The charge
of "abolitionism" was flung at me everywhere,
and it is impossible now to realize the odium then
attaching to that term by the general opinion. I
was an "amalgamationist" and a "woolly-head."
I was branded as the "apostle of disunion" and
"the orator of free-dirt." It was a standing charge
of the Whigs that I carried in my pocket a lock
of the hair of Frederick Douglass, to regale my
senses with its aroma when I grew faint. They declared that my audiences consisted of "eleven men,

5

three boys, and a negro," and sometimes I could not deny that this inventory was not very far from' the truth. I was threatened with mob violence by my own neighbors, and treated as if slavery had been an established institution of the State, with its machinery of overseers and background of pauperized whites ; while these same Whigs, as if utterly unconscious of the irony of their professions, uniformly resolved, in their conventions, that "the Whig party is the only true Free Soil party."

I was not, of course, a non-resistant in this warfare, and for two months I gave myself up to the work absolutely. I was seriously embarrassed in the outset by the question of transportation, having neither horse nor carriage, nor the financial ability to procure either ; but an anti-slavery Quaker, and personal friend, named Jonathan Macy, came to my rescue. He furnished me an old white horse, fully seventeen hands high, and rather thin in flesh, but which served my purpose pretty well. I named him "Old Whitey," in honor of General Taylor's famous war steed, and sallied forth in the work of the campaign. Having a first-class pair of lungs and much physical endurance, I frequently spoke as often as three times a day, and generally from two to three hours at each meeting. I spoke at cross-roads, in barns, in pork houses, in saw-mills, in any place in which a few or many people would hear me ; but I was rarely permitted to enter any of the churches. I was so perfectly swallowed up in my work and dominated by the singleness of my purpose, that I took no thought of anything else; and the vigor of my invective in dealing with the scurrilous attacks of my assailants was very keenly realized, and, I believe, universally acknowledged. With the truth on my side, I was delighted to find myself perfectly able, single-handed, to fight my battle against the advantages of superior talent and the trained leadership of men of established reputation on the stump. But the fight, as I have said, was unspeakably relentless, vitriolic and exhausting, and nothing could redeem it but an overmastering sense of duty and self-respect. The worst passions of humanity were set on fire among the Whigs by this provoking insurrection against their party as the mere tool of slavery, while animosities were engendered that still survive, and which many men have carried to their graves. This is only a single illustration of the spirit of the canvass, for similar conflicts marked the struggle in Ohio, Massachusetts and other States, and they were made inevitable by the desperation of a party already dead in its trespasses, and which deserved a funeral instead of a triumph.

The results of this contest were most remarkable. General Taylor was elected, but his triumph was the death of the Whig party. The long-coveted prize of the presidency was snatched from General Cass, and the Democratic party divided and humiliated by its struggle to serve two masters, while the friends of Mr. Van Buren had their longed-for revenge. The Free Soil ticket received a little less than three hundred thousand votes, and failed to carry the electoral vote of a single State; but the effect of the movement was inestimably important. It seated Chase in the United States Senate from Ohio, and sent to the lower branch of Congress a sufficient number of anti-slavery men from different States to hold the balance of power in that body. It was very savingly felt in Congress in July of this year, on the vote by which Oregon, with a territory nearly equal to that of the thirteen original States, narrowly escaped the damnation of slavery. It emphasized the demand of the million for " cheap postage," and the freedom of the public domain, and thus helped stereotype these great measures into law; and it played its part in creating the public opinion which compelled the admission of California as a free State. These were great achievements, but they were mere preliminaries to the magnificent and far-reaching work of succeeding years, of which the revolt of 1848 was the promise and pledge.

CHAPTER IV.

REMINISCENCES OF THE THIRTY-FIRST CONGRESS.

Novel political complications—The Compromise Measures—First
election to Congress—Sketch of the "immortal nine"—The
speakership and Wm. J. Brown—Gen. Taylor and the Wilmot proviso—Slave-holding bluster—Compromise resolutions
of Clay, and retreat of Northern Whigs—Visit to Gen. Taylor
—To Mr. Clay—His speeches—Webster's seventh of March
speech—Character of Calhoun—Speech on the slavery question.

THE scheme of "pacification" and "final settlement," which was launched in 1850, under the
leadership of Henry Clay, constitutes one of the
chief landmarks in the history of the great conflict
between freedom and slavery. It was the futile
attempt of legislative diplomacy to escape the fatal
logic of antecedent facts. The war with Mexico,
like the annexation of Texas which paved the way
for it, was inspired by the lust for slave territory.
No sophistry could disguise this fact, nor could its
significance be overstated. The prophets of slavery
saw clearly that restriction meant destruction.
They girded themselves for battle on this issue,
and were not at all placated by Northern disclaimers of "abolitionism," and reiterated disavowals
of any right or purpose to intermeddle with

(69)

slavery as the creature of State law. Its existence was menaced by the policy of confinement
and ultimate suffocation ; and therefore no compromise of the pending strife over its prohibition in
New Mexico, Utah and California was possible.

This strife was aggravated by its peculiar relations to the dominant political parties. The sacrifice of Martin Van Buren in 1844, because of his
manly letter on the annexation of Texas, had been
a sore trial to his devoted friends. They could
neither forgive nor forget it ; and when the opportunity for revenge finally came in 1848, they laid
hold of it with the sincerest and most heartfelt
satisfaction. As we have seen, they bolted from
their party, threw themselves into the Free Soil
movement, and thus made the defeat of Gen. Cass
inevitable by the election of Gen. Taylor. Thousands of these bolting Democrats, particularly in
the State of New York, cared more for the personal and political fortunes of Mr. Van Buren than
for the slavery question, as their subsequent return
to their party allegiance made manifest ; but their
action was none the less decisive in the emergency
which called it forth. The trouble in the Whig
camp was also serious. The last hopes of Mr.
Clay and his worshipers had perished forever in
the nomination of the hero of the Mexican war
and the owner of two hundred slaves, by a Convention which became famous as " the slaughter house
of Whig principles." Very many of these Clay

Whigs, like the devotees of Mr. Van Buren, would have been satisfied with almost any disposition of the slavery issue if their chief had been nominated, but they were now enlisted in the anti-slavery army, and, like Joseph L. White, of Indiana, vociferously shouted for " liberty and revenge." Mr. Webster and his friends were also profoundly disgusted, and lent a strong hand to the work of party insubordination, while the election of Gen. Taylor was quite naturally followed by formidable party coalitions. One of these, as already stated, made Salmon P. Chase a senator of the United States from Ohio, as John P. Hale had been chosen from New Hampshire some time before, and Charles Sumner came in a little later from Massachusetts; and the House of Representatives now contained nine distinctively anti-slavery men, chosen from different States by kindred combinations, who had completely renounced their allegiance to the old parties, and were able to wield the balance of power in that body. Such were the complications of the great problem which confronted the Thirty-first Congress at the opening of its first session, on the third day of December, 1849.

In this Congress I was a representative, for the first time, of the Fourth Indiana District. This district contained a large Quaker population, and in the matter of liberality and progress was in advance of all other portions of the State; and yet

the immeasurable wrath and scorn which were
lavished upon the men who deserted the Whig
party on account of the nomination of General
Taylor can scarcely be conceived. The friends
of a life-time were suddenly turned into enemies,
and their words were often dipped in venom. It
seemed as if a section of Kentucky or Virginia had
in some way usurped the geography of Eastern
Indiana, bringing with it the discipline of the slave-
master, and a considerable importation of " white
trash." The contest was bitter beyond all precedent; but after a hard fight, and by a union of
Free Soilers, Democrats, and Independent Whigs,
I was elected by a small majority. Owing to serious illness, resulting from the excitement and over-
work of the canvass, I did not reach Washington
till the 19th of December—just in time to cast my
vote for speaker on the fifty-sixth ballot in this
first important " dead-lock " in the organization of
the House. With the exception of two Indiana
members, I had no personal acquaintance in either
branch of Congress, and, on entering the old Hall
of Representatives, my first thought was to find
the Free Soil members, whose political fortunes
and experience had been so similar to my own.
The seat of Mr. Giddings was pointed out to me
in the northwest corner of the Hall, where I found
the stalwart champion of free speech busy with his
pen. He received me with evident cordiality, and
at once sent a page for the other Free Soil mem-

bers. Soon the " immortal nine," as we were often
sportively styled, were all together: David Wilmot, of Pennsylvania, then famous as the author
of the " Proviso," short and corpulent in person,
and emphatic in speech ; Preston King, of New
York, with his still more remarkable rotundity of
belt, and a face beaming with good humor ; the
eccentric and witty " Jo Root," of Ohio, always
ready to break a lance with the slave-holders ;
Charles Allen, of Massachusetts, the quiet, digni-
fied, clear-headed and genial gentleman, but a
good fighter and the unflinching enemy of slavery ;
Charles Durkee, of Wisconsin, the fine-looking and
large-hearted philanthropist, whose enthusiasm
never cooled ; Amos Tuck, of New Hampshire,
amiable and somewhat feminine in appearance, but
firm in purpose ; John W. Howe, of Pennsylvania,
with a face radiant with smiles and good will, and
full of anti-slavery fervor ; and Joshua R. Giddings,
of Ohio, with his broad shoulders, giant frame,
unquenchable love of freedom, and almost as
familiar with the slavery question, in all its aspects,
as he was with the alphabet. These, all now gone
to their reckoning, were the elect of freedom in
the lower branch of this memorable Congress.
They all greeted me warmly, and the more so,
perhaps, because my reported illness and doubtful
recovery had awakened a peculiar interest in my
fortunes at that time, on account of the political
situation, and the possible significance of a single

vote. John P. Hale happened to enter the hall during these congratulations, and still further lighted up the scene by his jolly presence ; while Dr. Bailey, of the " National Era," also joined in the general welcome, and at once confirmed all the good opinions I had formed of this courageous and single-minded friend of the slave. I was delighted with all my brethren, and at once entered fully into their plans and counsels.

An incident connected with the organization of the House, which caused intense excitement at the time, seems to deserve some notice. It occurred on the 12th of December, while William J. Brown, of Indiana, was being voted for as the Democratic candidate for Speaker. He was a pro-slavery Democrat, through and through, and commanded the entire and unhesitating confidence of Southern members ; and yet, on the last ballot for him, he received the votes of Allen, Durkee, Giddings, King, and Wilmot, and came within two votes of an election. The support of Mr. Brown by the leading Free Soilers was a great surprise to both sides of the House, and the suspicion that some secret arrangement had been made gave birth to a rumor to that effect. After the balloting, while Mr. Bailey, of Virginia, was on the floor, Mr. Ashmun, of Massachusetts, asked him whether a secret correspondence had not taken place between some member of the Free Soil party and Mr. Brown, by which the latter had agreed to constitute the Com-

mittees on the Judiciary, on Territories, and on
the District of Columbia, in a manner satisfactory
to that party. Mr. Bailey scouted the idea, and
asked Mr. Ashmun what authority he had for the
statement. Mr. Ashmun replied, "Common rumor"; to which Mr. Bailey rejoined, " Does not the
gentleman know that common rumor is a common
liar ? " Turning to Mr. Brown he said, " Has any
such correspondence taken place ? " Mr. Brown
shook his head, and Mr. Bailey became more emphatic than ever in his denial. But the fever was
now up, and the Southern members scented treason. Several of them withheld their votes from
Mr. Brown because of his Free Soil support, and
thus prevented his election. He was in a very
trying dilemma with his Southern friends, while
the Free Soilers who had supported him were also
placed in a novel predicament, and subjected to
catechism. The fact was finally revealed in the
course of a long and exciting debate, that Mr. Wilmot *had* entered into a correspondence with Mr.
Brown on the subject of the organization of the
Committees named, and that the latter *had* promised in writing to constitute them as stated in Mr.
Ashmun's inquiry—declaring that he had "always
been opposed to the extension of slavery," and
believed that "the Federal Government should be
relieved from the responsibility of slavery where it
had the constitutional right to abolish it." This,
in substance, was the whole Free Soil gospel; and

the disappointment and rage of Southern members, when the letter was produced, can be more easily imagined than described. Mr. Brown labored very painfully to explain his letter and pacify his South - ern friends, but the effort was utterly vain. He was branded with treachery and duplicity by Bailey, Harris, Burt, Venable, Stanton, and McMullen, while no man from the South pretended to excuse him. In the midst of great excitement he withdrew from the contest for Speaker, and the catastrophe of his secret maneuver was so unspeakably humiliating that even his enemies pitied him. But he was unjustly dealt with by his Southern brethren, whose fear of betrayal and morbid sensitiveness made all coolness of judgment impossible. While he possessed very social and kindly personal traits of character, no man in this Congress was more inflexibly true to slavery, as his subsequent career amply demonstrated. If he had been chosen Speaker he would doubtless have placed some of the Free Soil members on the Committees specified, but the whole power of his office would have been studiously subservient to the behests of the slave oligarchy ; and nothing could excuse the conduct of Mr. Wilmot and his associates but their entire ignorance of his political character and antecedents. I regretted this affair most sincerely, for I knew Mr. Brown well, and could undoubtedly have prevented the negotiation if I had been present.

The Speakership was obviously the first question
on which the slave power must be met in the
Thirty-first Congress. No question could more
completely have presented the entire controversy
between the free and slave States which had so
stirred the country during the previous eighteen
months. In view of the well-nigh autocratic
power of the Speaker over legislative measures, no
honest Free Soiler could vote for a candidate who
was not known to be sound on the great issue.
We could not support Howell Cobb, of Georgia,
the nominee of the Democratic party, however
anxious our Democratic constituents might be to
have us do so ; nor could we vote for Robert C.
Winthrop, of Massachusetts, to please the Whigs
and semi-Free Soilers who affiliated with them,
since Giddings, Palfrey and others had demonstrated that he was wholly untrustworthy in facing
the ragged issue of slavery. This had been proved
by his acts as Speaker in the preceding Congress.
We therefore united in the determination to vote
for neither of these candidates. The contest was
protracted till December 22d, when, on the sixty
third ballot, Mr. Cobb was chosen. The result
was effected, by adopting, at the instigation of the
Whigs, what was called the "plurality rule," the
operation of which enabled a minority to choose
the speaker. The Whigs, when they entered upon
this proceeding, well knew that the Free Soilers
were willing and anxious to vote for Thaddeus

Stevens, or any other reliable member of the party. They well knew that none of us would vote for Mr. Winthrop, under any circumstances, and for excellent reasons which we had announced. Further, they well knew that without Free Soil votes Mr. Cobb would certainly be chosen; and yet the angry cry went up from the Whigs in Congress and throughout the Northern States that the Free Soilers had elected a slave-holder to be speaker of the House! For a time the ridiculous charge served the purpose of its authors, but the subsequent career of Mr. Winthrop finally and entirely vindicated the sagacity of the men whose resolute opposition had thwarted his ambition.

In the further organization of the House Mr. Campbell, a Tennessee slave-holder, was chosen clerk on the twentieth ballot, by the help of Southern Democrats, over John W. Forney, who was then the particular friend of James Buchanan, and who had made himself so conspicuous by his abuse of anti-slavery men that the Free Soil members could not give him their support. On the eighth ballot Mr. Glossbrenner, of Pennsylvania, the nominee of the Democrats, was chosen sergeant-at-arms, and after fourteen ineffectual ballots for doorkeeper, Mr. Horner, the Whig incumbent in the preceding Congress, was continued by resolution of the House. This was on January 18th, and the organization of the House was not yet completed, but further proceedings in this direction were now postponed till the first of March.

In the meantime the slavery question had been receiving daily attention. The strife over the Speakership had necessarily involved it, and constantly provoked its animated discussion. The great issue was the Congressional prohibition of slavery in the Territories, then popularly known as the " Wilmot proviso"; and the first vote on it was taken December 31st, upon the motion to lay on the table Mr. Root's resolution which embodied it. The yeas were 83, nays 101; being a majority of only 18 in its favor. The Southern men seemed to gather hope and courage from this vote. On January 4th, the President sent in his special message relative to California and New Mexico, announcing his famous " Non-action " policy, which was simply another name for the " Non-intervention " dogma of Gen. Cass. A year before he had declared that the new Territories must not be " surrendered to the pistol and the bowie-knife "; but a new light now dawned on him, and he advised Congress to leave the Territories to themselves till their people should be prepared to ask admission into the Union as States. He talked as glibly about " geographical parties " and the " operation of natural causes " as any trained Whig politician, and seemed to have totally forgotten his repeated pledges not to interfere with the action of Congress respecting " domestic questions." While the hand

of the Executive was thus at work, extreme men in
both Houses led the way in violent and inflamma-
tory speeches.   "When we ask for justice, and to
be let alone," said Mr. Clingman, of North Carolina, "we are met by the senseless and insane cry
of Union, Union!   Sir, I am disgusted with it.
When it comes from Northern gentlemen who are
attacking us, it falls on my ear as it would do if a
band of robbers had surrounded a dwelling, and
when the inmates attempted to resist, the assailants
should raise the cry of peace, union, harmony!"
He gave out the threat, that unless the slave-holders were allowed to extend their system over the
virgin soil of our Territories, they would block the
wheels of Government, and involve the nation in
the horrors of civil war.   He charged that the free
States "keep up and foster in their bosoms Abolition Societies, whose main purpose is to scatter
fire-brands throughout the South, to incite servile
insurrections, and stimulate by licentious pictures
our negroes to invade the persons of our white
women."   Mr. Brown, of Mississippi, said he regarded slavery "as a great moral, social, and *religious* blessing,—a blessing to the slave, and a
blessing to the master."   He graciously admitted
that Northern people thought slavery an evil; but
he added, "Very well, think so; *but keep your
thoughts to yourselves.*"   Jefferson Davis, then as
ever afterward, the apostle of disunion, declared
that "slavery existed in the tents of the patriarchs,

and in the households of His own chosen people ";
that " it was established by decree of Almighty
God," and " sanctioned in the Bible—in both Testa-
ments—from Genesis to Revelations." Southern
members pointed to the battle-fields of the Revolution, and warned the people of the free States to
beware ; while the menace was uttered that if the
representatives of the Northern States should vote
California into the Union as a free State, without
some compensating measures to the South, their
numbers would be decimated by violence. Mr.
Toombs, in referring to the exclusion of slavery
from the common territory, said, " I will then, if I
can, bring my children and my constituents to the
altar of liberty, and like Hamilcar, I will swear
them to eternal hostility to your foul domination."
On January 29th, Mr. Clay introduced his eight
resolutions of compromise, which still further weak-
ened the anti-slavery policy of Northern Whigs ;
and when, on February 4th, another vote was taken
on the Wilmot proviso, it was laid on the table by
yeas 104, nays 75;—showing a majority of 29, and
a change of 47 votes in a little more than one month !
Thus began the sickening career of political apos-
tacy, which so gathered momentum during the
spring and summer months that it became impossible to admit the free State of California into the
Union till the passage of the Texas Boundary Bill
and the new Fugitive Slave Act had been made
certain.

6

Early in the session I called on President Taylor
with Mr. Giddings and Judge Allen.   I had a very
strong curiosity to see the man whose name I had
used so freely in two exasperating political cam-
paigns, and desired to stand corrected in my estimate
of his character, if I should find such correction to
be demanded by the truth.   Our interview with the
old soldier was exceedingly interesting and amusing.   I decidedly liked his kindly, honest, farmer-
like face, and his old-fashioned simplicity of dress
and manners.   His conversation was awkward and
labored, and evinced a lack of self-possession ; while
his whole demeanor suggested his frontier life, and
that he had reached a position for which he was
singularly unfitted by training and experience, or
by any natural aptitude.   In the few remarks he
addressed to me about farming in the West, he
greatly amused us by saying, "I would like to
visit Indiana, and see your plows, hoes—and other
reaping implements "; failing, as he often did, to
find the word he wanted.   He frequently mispro-
nounced his words, hesitated and stammered, and
sometimes made a breakdown in the middle of a
sentence.   But although he seemed to be in the
hands of the slave-holders, and was about to proclaim his policy of non-intervention with slavery
in the Territories, he impressed me as being personally honest and patriotic.   In this impression I
was fully confirmed later in the session, when
he sorrowfully but manfully resisted the attempt

of Senator Davis, his son-in-law, and other extreme men, to bully him into their measures, and avowed his sympathy with the anti-slavery sentiment of the country. I believe his dying words in July, "I have tried to do my duty," were the key-note of his life, and that in the Presidential campaign of 1848, I did him much, though unintentional, injustice.

It was about the same time that I called with other Western members to see Mr. Clay, at the National Hotel. He received us with the most gracious cordiality, and perfectly captivated us all by the peculiar and proverbial charm of his manners and conversation. I remember nothing like it in the social intercourse of my life. One of our party was Hon. L. D. Campbell, then a prominent Whig politician of Ohio, and an old friend of Mr. Clay, who seemed anxious to explain his action in supporting Gen. Scott in the National Convention of 1848. He failed to satisfy Mr. Clay, whose eye kindled during the conversation, and who had desired and counted on the nomination himself. Mr. Clay, addressing him, but turning to me, said : "I can readily understand the position of our friend from Indiana, whose strong opinions on the slavery question governed his action ; but your position was different, and, besides, General Scott had no chance for the nomination, and you were under no obligation to support him." He spoke in kindly terms of the Free Soil men ; said they acted consistently in supporting Van Buren in preference to Taylor, and that the election of the latter would prove the ruin of the Whigs. I heard Mr. Clay's great speech in the Senate on the Compromise Measures, and although I believed him to be radically wrong, I felt myself at times drawn toward him by that peculiar spell which years before had bound me to him as my idolized political leader. I witnessed his principal encounters with Col. Benton during this session, in which I thought the latter had the better of the argument; but his reply to Mr. Barnwell, of South Carolina, on July 22d, in which he said: "I owe a paramount allegiance to the whole Union, a subordinate one to my State," and denounced the treasonable utterances of Mr. Rhett, was altogether inimitable and unsurpassed. In the same speech he showed as little quarter to the Abolitionists. Turning to Mr. Hale, he said, "They live by agitation. It is their meat, their bread, the air which they breathe; and if they saw in its incipient state, a measure giving them more of that food, and meat, and bread, and air, do you believe they would oppose themselves to its adoption? Do you not believe that they would *hail* [Hale] it as a blessing? * * * They see their doom as certain as there is a God in heaven, who sends his providential dispensations to calm the threatening storm, and to tranquilize agitated man. As certain as God exists in heaven, your business, your vocation is gone."

His devotion to the Union was his ruling passion, and in one of his numerous speeches during this session he held up a fragment of Washington's coffin, and with much dramatic effect pleaded for reconciliation and peace between the warring sections.

His scheme of compromise, or "omnibus bill," was the darling child of his political ambition and old age; and when, after lovingly nursing it and gallantly fighting for it through seven or eight weary months, he saw it cruelly dismembered on July 31st, and his sovereign remedy for our national troubles insulted by the separate passage of the bill providing a Territorial Government for Utah, I could not help feeling a profound personal sympathy with him. Beaten at last at every point, deserted by some senators in whom he had trusted implicitly, crushed and exhausted by labors which few young and vigorous men could have endured, he bowed to the inevitable, and retired from the Senate Chamber. But the next morning, prior to his departure for the sea-shore, he was in his seat ; and with lightning in his eye, and figure erect as ever, he paid his respects to the men whose work of political havoc he deplored. His impassioned arraignment of the disunionists was loudly applauded by the galleries, and clearly indicated the part he would have played in the late Rebellion had his life been spared to witness that direful event. " So long," said he, " as it pleases God to give me a voice to express my sentiments, or an arm, weak and enfeebled as it may be by age, that voice and that arm will be on the side of my country, for the support of the general authority, and for the maintenance of the powers of this Union."

I heard the famous "Seventh of March Speech" of Mr. Webster. To me his oratory was a perfect surprise and curiosity. He not only spoke with very unusual deliberation, but with pauses having no relation whatever to the sense. His sentences were broken into the oddest fragments, and the hearer was perplexed in the endeavor to gather his meaning. In declaring, for example, that he " would put in no Wilmot proviso for the purpose of a taunt," etc., he made a long pause at " Wilmot," perhaps a half minute, and finally, having apparently recovered his breath, added the word " proviso "; and then, after another considerable pause, went on with his sentence. His speaking seemed painfully laborious. Great drops of perspiration stood upon his forehead and face, notwithstanding the slowness of his utterance, suggesting, as a possible explanation, a very recent and heavy dinner, or a greatly troubled conscience over his final act of apostasy from his early New England faith. The latter was probably the truth, since he is known to have long and seriously pondered the question of his ultimate decision; and with his naturally great and noble traits of character he could not have announced it without manifest tokens of uneasiness. I was greatly interested in the brief dialogue between him and Mr. Calhoun, which followed this speech. Reference was made to their famous passage-at-arms twenty years before; and Mr. Calhoun, while taking exception to some of Mr. Webster's positions, congratulated him on his strong deliverance in the interest of slavery. The great Carolinian was then wrestling with the disease which soon afterward terminated his life, and was thin, pale, and feeble of step; but his singularly intellectual face, and the peculiar light which flashed from his eye while speaking, made him the most strikingly picturesque figure in the Senate. No man can compute the evils wrought by his political theories; but in private life he was thoroughly upright and pure, and no suspicion of political jobbery was ever whispered in connection with his name. In his social relations he was most genial and kindly, while he always welcomed the society of young men who sought the aid of his friendly counsel. Politically, he has been singularly misunderstood. He was not, as has been so generally thought, a disunionist. He was the champion of State Sovereignty, but he believed that this was the sure basis and bond of Union. He thought the right of State nullification, if recognized, would hold the central power in check, and thus cement the Union; while his devotion to African slavery as a defensible form of society, and a solution of the conflict between capital and labor, was doubtless as sincere as it was fanatical.

During the first months of this session my spare time was devoted to the preparation of a speech on the slavery question. My constituents expected this, and so did my anti-slavery and Free Soil friends generally. It was my darling purpose, and I resolved to do my best upon it. I not only meant that they should not be ashamed of it, but that, if possible, it should stand the test of criticism, both as to matter and diction. I re-examined the question in its various aspects, and more thoroughly than I had been able to do before, giving special attention to the speeches of Southern members in both Houses, and carefully noting their vulnerable points. I overhauled the question of "Northern aggression" pretty thoroughly, and endeavored to expose the absurdity of that complaint, while crowding into my task such facts and arguments as would help educate the people in right thinking. I had my task completed in March, and now anxiously waited the opportunity for its delivery. I was very curious to know how it would sound, and what would be thought of it, while my constitutional self-distrust made me dread the experiment unspeakably. My scuffle for the floor was a sore trial of patience, and it was not until the fourteenth of May that the competitive contest was ended. I got through with the work better than I anticipated, was handsomely listened to, and went

home in triumph. A great burden of anxiety had
been lifted, while I received letters from the leading Abolitionists of New England and elsewhere,
very cordially commending the speech, which was
copied into the principal anti-slavery newspapers,
and quite favorably noticed. I was flattered beyond measure, and found my self-esteem germi-
nating into new life under these fertilizing dews.

CHAPTER V.

REMINISCENCES OF THE THIRTY-FIRST CONGRESS (CONTINUED).

Fracas between Col. Benton and Senator Foote—Character of Benton—Death of Gen. Taylor—The funeral—Defeat of the "Omnibus Bill"—Its triumph in detail—Celebration of the victory—"Lower law" sermons and "Union-saving" meetings—Slave-holding literature—Mischievous legislation—Visit to Philadelphia and Boston—Futile efforts to suppress agitation—Andrew Johnson and the homestead law—Effort to censure Mr. Webster—Political morality in this Congress—Temperance—Jefferson Davis and other notable men—John P. Hale—Thaddeus Stevens—Extracts from speeches—The famous men in both Houses—The Free Soilers and their vindication.

I HAPPENED to be in the Senate on April 17th, just before the memorable fracas between Foote, of Mississippi, and Col. Benton. They had had an unfriendly encounter not long before, and it was well understood that Benton had made up his mind that Foote should not henceforward name him or allude to him in debate. Foote had said: "I do not denounce him as a *coward*—such language is unfitted for this audience—but if he wishes to *patch up* his reputation for courage, now greatly on the wane, he will certainly have an opportunity of doing so whenever he makes known his desire in the premises." Benton replied: "Is a senator to be blackguarded in the discharge of his duty, and the culprit go unpunished? Is language to be used here which would not be permitted to be used in the lowest pot-house, tavern, or oyster cellar, and for the use of which he would be turned out of any tavern by a decent landlord?" Benton's wrath had not in the least cooled since this altercation. Foote was on the floor, and in speaking of the late "Southern address," referred to Benton in terms which everybody understood. In an indirect way he became more and more personal as he proceeded. Col. Benton finally arose from his seat with every appearance of intense passion, and with a quick pace moved toward Foote, who was addressing the Senate from his desk near the main aisle. The Vice President demanded "order," and several senators tried to hold Benton back, but he broke loose from his keepers, and was moving rapidly upon his foe. When he saw Benton nearing him, Foote sprang into the main aisle, and retreated toward the Vice President, presenting a pistol as he fled, or, as he afterward expressed it, "advanced backward." In the meantime Benton had been so obstructed by the sergeant-at-arms and others that Foote, if disposed to shoot, could not have done so without firing through the crowd. But Benton, with several senators hanging to him, now proceeded round the lobby so as to meet Foote at the opposite side of the Chamber. Tearing himself away from those who sought to hold him, and throwing open his bosom, he said: " Let him shoot me! The cowardly assassin has come here to shoot me; let him shoot me if he dares! I never carry arms, and he knows it; let the assassin fire!" He was an embodied fury, and raged and raved, the helpless victim of his passions. I had never seen such an uproar in a legislative body; but the sergeant-at-arms at last restored order, when Mr. Clay suggested that both parties should voluntarily enter into bonds to keep the peace, upon which Benton instantly rose and said: "I'll rot in jail, sir, before I will do it! No, sir! I'll rot in jail first. I'll rot, sir!" and he poured forth a fresh torrent of bitter words upon the man who was then so well known throughout the Northern States as "Hangman Foote."* Benton was not only a man of tremendous passions, but unrivaled as a hater. Nor did his hatred spend itself entirely upon injustice and meanness. It was largely personal and unreasoning. He was pre-eminently unforgiving. He hated Calhoun with a real vengeance, styling him "John Cataline Calhoun," and branding him as a "coward cur that sneaked to his kennel when the Master of the Hermitage blew his bugle horn." He seemed to relent a little, however, when he saw the life of the great Carolinian rapidly ebbing away, and on one occasion declared that, "When God lays his hand on a man, I take

---

* So named because of his declaration in the Senate the year before, that if John P. Hale would come to Mississippi he would be hung to "one of the tallest trees of the forest," and that he (Foote) would himself "assist in the operation."

mine off." His wit was sometimes as pungent as his invective. In his famous speech on the Compromise measures, he gave Mr. Clay a telling hit by comparing the boasted panacea of his "Omnibus Bill," or "five old bills tacked together," to "old Dr. Jacob Townsend's sarsaparilla," and contrasting it with the alleged worthlessness of the same measures when separately proposed, which he likened to "young Dr. Samuel Townsend's" extract from the same vegetable. "Sarsaparilla" was thus more widely advertised than ever before, but it aided the triumph of the "young Dr.," and the defeat of Mr. Clay's pet scheme.

The sudden death of Gen. Taylor, July 9, 1850, produced a very profound impression. The shock to the people of the Northern States was felt the more keenly because of the peculiarly threatening aspect of public affairs, and of the unexpectedly manly course of the President in withstanding the imperious and insolent demands of the extreme men of his own section. Millard Fillmore then stood well before the country, and was quite as emphatically committed to the growing anti-slavery sentiment of the Free States as Gov. Seward himself; but he was now to be severely tried, and no one could tell whether he would be true to the policy of his predecessor in resisting the ultra demands of the South, or repeat the perfidy of John Tyler by flagrantly turning his back on his past life. For the time, however, the national bereavement seemed too absorbing for any political speculations. The funeral pageant, which took place on the 13th, was very imposing. The funeral car was a long-coupled running gear, with wheels carved from solid blocks of wood. Over this was raised a canopy covered with broadcloth, and surmounted by a magnificent eagle. Curtains of black and white silk in alternating festoons hung from the canopy, with rosettes, fringes, and tassels. The car was drawn by eight white horses, richly caparisoned, and led by as many grooms, who were all white men. " Old Whitey," the venerable war steed of the President, followed immediately behind the remains of his master, and attracted universal attention. The procession was accompanied by the tolling of bells, the firing of heavy ordnance, and plaintive strains of music; and the whole affair exceeded anything of the kind that had ever taken place in Washington, although the outpouring of people would bear no comparison with that of several notable funerals of later years.

The dreadful heat of the summer months, and the monotonous " ding-dong " of the debate on the Compromise measures, made life dreary enough. The " rump-session," as it was then called, became more and more dismal as it dragged its slow length into the fall months. Members grew pale and thin, and sighed for their homes; but the Congressional mill had to be kept running till the grists of the slave-power could be got fully ready for the hopper, and ground in their regular order. Mr. Clay's

Omnibus Bill having gone to pieces, the "five gaping wounds" of the country, about which he had talked so eloquently, called for treatment in detail ; and by far the most threatening of these was the dispute between Texas and New Mexico. The remedy was the Texas Boundary Bill, which surrendered a large belt of country to Texas and slavery, and gave her ten million dollars besides. It was vehemently opposed in the House, and its fate seemed to hang in doubt up to the final vote upon it; but its passage was really assured from the beginning by the corrupt appliances of its friends. Texas bonds, which were then worth ten cents on the dollar, would be lifted nearly to par by this measure, and its success was undoubtedly secured by the bribery of members. The territorial question was disposed of by the legislative covenant that new States might be admitted from our Mexican acquisitions, either with or without slavery, as their people might determine. This was not only an open abandonment of the Wilmot proviso, but a legislative condemnation of the Missouri compromise line, as a violation of the principle of "popular sovereignty," and was sure to breed the mischiefs which followed four years later. But of the several compromise or "healing measures" of this session, the Fugitive Slave Bill was by far the most atrocious. It made the *ex parte* interested oath of the slave-hunter final and conclusive evidence of the fact of escape, and of the identity of the party

pursued, while the simplest duties of humanity were
punished as felonies by fine and imprisonment.
The method of its enactment perfectly accorded
with its character.   It was reached on the Speaker's
table on September 12th, and on motion of Mr.
Thompson, of Pennsylvania, who served as the
parliamentary hangman of his employers, the previous question was seconded on its passage ; and
thus, without reference to any committee, without
even being printed, and with no opportunity whatever for debate, it became a law.   It is needless to
say that these pretended measures of final adjustment paved the way for the repeal of the Missouri
restriction, the bloody raid into Kansas, the Dred
Scott decision, and the final chapter of the Civil
War ; while they completely vindicated the little
party of Independents in this Congress in standing
aloof from the Whig and Democratic organizations,
and warning the country against further submission
to their rule.   One hundred guns were fired in
Washington over the final triumph of slavery in
this memorable struggle ; and Congress adjourned,
at last, on September 30th, the session having
lasted nearly ten months, and being considerably
the longest thus far since the formation of the Government.

The adjournment was followed by great " Union-
saving " meetings throughout the country, which
denounced "abolitionism " in the severest terms,
and endorsed the action of Congress.   Multitudes

of "lower law" sermons by conservative Doctors of Divinity were scattered over the Northern States through the mails, and a regular system of agitation to *suppress* agitation was inaugurated. The sickly air of compromise filled the land, and for a time the deluded masses were made to believe that the Free Soilers had brought the country to the verge of ruin. Both clergy and laity zealously dedicated themselves to the great work of sectional pacification. The labors of Dr. Nehemiah Adams and Dr. Lord in this direction will not be forgotten. The Rev. Moses Stuart, of Andover Theological Seminary, in a work in the interest of peace, spoke of the "blessings and comforts" of slavery, and declared that "Christ doubtless felt that slavery might be made a very tolerable condition—aye, even a blessing—to such as were shiftless and helpless." Another book, entitled ."Aunt Phillis's Cabin ; or Southern Life as it is," was issued from the press, in which it was said that slavery was "authorized by God, permitted by Jesus Christ, sanctioned by the Apostles, and maintained by good men in all ages." A very remarkable book made its appearance, entitled, " A Choice of Evils ; or Thirteen Years in the South. By a Northern man." Its author was a Mr. Hooker, of Philadelphia. In this work he announced the discovery that slavery is not only an unspeakable blessing, but a great " missionary institution for the conversion of the heathen." One of the chapters of this book is

7

on " The Pleasures of Slavery." He declared that
the Southern slave is not merely contented, but a
" joyous fellow "; and that " in willing and faithful
subjection to a benignant and protecting power,
and that visible to his senses, he leans upon it in
complete and sure confidence, as a trusting child
holds on to the hand of his Father, and passes joy-
ously along the thronged and jostling way, where
he would not dare to be left alone." Mr. Hooker
declared that " his are the thoughts that make glad
the cared-for child, led by paternal hand "; and
that " of all people in the world, the pleasures of
the Southern slaves seem, as they really are, most
unalloyed." The press teemed with kindred publications, while "Graham's Magazine," Harper's
"Journal of Civilization," the "Literary World,"
"Godey's Ladies' Book," and other periodicals,
joined in the united effort to shout the anti-slavery
agitation into silence.

During this session some laws were passed having no connection with the slavery question, which
were pregnant with very great mischief, and have
only yielded up their meaning as they have been
practically applied and extended. The act of September 28th, granting land bounties to the soldiers
of the Mexican war, opened the way for the monopoly of many millions of acres of the public domain
by sharks and speculators, while proving a wretched
mockery of the just claims of the men in whose
name it was urged. The Swamp Land Act of the

same date, owing to its loose and unguarded provisions and shameful mal-administration, has been
still more fruitful of wide-spread spoliation and
plunder. The act of September 20th, granting
alternate sections of land in aid of the Illinois Central Railway, inaugurated our famous land-grant
policy, which, becoming more and more reckless
and improvident in its exactions, and cunningly
combining the power of great corporations with
vast monopolies of the public domain, has signally
eclipsed all other schemes of commercial feudalism,
and left to coming generations a problem involving the very life of our popular institutions. The
fruits of this legislation were not foreseen at the
time, but the legislation itself fitly belongs to the
extraordinary work of this Congress.

The events of this session formed a new bond
of union among anti-slavery men everywhere,
and naturally strengthened the wish I had long
cherished to meet some of the famous people with
whose names I had been most familiar. Accordingly, I paid a visit to James and Lucretia Mott in
Philadelphia, which I greatly enjoyed, meeting
there Dr. Elder, J. Miller McKim, Dr. Furness,
and other well known friends of freedom. Oddly
enough, I was invited to dine with Judge Kane,
then conspicuous through his remarkable rulings in
fugitive slave cases, and I found his manners and hos-
pitality as charming as his opinions about slavery
were detestable. From Philadelphia I went to Bos-

ton, and attended the Free Soil State Convention
which met there early in October, 1850, where Sumner and Burlingame were the principal speakers.
The latter was extremely boyish in appearance, but
was counted a marvel in native eloquence. Mr.
Sumner was then comparatively a young man,
apparently somewhat fastidious, with a winning
face, commanding figure, and a voice singularly
musical. At this time he was only famous through
his orations, and I think knew relatively little of
American life and society outside of Boston and
his books. He told me he had recently been lect-
uring at several points out of the city, and had
been delighted to find the people so intelligent
and so capable of understanding him. He seemed
much surprised when I told him how many admir-
ers he had in Indiana, and I found that others
shared his unflattering impressions respecting the
general intelligence of the West. At this convention I met Dr. Palfrey, then actively interested in
anti-slavery politics, and Charles Francis Adams,
the Free Soil nominee for Vice President in 1848,
with whom I dined at the old Adams mansion in
Quincy a few days later. I enjoyed the honor of a
call from Theodore Parker while in the city, but
failed to meet Mr. Garrison, who was absent. At
the " Liberator " office, however, I met Stephen S.
Foster, who entertained me with his views on
"non-resistance." I attended a spirited anti-fugi-
tive-slave-law meeting in Lynn, where I first met

Wendell Phillips, and enjoyed the long-coveted pleasure of hearing him speak. The music of his voice so charmed me that I became completely his captive. From Boston I went to Worcester, and after a delightful visit with my excellent friend, Judge Allen, returned to my home in the West.

After a vacation of two months, the work of the Thirty-first Congress was resumed at the opening of its second session. Members returned so refreshed and invigorated that they did not appear like the same men. All parties seemed more friendly, but the agitation of the slavery question had not been suppressed. Thousands of fugitive slaves had fled to Canada or to remote sections of the Northern States, through the fear of recapture under the harsh features of the new Fugitive Slave Act. The method of enforcing it in different States, involving the intervention of the army and navy, had stirred the blood of thousands who had else remained unmoved by the slavery issue. The effort of the National Government to make the harboring of a fugitive constructive treason, was the farthest thing possible from a peace-offering to the Abolitionists, but the friends of the Compromise measures failed to see that their scheme had proved entirely abortive, and made one further effort to silence the voice of humanity. They entered into a solemn compact in writing to support no man for President or Vice President of the United States, or for senator or representative in

Congress, or member of a State legislature, who was not known to be opposed to disturbing their "final settlement" of the slavery question. The signature of Henry Clay was the first on this document, and was followed by those of various prominent men of the free and slave States, and of different political parties. But the extreme men of the South and most of the moderate men of the North refused to assume this obligation, while the Free Soilers felt perfectly sure that their cause would be advanced by the very measures which had been taken to defeat it. In this they were not mistaken. "Uncle Tom's Cabin," born of the Fugitive Slave Act, was then making its first appearance in weekly numbers of Dr. Bailey's "National Era." Hildreth's "White Slave" and Sumner's "White Slavery in the Barbary States" were widely circulated, and exerted a powerful influence. The writings of Judge Jay and William Goodell on the slavery question found more readers than ever before, while the pro-slavery literature and "south side" theology, already referred to, called forth replies from various writers, and contributed largely to the general ferment which the friends of the Compromise measures were so anxious to tranquilize. Indeed, while the champions of slavery were exerting themselves as never before to stifle the anti-slavery spirit of the free States, the Abolitionists were delighted with the tokens of progress which everywhere saluted their vision and animated them with new courage and hope.

It was early in the first session of this Congress that several members of the House introduced bills providing homesteads of one hundred and sixty acres each to actual landless settlers, without cost, on prescribed conditions of occupancy and improvement. The first of these bills in the order of time was that of Andrew Johnson, which was referred to the Committee on Agriculture, and subsequently reported favorably, and debated at different times. Similar propositions were offered in the Senate by Mr. Webster, and by Senator Walker, of Wisconsin. The fact is also worthy of note, that Horace Greeley, during his short term of service in the previous Congress, had offered a bill giving to landless men the right to pre-empt one hundred and sixty acres for seven years, and, on condition of occupancy and improvement, the " right of unlimited occupancy " to forty acres of the same, without price, by a single man, or eighty acres by the married head of a family. But the legislative initiation of the Homestead law, substantially as we now have it, belongs to the House of Representatives of the Thirty-first Congress, and its policy was borrowed from the Free Soil platform of 1848 and the Land Reformers of New York. This measure completely reversed the early policy of the Government, when settlers on the public lands were dealt with as trespassers, while its triumph, years afterward, marked an epoch in our legislation, and has done more to make the Ameri-

can name honored and loved at home and abroad
than any single enactment since the year 1789.
Having earnestly espoused this policy years before,
I sought the acquaintance of Mr. Johnson for the
purpose of co-operating with him in urging it,
and found him its sincere friend. Although loyal
to his party, he seemed to have little sympathy
with the extreme men among its leaders, and no
unfriendliness to me on account of my decided
anti-slavery opinions. When my homestead speech
was ready for delivery, he was anxious that I
should be recognized, although the slave-holders
hated its doctrines as heartily as they hated
" abolitionism " itself, and it was through his
friendly tactics that I finally obtained the floor, in
opposition to the earnest wish and determined
purpose of Speaker Cobb.

Near the close of this session, at the instance
of Charles Allen, of Massachusetts, a man of real
ability and stainless life, a preamble and resolutions
were offered by myself calling for a committee to
inquire into the alleged corrupt conduct of Daniel
Webster in accepting the office of Secretary of
State as the stipendiary of Eastern capitalists.
On the motion to suspend the rules to allow this
to be done, the yeas were only thirty-five; but this
vote was quite as large as could have been expected,
considering the excellent standing of Mr. Webster
at that time with the pro-slavery sentiment of the
country. I think it is not doubted that, being

then poor, he accepted office, as he had done before, on condition of pecuniary indemnity by his
rich friends in Wall street and State street; but in
the light of the far greater immoralities and profli-
gacies of later times, it now seems a relatively
small matter.

Political morality was at a very low ebb during
the period covered by the Thirty-first Congress.
The Whigs, now that they were in power, saw
nothing amiss in the spoils system inaugurated by
Gen. Jackson, which was in full blast. The President had declared that he had " no friends to reward
and no enemies to punish," but under the party
pressure he totally lost sight of these words, and
seemed almost as powerless to withstand it as did
Gen. Grant in later years. Thousands of officials
were turned adrift for no other than party reasons,
while political nepotism was the order of the day.
Under the brief administration of Gen. Taylor, unprecedented political jobbery prevailed, both in the
legislative and executive departments of the Government, and these evils seemed to be aggravated by
the accession of Mr. Fillmore, and to gather strength
as the spirit of liberty declined. Nor was the personal morality of members more to be commended
than their political. The vice of intemperance was
not, as now, restricted to a few exceptional cases,
but was fearfully prevalent. A glass of wine could
sometimes be seen on the desk of a senator while
engaged in debate, and the free use of intoxicating

drinks by senators was too common to provoke remark. It was still more common in the House; and the scenes of drunkenness and disorder in that body on the last night of the last session beggared description. Much of the most important legislation of the session, involving the expenditure of many millions, remained to be disposed of at that sitting; and, as a preparation for the work, a large supply of whisky had been deposited in a room immediately connected with the Hall of Representatives, which was thronged by members at all hours of the night. The chairman of the Ways and Means Committee became so exhilarated that he had to be retired from his post; and some of his brethren, who had been calling him to order in a most disorderly manner, were quite as incapable of business as himself, while order had sought her worshipers elsewhere. The exhibition was most humiliating, but it now pleasantly reminds us of the wonderful changes which have been wrought by thirty years.

In this Congress, the men who afterward became the chief leaders of the Rebellion were conspicuous, and foreshadowed their future course. Jefferson Davis had a military and magisterial look. His estimate of himself was so exalted that his ordinary demeanor toward others seemed like a personal condescension, if not an insinuation of contempt. One of the most striking personalities in the Senate was A. P. Butler, the colleague of Mr. Calhoun,

and uncle of Preston S. Brooks, of infamous memory. His robust physique, florid complexion,
sparkling eye, heavy bushy suit of snow-white hair,
and a certain indefinable expression of mischievous
audacity, made him a very attractive figure. In his
eulogy upon Calhoun he marred the solemnity of
the occasion by pronouncing the word "always" as
if written "allers," and by kindred evidences of
"life among the lowly." The wit of John P. Hale
was effective and unfailing, and gave him a decided
advantage over Mr. Chase, who had nothing but
his dignity and power of argument with which to
confront the tremendous odds against him. This
was happily illustrated early in the first session of
this Congress, in his reply to Mr. Clemens, of
Alabama, who, in a furious tirade against the Abolitionists, had pronounced the Union dissolved
already. "There are many timid people at the
North," said Hale, "who have looked forward with
excited nerves and trembling fears at the 'wreck
of matter and the crush of worlds' which they
believed would be the result of the dissolution of
this Union. I think they will be exceedingly
quiet now, when they find it has already taken
place and they did not know it, for the honorable
senator from Alabama tells us it is already dissolved. If it is not a matter too serious for a pleasant illustration, let me give you one. Once in my
life, in the capacity of a justice of the peace—for I
held that office before I was a senator—I was

called on to officiate in uniting a couple in the
bonds of matrimony. They came up, and I made
short work of it. I asked the man if he would take
the woman whom he held by the hand to be his
wedded wife ; he replied, ' To be sure I will, I came
here to do that very thing.' I then put the question to the lady, whether she would have the man
for her husband. And when she answered in the
affirmative, I told them they were man and wife.
She looked up with apparent astonishment, and
inquired ' Is that all ?' ' Yes,' I said, ' that is all.'
' Well,' said she, ' it is not such a mighty affair as
I expected it to be, after all.' "

Some of the finest of Mr. Seward's speeches
were delivered during the first session of this Congress, but in the same husky voice which marked
his later efforts. Decidedly the finest looking man
in the Senate was General Shields, of Illinois, then
in his prime, and crowned with the laurels he had
won in the Mexican War. The appearance of Mr.
Douglas, familiarly known as the "little giant,"
was in striking contrast with that of his colleague.
He cared nothing about dignity and refinement,
and had a slovenly and " unwashed " appearance.
The towering and erect form of General Houston
always commanded attention in the Senate, and he
added to his attractiveness by wearing an old-
fashioned knit cap, and always devoting a portion
of his time to whittling a pine board. The most
fascinating member of the Senate was Soule, of

Louisiana. There was a tropical charm about his oratory, which was heightened by his foreign accent and his singularly striking presence and physiognomy. Winthrop was the most accomplished gentleman in the House. Edward D. Baker, since so famous, was a member from Illinois, but made no mark. Stephens, of Georgia, looked like a corpse, but his clear and ringing voice always commanded attention, and his words went directly to the mark. Toombs was recognized as a leader of Southern opinion, but disfigured his speeches by his swagger and defiance. Among the notable men from the Northern States, Hannibal Hamlin, lately retired from public life, was in the Senate. He was then a young man, erect, fine looking, a thorough Democrat, but not the tool of slavery. Thaddeus Stevens was in the House, and just at the beginning of his remarkable congressional life; but the slave power, then in the full sweep of its despotism, took good care to keep him in the background in the organization of the committees. He made several speeches, in which he displayed his rare powers of invective, irony, and sarcasm, in dealing with the Southern leaders; and no one who listened to his speech of Feb. 20, 1850, could ever forget his withering reply to Mr. Mead, of Virginia, who had argued against the prohibition of slavery in the Territories because it would conflict with the interests of Virginia as a breeder of slaves. I quote the following:

"Let us pause a moment over this humiliating confession. In plain English, what does it mean? That Virginia is now only fit to be the breeder, not the employer, of slaves! That she is reduced to the condition that her proud chivalry are compelled to turn slave-traders for a livelihood! Instead of attempting to renovate the soil, and by their own honest labor compelling the earth to yield her abundance; instead of seeking for the best breed of cattle and horses to feed on her hills and valleys, and fertilize the land, the sons of that great State must devote their time to selecting and grooming the most lusty sires and the most fruitful wenches, to supply the slave barracoons of the South! And the learned gentleman pathetically laments that the profits of this genteel traffic will be greatly lessened by the circumscription of slavery! This is his picture, not mine."

Mr. Stevens was equally merciless in dealing with the tribe of "dough-faces." This was illustrated in a speech later in the session, in which he alluded to his colleague from Bucks County, Mr. Ross, who had attacked him in a violent pro-slavery harangue:

"There is," said Mr. Stevens, "in the natural world, a little, spotted, contemptible animal, which is armed by nature with a fetid, volatile, penetrating *virus*, which so pollutes whoever attacks it as to make him offensive to himself and all around him for a long time. Indeed, he is almost incapa-

ble of purification. Nothing, sir, no insult, shall
provoke me to crush so filthy a beast." As these
words were being uttered, Mr. Ross was seen pre-
cipitately making his way out of the hall under
this return fire of his foe. But Mr. Stevens then
gave no clear promise of the wonderful career as a
parliamentary leader which awaited him in later
years, when perfectly unshackled by the power
that at first held him in check.

The Thirty-first Congress was not alone remark-
able for the great questions it confronted and its
shameless recreancy to humanity and justice; it
was equally remarkable for its able and eminent
men. In the Senate, the great triumvirate of
Webster, Clay, and Calhoun, appeared in public
life for the last time. With them were associated
Benton, Cass, Douglas, Seward, Chase, Bell,
Berrien, Soule, Davis of Mississippi, Dayton, Hale,
Ewing, Corwin, Hamlin, Butler, Houston, and
Mason. In the House were Thaddeus Stevens,
Winthrop, Ashmun, Allen, Cobb of Georgia,
McDowell, Giddings, Preston King, Horace Mann,
Marshall, Orr, Schenck, Stanley, Toombs, Alexander H. Stephens, and Vinton. If mere talent could
have supplemented the lack of conscience, the
slave power might have been overborne in 1850,
and the current of American history turned into
the channels of liberty and peace. But the better
days of the Republic, when high integrity and un-
selfish devotion to the country inspired our states-

men, were past, and we had entered upon the era
of mean ambitions and huckstering politics. "The
bulk of the nation," as Harriet Martineau said, a
little later, "was below its institutions," and our
fathers "had laid down a loftier program than their
successors were able to fulfill." It was not strange,
therefore, that the little band of Free Soilers in this
Congress encountered popular obloquy and social
outlawry at the Capital. Their position was offensive, because it rebuked the ruling influences of the
times, and summoned the real manhood of the
country to its rescue. They were treated as pesti-
lent fanatics because they bravely held up the ideal
of the Republic, and sought to make it real. But
they pressed forward along the path of their aspirations. They found a solace for their social ostra-
cism in delightful gatherings which assembled
weekly at the residence of Dr. Bailey, where they
met philanthropists, reformers, and literary notables. They had the courage of their opinions, and
the genuine satisfaction which accompanies manli-
ness of character; and they lived to see their principles vindicated, and the political and social tables
turned upon the men who had honored them by
their scorn and contempt. The anti-slavery revolt
of 1848, which they represented, saved Oregon
from slavery, made California a free State, and
launched the policy of free homes on the public
domain which finally prevailed in 1862; and it was
the prophecy and parent of the larger movement

which rallied under Fremont in 1856, elected Lincoln in 1860, and played its grand part in saving the nation from destruction by the armed insurgents whom it had vanquished at the ballot-box   This will be the sure award of history ; but history will find another parentage for the party despotism and political corruption which have since disgraced the administration of the Government.

CHAPTER VI.

THE EVOLUTION OF THE REPUBLICAN PARTY.

Pro-slavery reaction—Indiana and Ohio—Race for Congress—
Free Soil gains in other States—National Convention at Cleveland—National canvass of 1852—Nomination of Pierce and
Scott, and the "finality" platforms—Free Soil National Convention—Nomination of Hale—Samuel Lewis—The Whig
canvass—Webster—Canvass of the Democrats—Return of
New York "Barnburners" to the party—The Free Soil campaign—Stumping Kentucky with Clay—Rev. John G. Fee—
Incidents—Mob law in Indiana—Result of the canvass—
Ruin of the Whigs—Disheartening facts—The other side of
the picture.

THE reaction which followed the passage of the
compromise acts of 1850 was quite as remarkable
as the anti-slavery revolt of 1848, which fright-
ened the champions of slavery into the espousal
of these desperate measures. Immense meetings
were held in Philadelphia, New York, Boston, and
other cities and towns throughout the country, in
which leading Whigs and Democrats united in
pledging themselves to make the suppression of
abolitionism paramount to any question of party
allegiance. These demonstrations were vigorously seconded by leading clergymen and doctors of
divinity, whose sermons were plentifully scattered
over the land under the frank of members of Con-

(114)

gress and otherwise. The press put forth its whole power on the side of anti-slavery submission and peace, while the Executive and Judicial departments of the Government made haste to abase themselves by their super-serviceable zeal in the enforcement of the new Fugitive Slave law. The tables seemed to be completely turned, and the time-honored rule of our slave-masters impregnably re-established. The anti-slavery commotion which a little while before had rocked the country from one end of the Union to the other was hushed in the restored order which succeeded, and gave promise of that longed-for " finality " for which the two great parties had so ardently labored.

In no section of the non-slaveholding States was this reaction more strikingly felt than in the West, and especially in Illinois and Indiana. These States were outlying provinces of the empire of slavery. Their black codes and large Southern population bore witness to their perfect loyalty to slave-holding traditions. Indiana, while a Territory, had repeatedly sought the introduction of slavery into her borders. Her black laws had disfigured her legislation from the beginning, and in 1850 were made still blacker by her new Constitution, the 13th article of which, forbidding negroes from coming into the State and white men from encouraging them to remain, was submitted to the people separately, and ratified by a popular majority of nearly ninety thousand votes. Ten years before, in the Harrison campaign, Mr. Bigger, the Whig candidate for Governor, made himself very popular by proving that Van Buren had favored negro suffrage in New York. In 1842, four of the Indiana delegation in Congress—namely, Lane, Wallace, Thompson, and Kennedy—voted for the censure of Mr. Giddings, which Mr. Clay indignantly denounced at the time, and two only—namely, White, and Cravens—voted in the negative. Although the execution of the Fugitive Slave Act of 1793 was a matter of Federal cognizance exclusively, yet the State code made the harboring of a fugitive an offense against its peace and dignity, punishable by fine and imprisonment. The colored people were denied any share in the school fund, but were taxed for its support; and under the law forbidding them to testify in cases where white men were parties, they were at the mercy of any white villain who might take the precaution to perpetrate an outrage upon them in the absence of white witnesses. Of course, the organization of an anti-slavery party strong enough to rule such States as these, was to be the work of time, toil, and patience. It was only possible to lay the foundation, and build as the material could be commanded; but the Free Soilers, whether in the East or in the West, were undismayed by the crisis, and fully resolved upon keeping up the fight. In compliance with the wishes of my anti-slavery friends, and by way of doing my part in the work, I decided to stand for a re-election from the Fourth Indiana District in the spring of 1851. The Wilmot proviso Democrats who had been chosen with me two years before on the strength of their Free Soil pledges, including such men as Joseph E. McDonald and Graham N. Fitch, now stood squarely on the Compromise measures.

The Whigs of the State, following the lead of Webster and Clay, and including Edward W. McGaughey, their only delegate in Congress, had also completely changed their base. My competitor, Samuel W. Parker, whom I had defeated two years before, and who had then insisted that the Whigs were better anti-slavery men than the Free Soilers themselves, now made a complete somersault, fully committing himself to the Compromise acts, and especially the Fugitive Slave law, which he declared he approved without changing the dotting of an *i* or the crossing of a *t*. Foote, Cass, and Webster were now the oracles of the Whig faith ; but, oddly enough, the Democrats, who had formed by far the larger portion of my support two years before, now stood firm, and I would undoubtedly have been re-elected but for very vigorous outside interference. Wm. J. Brown, who had intrigued with the leading Free Soilers for the Speakership in 1849, as I have already shown, and favored the passage of the Wilmot proviso in order to " stick it at old Zach," was now the editor of the "Sentinel," the State organ of the Democracy, which was sufficiently orthodox on the slavery question to pass muster in South Carolina. It was this organ which afterward insisted that my abolitionism entitled me to at least five years service at hard labor in the penitentiary. Mr. Brown's dread of this fearful heresy seemed as intense as it was unbounded, and he resolved, at all hazards, to avert any further alliance with it by Democrats in any portion of the State. By very hard work and the most unscrupulous expedients he succeeded in enlisting a few ambitious local magnates of his party in the district, who were fully in sympathy with his spirit and aims, and of whom Oliver P. Morton was the chief; and by thus drawing away from the democracy from two to three hundred pro-slavery malcontents and turning them over to my Whig competitor, my defeat was accomplished.

But the effort to stem the tide of slavery fared better elsewhere. While Mr. Webster was publicly ridiculing the "higher law," and blurting his contempt upon one of the noted anti-slavery strongholds of the country as "a laboratory of abolitionism, libel, and treason," Massachusetts sent Charles Sumner to the Senate of the United States, and elected Horace Mann, Charles Allen and Robert Rantoul as members of the House. Amos Tuck was returned from New Hampshire, Preston King from New York, Thaddeus Stevens and John W. Howe from Pennsylvania, Charles Durkee from Wisconsin, and Giddings and Townsend from Ohio. These events were exceedingly gratifying, and lent

new life to the cause throughout the Northern States.
During the summer of this year Mr. Sumner moved
the repeal of the Fugitive Slave Act, and although
it received but ten votes, it led to an angry and
protracted discussion, which showed how signally
the attempt to suppress anti-slavery agitation had
failed. In the latter part of September of this
year a Free Soil National Convention met at Cleveland, to take into consideration the state of the
country and the duty of anti-slavery men. It was
large and enthusiastic. It adopted a series of
spirited resolutions and a timely public address, and
admirable speeches were made by Cassius M. Clay,
Joshua R. Giddings, Samuel Lewis, George Brad-
burn, and others. The only drawback to the prevailing spirit of hopefulness and courage was the
absence of Mr. Chase, who had just withdrawn
from the Free Soil party and united his fortunes
with the Democrats of Ohio, who had adopted a
platform which admitted an interpretation covering,
substantially, the principles of the Free Soil creed.

As the time for another Presidential election drew
near, Whigs and Democrats were alike engrossed
with the consideration of their " final settlement "
of the slavery question, and their attitude respecting it in the impending struggle. Among the latter there was substantially no division. Their experience in 1848 with Gen. Cass and his " Nicholson letter," had convinced them that nothing was
to be gained by mincing matters, and that a hearty,

complete and unhesitating surrender to slavery was
the surest means of success. The Democrats in
Congress, both North and South, had very generally favored this " settlement," and there was now
no division in the party except as to men. The
candidates were Cass, Buchanan, Douglas, and
Marcy; and the National Convention assembled on
the first of June. The platform of the party began
with the declaration of its "trust in the intelligence,
the patriotism, and the discriminating justice of
the American people"; and then, in the fourth
and fifth resolutions, pronounced the Fugitive Slave
Act equally sacred with the Constitution, and
pledged the party to " resist all attempts at renew-
ing, in Congress or out of it, the agitation of the
slavery question, under whatever shape or color the
attempt may be made." So far as slavery was concerned it thus became a recognized and authorita-
tive principle of American Democracy to muzzle
the press and crush out the freedom of speech, as
the means of upholding and perpetuating its power.
On this platform Franklin Pierce was nominated on
the forty-ninth ballot; and in his letter of acceptance he declared that "the principles it embraces
command the approbation of my judgment, and
with them I believe I can safely say that no word
nor act of my life is in conflict." It is difficult to
conceive of any words by which he could more
completely have abdicated his manhood and self-
respect, and sounded the knell of his own con-

science. There was no lower deep, and he was evidently the right man in the right place.

The Whig National Convention assembled on the sixteenth of June, with Scott, Fillmore and Webster as the candidates. There was yet a considerable anti-slavery element in the party, but it was paralyzed and powerless. It had made a fatal mistake in submitting to the nomination of Gen. Taylor, and became still more completely demoralized by the accession of Fillmore, who turned his back upon his past life, and threw himself into the arms of the slave-holders. The old party had gone astray too long and too far to return, and now determined to seek its fortunes in the desperate effort to outdo the Democrats in cringing servility to the South. The platform of the Convention expressed the reliance of the Whigs " upon the intelligence of the American people," but in its eighth resolution declared their acquiescence in the Compromise Acts of 1850 " as a final settlement, in principle and substance, of the subjects to which they relate "; and it deprecated " all further agitation of the questions thus settled, as dangerous to our peace," and pledged the party " to discountenance all efforts to continue or renew such agitation, whenever, wherever, or however made." On this platform, which is well understood to have been the work of Mr. Webster, Gen. Scott was nominated on the fifty-ninth ballot by a vote of two hundred and twenty-seven to sixty-six, while the highest vote

received by Mr. Webster was twenty-nine. Here
at last, the Whig party had made a complete surrender of its integrity, and verified all that had ever
been said by Free Soilers as to its treachery to freedom; and here, finally, these rival parties were
tumbled together into the ditch of slavery, and
wallowing in the mire of their degradation and
shame. The only issue of the canvass was slavery,
and on this they were perfectly agreed, while each,
for the sake of the spoils of office, was trying to
surpass the other in the damning proofs of its
treason to humanity and its contempt for the fundamental truths of republican government.

The spectacle was most pitiably humiliating, but
I counted it an omen of progress. The old parties
were now unequivocally committed to the policy of
nationalizing the sectional interest of slavery, and
the way thus opened for a fair fight. The lines
were clearly drawn, and the issue unmistakably
made between freedom and free speech on the one
side, and slavery and the gag on the other. I
thought we should have no more anti-slavery professions from Whigs and Democrats, no further
courting of Free Soilers, and no more mutual up-
braidings of servility to the South; and that thus
the way would be smoothed for intelligent and effective anti-slavery work.

The Free Soil National Convention met in Pittsburg on the eleventh of August, and I believe an
assemblage of purer men never convened for any

political purpose. All the compromising and trading elements that had drifted into the movement in 1848 had now gravitated back to the old parties, leaving a residuum of permanent adherents of the cause, who were perfectly ready to brave the frowns of public opinion and the proscription and wrath of the old parties. Henry Wilson was made president of the convention, and the platform adopted was substantially that of 1848. A few additional resolves, however, were added, including the declaration " that emigrants and exiles from the old world should find a cordial welcome to homes of comfort and fields of enterprise in the new," and that " every attempt to abridge their privilege of becoming citizens and owners of the soil among us ought to be resisted with inflexible determination." It was also declared " that the Free Democratic party was not organized to aid either the Whig or Democratic wing of the great Slave Compromise party of the Nation, but to defeat them both; and that, repudiating and renouncing both as hopelessly corrupt and utterly unworthy of confidence, the purpose of the Free Democracy is to take possession of the Federal Government, and administer it for the better protection of the rights and interests of the whole people." On this platform John P. Hale was nominated for the Presidency. My own nomination for the second place on the ticket was to me a complete surprise. I fully expected this honor would

fall upon Samuel Lewis, of Ohio, and the delegation from my own State was unitedly for him. He
coveted the nomination, and so did his many devoted friends, simply as a fitting recognition of his
faithful service in the cause of freedom, to which he
had been unselfishly devoted since the year 1841.
He had made himself a public benefactor by his
long and powerful championship of the cause of
education in Ohio. He was a man of brains, and
enthusiastically devoted to every work of practical
philanthropy and reform. As an impassioned,
eloquent, and effective popular orator, he had no
equal in the country. His profound earnestness,
perfect sincerity, and religious fervor conquered all
hearts, and made his anti-slavery appeals irresistible.
He was a strong and brave old man, who richly
deserved whatever distinction his nomination could
confer; but for reasons unknown to me he encountered in the convention the formidable opposition
of Mr. Chase, and he wrote me very touchingly
a few days afterward that "among the thousands
who have given their lives and fortunes to this
cause, my name will be forgotten, while those who
have coolly stood by and watched the signs of the
times, and filled their sails with the wind that others
have raised, will go down to history as heroes and
martyrs in a cause for which they never fought a
battle nor suffered a sacrifice."

The canvass of the Whigs was totally without
heart or enthusiasm. The Southern wing of the

party had dictated the platform, but did not like Gen. Scott. Stephens and Toombs, of Georgia, and Jones and Gentry, of Tennessee, refused to support him. The Northern Whigs were greatly embarrassed, and while they felt constrained to support the candidate, tried to relieve their consciences by " spitting upon the platform" on which he stood. Mr. Webster did not disguise his hostility to the ticket, and predicted the speedy dissolution of the party. The Democrats were united in this contest. Notwithstanding their atrocious platform they succeeded in persuading the leading Barnburners of 1848 to return to the party and muster again in the army of slavery. Dix, the Van Burens, David Dudley Field, Tilden, and a host of others, including even Robert Rantoul and Preston King, were now fighting for Pierce, while Bryant's " Evening Post " and Greeley's " Tribune " cravenly submitted to the shackles of slavery. In the light of such facts as these it was easy to forecast the result of the contest.

The real enthusiasm of this campaign was in the ranks of the Free Soilers. They had, of course, no dream of success, or even of carrying a single electoral vote ; but they were profoundly in earnest, and united as one man against the combination of the old parties in behalf of slavery. I took the stump, and early in the campaign accepted an invitation to join Cassius M. Clay in the canvass of the counties of Lewis, Bracken, and Mason, in

Kentucky.   On my way to our first appointment I
stopped at Maysville, where I found myself in the
midst of a considerable excitement about some
thirty or forty slaves who had just crossed the Ohio
on their way to Canada.   I met Mr. Clay at the
residence of the Rev. John G. Fee, some eight miles
distant in Lewis county, where we talked over the
plan of our campaign.   Mr. Fee was the founder
of an anti-slavery colony, a free school, and a free
church, in that region, and was a scholar, philanthropist, and reformer.   His whole heart was in
the anti-slavery cause, and his courage had never
failed him in facing the ruffianism and brutality
which slavery employed in its service; but I would
not have felt very safe in this enterprise without the
presence of Mr. Clay, who was known in Kentucky,
and everywhere else, as "a fighting Christian,"
who would defend the freedom of speech at any
hazard.   Our first meeting was in Mr. Fee's
church, in the rocky and mountainous region of
the county, where we had perfect order and an at-
tentive and sympathetic audience.   From this
point we proceeded the next day to our appointment in Maysville, finding a good deal of excitement in the city as to the propriety of allowing us
to speak in the court house.   It was finally thrown
open to us, and in the afternoon I was handsomely
introduced by Mr. Clay to a fine audience, speaking at length, and with great plainness, on the
issues of the canvass, and being frequently ap-

plauded. Mr. Clay spoke at night to a still larger audience, while perfect order prevailed. So far our success seemed gratifying, and Mr. Fee was delighted ; and we proceeded the following morning to our next appointment at Brooksville, in Bracken county. Here we found assembled a large crowd of that brutalized rabble element which formed the background of slavery everywhere. The aboriginal creatures gazed at us like so many wild animals, but showed not the slightest disposition to enter the house in which we were to speak. Mr. Clay remarked that they must be Whigs, since they did not seem inclined to " resist," but only to " discountenance " our agitation ; but we had come to speak, and with Mr. Fee's family and a few friends who had come with us for an audience, we spoke about an hour and a half each, just as if the house had been filled. A few straggled in during the speaking, and several hung about the windows and listened, though they tried to seem not to do so ; but the most remarkable and praiseworthy thing about this congregation of Yahoos was that they did not mob us. It must have seemed to them a strange waste of power to spare such notorious disturbers of the peace, and return to their homes without any laurels. This ended our work in Kentucky, where we could boast that the "finality" platform had been openly set at defiance, and I returned to my work on the other side of the Ohio.

Later in the canvass, on my return from Wisconsin and Illinois, I learned that Andrew L. Robinson, the Free Soil candidate for Governor of Indiana, had been mobbed in the city of Terre Haute, and prevented from making an anti-slavery speech. This was not surprising, as this section of the State was largely settled by people from Maryland, Virginia and Kentucky, who were as intolerant of abolitionism as those of Bracken county already described. I immediately sent a telegram making an appointment to speak in that city, and on the day appointed reported for duty. I found my friends uneasy and apprehensive. They evidently regretted my coming, and some of them advised me quietly to return home. The town was full of rumors that I was not to be allowed to speak, and was to be "wabashed," as the rowdies phrased it. But I had no thought of returning without being heard; and accordingly, at the appointed hour, I repaired to the court house, where I found a small crowd assembled, with restless countenances, and a gang of ruffians outside, armed with stones and brickbats. The audience gradually increased, and as I began to speak I noticed that the roughs themselves began to listen, which they continued to do during the hour and a half I devoted to the most unmistakable utterances on the slavery question. The ringleader of the mob, for some reason, failed to give the signal of attack, and free speech was vindicated. Timid men grew brave, and boasted of the love of order that

had prompted the people of the town to stand by my
rights; yet the mob would probably have triumphed
but for the presence of Joseph O. Jones, the postmaster of the city, himself a Kentuckian, but a
believer in the right of free speech and the duty of
defending it at all hazards.

The result of this Presidential canvass was a surprise to all parties. The triumph of the Democrats
was anticipated, but it was far more signal than
they expected. Pierce received two hundred and
fifty-four electoral votes, and Scott only forty-two,
representing only four States of the Union. So
far as the Whig party was concerned, the result
was overwhelming and final. The party was buried forever in the grave it had dug for itself. Hale
received a little more than one hundred and fifty-
six thousand votes, being about one-twentieth of
the entire popular vote cast at this election; so that
nineteen-twentieths of the people of the United
States in 1852, and only a little more than a dozen
years before slavery was swept from the land, voted
themselves bound and dumb before this Moloch of
American politics, while only one-twentieth had
the courage to claim their souls as their own.
These were very startling facts after more than a
quarter of a century of anti-slavery agitation, and
they were naturally interpreted by the victorious
party everywhere as clearly foreshadowing the
complete triumph of the " final settlement " made
by Congress in 1850. Certainly they seemed very

9

disheartening to anti-slavery men ; for, however confidently they might believe in the final success of their struggle, they could not fail to see the immense odds and fearful obstacles against which they would have to contend. The debauched masses who had been molded and kneaded by the plastic touch of slavery into such base uses, were the only possible material from which recruits could be drawn for a great party of the future, which should regenerate our politics and re-enthrone the love of liberty ; and this should be remembered in estimating the courage and faith of the men who in that dark hour held aloft the banner of freedom, in spite of all temptations to go with the multitude.

But there was another view of the situation which thoughtful anti-slavery men did not fail to enforce. The overwhelming triumph of Pierce was not an unmixed victory for slavery. It had another explanation. It was to be remembered, to the credit of the Whig party, that thousands of its members, notwithstanding their dislike of Pierce and their admiration of Gen. Scott as a man and a soldier, and despite the attempted drill of their leaders and the influence of Greeley and Seward, could not be induced to support the ticket, and were now ready for further acts of independence. It was likewise to be remembered that in the complete rout and ruin of the party a great obstacle to anti-slavery progress had been removed. The

slave-holders at once recognized this fact. They
had aimed to defeat the party, not to annihilate it.
They saw clearly that what slavery needed was
two pretty evenly divided parties, pitted against
each other upon economic issues, so that under
cover of their strife it could be allowed to have its
way; and they were justly alarmed at the prospect
of a new movement, basing its action upon moral
grounds, and gathering into its ranks the unshackled conscience and intelligence of the Northern States. The "Washington Union," then the
National organ of the Democracy, deplored the
death of the Whig party, and earnestly hoped for
its resurrection. The fact had always been patent
to anti-slavery men that these parties were alike
the bulwarks of slavery, since the Southern wing
of each gave law to the whole body, and that until
one or the other could be totally destroyed, a really
formidable anti-slavery party was impossible.
There was also great cause for encouragement in
the evident signs of a growing anti-slavery public
opinion. "Uncle Tom's Cabin" had found its way
to the million on both sides of the Atlantic, and the
rage for it among all classes was without parallel
in the history of literature. It was served up for
the masses in sixpenny editions, dramatized and
acted on the stage, and coined into poetry and
song. Slave-holders were alarmed at its wonderful
success, because they saw the grand part it was
playing in creating that "public opinion of the

civilized world" which Mr. Webster had declared to
be " the mightiest power on earth." The replies to
this wonderful book, and the anti-slavery and pro-
slavery literature to which it gave birth, largely
contributed to the progress of freedom, and the
final repudiation of the " finality " which the great
parties had combined to establish.

Nor was the small vote for Hale a matter of serious discouragement. It was much smaller than
that cast for Van Buren in 1848; but that was a
deceptive epoch. Multitudes, and especially in
the State of New York, then voted the Free Soil
ticket who had never before shown any interest in
the slavery question, and did not manifest it afterward. They were not Free Soil men, but Van
Buren men, who hated Gen. Cass. The vote for
Hale represented the *bona fide* strength of our
cause after this element had been eliminated, and
its quality went far to atone for its quantity. The
proper test of anti-slavery progress was a comparison of the anti-slavery vote of 1844 with that of
1852, and this showed an increase of nearly three-
fold in the intervening space of eight years. This
steady evolution of anti-slavery opinion from the
deadening materialism and moral inertia of the
times could not go backward, but in the very
nature of things would repeat itself, and gather
fresh momentum from every effort put forth to
stay its advance.

CHAPTER VII.

THE EVOLUTION OF THE REPUBLICAN PARTY (CONTINUED).

It was early in the year 1853 that a notable fugitive slave case occurred in Indiana. The alleged fugitive was John Freeman, who had once resided in Georgia, but for many years had been a resident of Indianapolis and had never been a slave. The marshal of the State, though he had voted against the passage of the Fugitive Act of 1850, entered upon the service of Ellington, the claimant, with a zeal and alacrity which made him exceedingly odious to anti-slavery men. He accompanied

(133)

Ellington into the jail in which Freeman was con-
fined, and compelled him to expose his shoulders
and legs, so that the witnesses could identify him
by certain marks, and swear according to the pat-
tern, which they did.   The case became critical for
Freeman; but the feeling in Indianapolis was so
strong in his favor that a continuance of the hearing was granted to enable him to prepare his proofs.
He hired friends to go to Georgia, who succeeded
in bringing back with them several men who had
known him there many years before, and testified
that he was a free man.   On the day of the trial
Ellington became the fugitive, while Freeman was
preparing his papers for a prosecution for false imprisonment.   The large crowd in attendance was
quite naturally turned into an anti-slavery meeting,
which was made to do good service in the way of
" agitation."   The men from Georgia were on the
platform, and while they were complimented by the
speakers on their love of justice and humanity in
coming to the rescue of Freeman, no quarter was
given to the Northern serviles and flunkeys who had
made haste to serve the perjured villains who had
undertaken to kidnap a citizen of the State under
the forms of an atrocious law.   The meeting was
very enthusiastic, and the tables completely turned
on the slave-catching faction.

When President Pierce was inaugurated, on the
fourth of March, 1853, the pride and power of the
Democratic party seemed to be at their flood.   In

his inaugural message he expressed the fervent hope that the slavery question was "forever at rest," and he doubtless fully believed that this hope would be realized. In his annual message, in December following, he lauded the Compromise measures with great emphasis, and declared that the repose which they had brought to the country should receive no shock during his term of office if he could avert it. The anti-slavery element in the Thirty-third Congress was scarcely as formidable as in the preceding one, though there were some accessions. Benjamin F. Wade was now in the Senate, and De Witt of Massachusetts, Gerritt Smith of New York, and Edward Wade of Ohio, were members of the House. In the beginning the session gave promise of a quiet one, but on the twenty-third of January the precious repose of the country, to which the President had so lovingly referred in his message, was rudely shocked by the proposition of Senator Douglas to repeal the Missouri compromise. This surprising demonstration from a leading friend of the Administration and a champion of the compromise measures marked a new epoch in the career of slavery, and rekindled the fires of sectional strife. After a very exciting debate in both houses, which lasted four months, the measure finally became a law on the thirtieth of May, 1854. It was a sprout from the grave of the Wilmot proviso; for if, under the Constitution, it was the duty of Congress to abandon the policy of restric-

tion in 1850, and provide that Utah and New
Mexico should be received into the Union, with or
without slavery, according to the choice of their
people, the Missouri compromise line should never
have been established, and was a rock of offense
to the slave-holders.   The Compromise Acts of
1850 had not abrogated that line, and related only
to our Mexican acquisitions; but they had affirmed
a principle, and if that principle was sound, the
Missouri restriction was indefensible.   The whole
question of slavery was thus reopened, for the sacredness of the compact of 1820 and the wickedness of its violation depended largely upon the
character of slavery itself, and our constitutional
relations to it.   .

On all sides the situation was exceedingly critical and peculiar.   The Whigs, in their now practically disbanded condition, were free to act as they
saw fit, and were very indignant at this new demonstration in the interest of slavery, while they were
yet in no mood to countenance any form of "abolitionism." Multitudes of Democrats were equally
indignant, and were quite ready to join hands with
the Whigs in branding slavery with the violation
of its plighted faith.   Both made the sacredness of
the bargain of 1820 and the crime of its violation
the sole basis of their hostility.   Their hatred of
slavery was geographical, spending its force north
of the Missouri restriction.   They talked far more
eloquently about the duty of keeping covenants,

and the wickedness of reviving sectional agitation, than the evils of slavery, and the cold-blooded conspiracy to spread it over an empire of free soil. Their watch-word and rallying cry was " the restoration of the Missouri compromise "; but this demand was not made merely as a preliminary to other measures, which would restore the free States to the complete assertion of their constitutional rights, but as a means of propitiating the *spirit* of compromise, and a convenient retreat to the adjustment acts of 1850 and the " finality " platforms of 1852. In some States and localities the anti-slavery position of these parties was somewhat broader; but as a general rule the ground on which they marshaled their forces was substantially what I have stated.

The position of the Free Soilers was radically different. They opposed slavery upon principle, and irrespective of any compact or compromise. They did not demand the restoration of the Missouri compromise; and although they rejoiced at the popular condemnation of the perfidy which had repealed it, they regarded it as a false issue. It was an instrument on which different tunes could be played. To restore this compromise would prevent the spread of slavery over soil that was free; but it would re-affirm the binding obligation of a compact that should never have been made, and from which we were now offered a favorable opportunity of deliverance. It would be to recognize

slavery as an equal and honorable contracting
party, waiving its violated faith, and thus preclud-
ing us from pleading its perfidy in discharge of all
compromises. It would degrade our cause to the
level of those who washed their hands of all taint
of abolitionism, and only waged war against the
Administration because it broke up the blessed
reign of peace which descended upon the country
in the year 1850. These Free Soilers insisted that
the breach of this compact was only a single link
in a great chain of measures aiming at the absolute
supremacy of slavery in the Government, and thus
inviting a resistance commensurate with that policy;
and that this breach should be made the exodus of
the people from the bondage of all compromises.
They argued that to cut down the issue between
slavery and freedom to so narrow, equivocal, and
half-hearted a measure, at a time when every consideration pleaded for radical and thorough work,
was practical infidelity to the cause and the crisis.
It was sporting with humanity, and giving to the
winds a glorious victory for the right when it was
within our grasp.

The situation was complicated by two other political elements. One of these was Temperance, which
now, for the first time, had become a most absorbing political issue. The " Maine Law " agitation
had reached the West, and the demand of the
temperance leaders was " search, seizure, confiscation, and destruction of liquors kept for illegal

sale." Keenly alive to the evils of drunkenness, and too impatient to wait for the inevitable conditions of progress, they thought the great work could be accomplished by a legislative short-cut. They insisted that the "accursed poison " of the "rumseller," wherever it could be found, should be poured into the gutter along with other filth, while he should be marched off to answer to the charge of a crime against society, and take his rank among other great offenders. Instead of directing their chief attack against the appetite for drink and seeking to lessen the demand, their effort was to destroy the supply. They had evidently given no thought to the function of civil government in dealing with the problem, nor did they perceive that the vice of drunkenness is an effect, quite as much as a cause, having its genesis in unequal laws, in the domination of wealth over the poor, in the lack of general education, in inherited infirmities, physical and mental, in neglected household training; in a word, in untoward social conditions which must be radically dealt with before we can strike with effect at the root of the evil. They did not see that the temperance question is thus a many-sided one, involving the general uplifting of society, and that no legislation can avail much which loses sight of this truth. For these very reasons the agitation for a time swept everything before it. Its current was resistless, because it was narrow and impetuous. If the leaders had comprehended the logic of their work and its unavoidable limitations, and had only looked forward to the overthrow of the fabric of intemperance by undermining its foundations, the regular current of politics would not have been perceptibly affected, while the way would have been left open for a more perfect union on the really vital and overshadowing issue of slavery.

The other element referred to made its appearance in the closing months of 1853, and took the name of the Know-Nothing party. It was a secret oath-bound political order, and its demand was the proscription of Catholics and a probation of twenty-one years for the foreigner as a qualification for the right of suffrage. Its career was as remarkable as it was disgraceful. Thousands were made to believe that the Romish hierarchy was about to overthrow our liberties, and that the evils of "foreignism" had become so alarming as to justify the extraordinary measures by which it was proposed to counteract them. Thousands, misled by political knaves through the arts of the Jesuits believed that the cause of freedom was to be sanctified and saved by this new thing under the sun. Thousands, through their unbridled credulity, were persuaded that political hacks and charlatans were to lose their occupation under the reign of the new Order, and that our debauched politics were to be thoroughly purified by the lustration which it promised forthwith to perform. Thousands, eager to bolt from the old parties, but fearful of being shot down on the way as deserters, gladly availed themselves of this newly devised " underground railroad " in escaping from the service of their old masters. Under these various influences the Whigs generally, and a large proportion of the Free Soilers and Democrats, were enlisted in the service of this remarkable movement. Pretending to herald a new era in our politics in which the people were to take the helm and expel demagogues and traders from the ship, it reduced political swindling to the certainty and system of a science. It drew to itself, as the great festering centre of corruption, all the known rascalities of the previous generation, and assigned them to active duty in its service. It was an embodied lie of the first magnitude, a horrid conspiracy against decency, the rights of man, and the principle of human brotherhood.

Its birth, simultaneously with the repeal of the Missouri compromise, was not an accident, as any one could see who had studied the tactics of the slave-holders. It was a well-timed scheme to divide the people of the free States upon trifles and side issues, while the South remained a unit in defense of its great interest. It was the cunning attempt to balk and divert the indignation aroused by the repeal of the Missouri restriction, which else would spend its force upon the aggressions of slavery; for by thus kindling the Protestant jealousy of our people against the Pope, and enlisting them in a crusade against the foreigner, the South could all the more successfully push forward its schemes.

On this ground, as an anti-slavery man, I opposed it with all my might from the beginning to the end of its life. For a time it carried everything with a high hand. It was not only irresistible in numbers, but it fought in the dark. It pretended to act openly and in friendly conference with its enemies as to questions which it had already settled in secret conclave. Its opponents did not know how to wage war against it, because they did not know who were their friends. If a meeting was called to expose and denounce its schemes, it was drowned in the Know-Nothing flood which, at the appointed time, completely overwhelmed the helpless minority. This happened in my own county and town, where thousands of men, including many of my old Free Soil brethren, assembled as an organized mob to suppress the freedom of speech ; and they succeeded by brute force in taking possession of every building in which their opponents could meet, and silencing them by savage yells. At one time I think I had less than a dozen political friends in the State, and I could see in the glad smile which lighted up the faces of my old-time enemies that they considered me beyond the reach of political resurrection. But I never for a moment intermitted my warfare, or doubted that in the end the truth would be vindicated, although I did not dream that in less than two years I would be the recognized leader of the men composing this mob, who would be found denying their membership of this secret order, or confessing it with shame. It was a strange dispensation ; and no record of independent journalism was ever more honorable than that of the " New York Tribune " and " National Era," during their heroic and self-sacrificing fight against this organized scheme of bigotry and proscription, which can only be remembered as the crowning and indelible shame of our politics. It admits of neither defense nor palliation, and I am sorry to find Henry Wilson's " History of the Rise and Fall of the Slave Power " disfigured by his elaborate efforts to whitewash it into respectability, and give it a decent place in the records of the past.

Such were the elements which mingled and commingled in the political ferment of 1854, and out of which an anti-slavery party was to be evolved capable of trying conclusions with the perfectly disciplined power of slavery. The problem was exceedingly difficult, and could not be solved in a day. The necessary conditions of progress could not be slighted, and the element of time must necessarily be a large one in the grand movement which was to come. The dispersion of the old parties was one thing, but the organization of their fragments into a new one on a just basis was quite a different thing. The honor of taking the first step in the formation of the Republican party belongs to Michigan, where the Whigs and Free Soilers met

in State convention on the sixth of July, formed a
complete fusion into one party, and adopted the
name Republican. This action was followed soon
after by like movements in the States of Wisconsin
and Vermont. In Indiana a State "fusion" convention was held on the thirteenth of July, which
adopted a platform, nominated a ticket, and called
the new movement the "People's Party." The
platform, however, was narrow and equivocal, and
the ticket nominated had been agreed on the day
before by the Know-Nothings, in secret conclave,
as the outside world afterward learned. The ticket
was elected, but it was done by combining opposite
and irreconcilable elements, and was not only
barren of good fruits but prolific of bad ones,
through its demoralizing example; for the same
dishonest game was attempted the year following,
and was overwhelmingly defeated by the Democrats. In New York the Whigs refused to disband,
and the attempt to form a new party failed. The
same was true of Massachusetts and Ohio. The
latter State, however, in 1855, fell into the Republican column, and nominated Mr. Chase for Governor, who was elected by a large majority. A
Republican movement was attempted this year in
Massachusetts, where conservative Whiggery and
Know-Nothingism blocked the way of progress, as
they did also in the State of New York. In November of the year 1854 the Know-Nothing party
held a National Convention in Cincinnati, in which

the hand of slavery was clearly revealed, and the " Third Degree," or pro-slavery obligation of the order, was adopted; and it was estimated that at least a million and a half of men afterward bound themselves by this obligation. In June of the following year another National Convention of the order was held in Philadelphia, and at this convention the party was finally disrupted on the issue of slavery, and its errand of mischief henceforward prosecuted by fragmentary and irregular methods; but even the Northern wing of this Order was untrustworthy on the slavery issue, having proposed, as a condition of union, to limit its anti-slavery demand to the restoration of the Missouri restriction and the admission of Kansas and Nebraska as free States.

Indeed, the outlook as to the formation of a triumphant anti-slavery party was not so promising towards the close of the year 1855 as it had seemed in the spring of the preceding year. If the Free Soilers had been clear-sighted enough to distinguish between that which was transient and that which was permanent in the forces .which had roused the people of the free States, and, availing themselves of the repeal of the Missouri restriction as a God-send to their cause, had summoned the manhood of the country to their help, a powerful impulse would have been given in the right direction. But in the general confusion and bewilderment of the times many of them lost their way, and

10

were found mustering with the mongrel hordes of Know-Nothingism, and under captains who were utterly unworthy to lead them. Instead of inflexibly maintaining their ground and beckoning the people to come up and possess it, they meanly deserted it themselves, while vainly expecting others to occupy it. The Whigs were totally powerless to render any service without first disbanding their party, and this, in many localities, they declined to do. Both wings of the Know-Nothing movement were organized obstacles to the formation of a new party, while the bolters from the Democrats were as unprepared for radical anti-slavery work as the Whigs or Know-Nothings. But notwithstanding all these drawbacks, real progress had been made. In the Thirty-fourth Congress, Wilson, Foster, Harlan, Trumbull, and Durkee were chosen senators. In the House were Burlingame, Buffington, Banks, Hickman, Grow, Covode, Sherman, Bliss, Galloway, Bingham, Harlan, Stanton, Colfax, Washburn, and many others. These were great gains, and clearly pointed to still larger accessions, and the final subordination of minor issues to the grand one on which the people of the free States were to take their stand. An unprecedented struggle for the Speakership began with the opening of the Thirty-fourth Congress, and lasted till the second day of February, when the free States finally achieved their first victory in the election of Banks. Northern manhood at last was at a premium, and

this was largely the fruit of the " border ruffian "
attempts to make Kansas a slave State, which had
stirred the blood of the people during the year 1855.
In the meantime, the arbitrary enforcement of the
Fugitive Slave Act still further contributed to the
growth of an anti-slavery opinion. The famous
case of Anthony Burns in Boston, the prosecution
of S. M. Booth in Wisconsin, and the decision of
the Supreme Court of that State, the imprisonment
of Passmore Williamson in Philadelphia, and the
outrageous rulings of Judge Kane, and the case of
Margaret Garner in Ohio, all played their part in
preparing the people of the free States for organized political action against the aggressions of
slavery.

Near the close of the year 1855, the chairmen
of the Republican State Committees of Ohio, Massachusetts, Pennsylvania, Vermont, and Wisconsin,
issued a call for a National Republican Convention to be held at Pittsburg, on the 22d of February, 1856, for the purpose of organizing a National
Republican party, and making provision for a subsequent convention to nominate candidates for
President and Vice President. It was very largely
attended, and bore witness to the spirit and courage
which the desperate measures of the slave oligarchy had awakened throughout the Northern
States. All the free States were represented, and
eight of the slave-holding, namely: Maryland,
Virginia, Delaware, Kentucky, Missouri, Tennessee,

North Carolina, and Texas. The convention assembled in Lafayette Hall, and the Hon John A.
King, of New York, a son of Rufus King, was
made temporary chairman, and Francis P. Blair,
of Maryland, the intimate friend of President
Jackson, was made its permanent president. He
was most enthusiastically greeted on taking the
chair, and began his address with the remark that
this was the first time he had ever been called on
to make a speech. His views were too conservative in tone to satisfy the demands of the crisis,
but he was most cordially welcomed as a distinguished delegate from a slave State. The convention was opened by a prayer from Owen Lovejoy,
and there was a suppressed murmur of applause
when he asked God to enlighten the mind of the
President of the United States, and turn him from
his evil ways, and if this was not possible, to take
him away, so that an honest and God-fearing man
might fill his place. Horace Greeley was seen in
the audience, and was loudly and unitedly called
on for a speech. He spoke briefly, saying that he
had been in Washington several weeks, and friends
there "counseled extreme caution in our movements." This was the burden of his exhortation.
At the close of his remarks Mr. Giddings was
tumultuously called for, and responded by saying
that Washington was the last place in the world to
look for counsel or redress, and related an anecdote
of two pious brothers named Joseph and John,

who in early times had begun a settlement in the
West. Joseph prayed to the Lord: "O, Lord!
we have begun a good work; we pray thee to
carry it on thus,"—giving specific directions. But
John prayed: "O, Lord, we have begun a good
work; carry it on as you think best, and don't mind
what Joe says." Mr. Giddings then introduced
the Rev. Owen Lovejoy, of Illinois,—"not Joe,
but John." Mr. Lovejoy delighted the audience,
and was followed by Preston King and other
speakers; and it was quite manifest that this was
a *Republican* convention, and not a mere aggre-
gation of Whigs, Know-Nothings, and dissatisfied
Democrats. It contained a considerable Know-
Nothing element, but it made no attempt at leadership, while Charles Remelin and other speakers
were enthusiastically applauded when they denounced Know-Nothingism as a mischievous side
issue in our politics, which the new movement
should openly repudiate. The convention was in
session two days, and was singularly harmonious
throughout. Its resolutions and address to the
people did not fitly echo the feeling and purpose of
its members, but this was a preliminary movement, and it was evident that nothing could stay
the progress of the cause. As chairman of the
committee on organization, I had the honor to report the plan of action through which the new
party took life, providing for the appointment of a
National Executive Committee, the holding of a

National Convention in Philadelphia on the 17th of June, for the nomination of candidates for President and Vice President, and the organization of the party in counties and districts throughout the States.

The Philadelphia convention was very large, and marked by unbounded enthusiasm. The spirit of liberty was up, and side issues forgotten. If Know-Nothingism was present, it prudently accepted an attitude of subordination. The platform reasserted the self-evident truths of the Declaration of Independence, and denied that Congress, the people of a Territory, or any other authority, could give legal existence to slavery in any Territory of the United States. It asserted the sovereign power of Congress over the Territories, and its right and duty to prohibit it therein. Know-Nothingism received no recognition, and the double-faced issue of the restoration of the Missouri compromise was disowned, while the freedom of Kansas was dealt with as a mere incident of the conflict between liberty and slavery. On this broad platform John C. Fremont was nominated for President on the first ballot, and Wm. L. Dayton was unanimously nominated for Vice President. The National Republican party was thus splendidly launched, and nothing seemed to stand in the way of its triumph but the mischievous action of the Know-Nothing party, and a surviving faction of pro-slavery Whigs. The former party met in National Convention in

Philadelphia, on the twenty-second of February,
and nominated Millard Fillmore for President and
Andrew J. Donelson for Vice President. Some
bolters from this convention subsequently nominated Nathaniel P. Banks and William F. Johnson
as their candidates, and a remnant of the Whig
party held a convention in Baltimore on the seventeenth of September, and endorsed Fillmore and
Donelson; but a dissatisfied portion of the convention afterward nominated Commodore Stockton
and Kenneth Raynor. All these factions were destined soon to political extinction, but in a hand-to-
hand fight with the slave power they yet formed a
considerable obstacle to that union and harmony
in the free States which were necessary to success.

The Democratic National Convention met at
Cincinnati on the second of June. The candidates
were Buchanan, Pierce, and Douglas. On the
seventeenth ballot Buchanan was unanimously
nominated for President, and on the second ballot
John C. Breckenridge was nominated for Vice
President. The platform re-affirmed the action
of Congress respecting the repeal of the Missouri compromise and the compromises of 1850,
and recognized the right of the people of all the
Territories, including Kansas and Nebraska, whenever the number of their inhabitants justified it, to
form a Constitution with or without domestic slavery, and to be admitted into the Union upon terms

of equality with the other States. These declarations, coupled with the express denial to Congress
of the right to interfere with slavery in the Territories, were accepted as satisfactory to the South, and
were fairly interpreted to mean that the people of
the Territories, pending their territorial condition,
had no power to exclude slavery therefrom. In
Mr. Buchanan's letter of acceptance he completely
buried his personality in the platform, and Albert
G. Brown of Mississippi, and Governor Wise of Virginia, pronounced him as true to the South as Mr.
Calhoun himself. These were the tickets for 1856,
but the real contest was between Buchanan and
Fremont. It was pre-eminently a conflict of principles. The issues could hardly have been better
defined, and they were vital. It was a struggle
between two civilizations, between reason and
brute force, between the principles of Democracy
and the creed of Absolutism; and the case was
argued with a force, earnestness, and fervor, never
before known. No Presidential contest had ever
so touched the popular heart, or so lifted up and
ennobled the people by the contagion of a great
and pervading moral enthusiasm. The campaign
for Buchanan, however, was not particularly animated, at least in the Northern States. It illustrated the power of party machinery, and the desperate purpose to press forward along a path which
had been followed too far to call a halt. It was a
struggle for party ascendancy by continual and

most humiliating concessions to the ever-multiply-
ing demands of slavery ; and the ardor of the struggle must have been cooled by many troublesome
misgivings as to the final effect of these concessions, and the policy of purchasing a victory at
such a price.

The excitement of the canvass was aggravated by
very exasperating circumstances. The brutal and
cowardly assault of Brooks upon Sumner was the
counterpart of border ruffianism in Kansas, and
perhaps did more to stir the blood of the people of
the Northern States than any of the wholesale outrages thus far perpetrated in that distant border.
These outrages, however, were now multiplied in
all directions, and took on new shapes. They were
legislative, executive, and judicial, cropping out
in private pillage and assassination, in organized
marauding and murder, and in armed violence ;
and these horrid demonstrations enlivened the canvass to the end. Republican enthusiasm reached
its white heat, borrowing the self-forgetting devotion and dedicated zeal of a religious conversion.
Banks and tariffs and methods of administration
were completely forgotten, while thousands of
Democrats who had been trained in the school of
slavery, and hundreds of thousands of conservative
Whigs, caught the spirit of liberty which animated
the followers of Fremont and Dayton. The canvass had no parallel in the history of American
politics. No such mass-meetings had ever assem-

bled.   They were not only immense in numbers,
but seemed to come together spontaneously, and
wholly independent of machinery.   The proces-
sions, banners, and devices were admirable in all
their appointments, and no political campaign had
ever been inspired by such charming and soul-stir-
ring music, or cheered by such a following of
orderly, intelligent, conscientious and thoroughly
devoted men and women.   To me the memory of
this first great national struggle for liberty is a
delight, as the part I played in it was a real jubilee of the heart.   I was welcomed by the Republican masses everywhere, and the fact was as gratifying to me as it proved mortifying to the party
chiefs who, a little while before, had found such
comfort in the assurance that henceforward they
were rid of me.   With many wry faces they submitted, after all sorts of manœuvers early in the
canvass to keep me in the background, varied by
occasional threats to drive me out of the party.
As their own party standing became somewhat
precarious they completely changed their base, and
often amused the public by super-serviceable dis-
plays of their personal friendship.   Even the ringleader of the Know-Nothing mob of two years
before, standing up to his full height of " six feet
six," used to introduce me at mass-meetings as
" Your honored representative in Congress, and
war-worn veteran in the cause of liberty."

But Buchanan triumphed.   The baleful interposition of Know-Nothingism stood in the way of that union of forces which the situation demanded, and was thus chiefly responsible for the Republican defeat. The old Whigs who had so recently stepped from their "finality" platform, could not be unitedly rallied, and the Democratic bolters were only half converted. In my own State the opposition to the Democracy repudiated even the name Republican, and entered the field as "the People's party." It was a combination of weaknesses, instead of a union of forces. All the Fillmore Know-Nothings and Silver-Grey Whigs of the State were recognized as brethren. At least one man on the State ticket, of which Oliver P. Morton was the head, was a Fillmore man, while both Fillmore and anti-Fillmore men had been chosen as delegates to Philadelphia and electors for the State. The political managers even went so far as to suppress their own electoral ticket during the canvass, as a peace-offering to old Whiggery and Know-Nothingism, while the admission of Kansas as a free State was dealt with as the sole issue, and border ruffian outrages and elaborate disclaimers of "abolitionism" were the regular staple of our orators, who openly declared that the Republican party was a "white man's party." Anti-slavery speakers like Clay and Burlingame were studiously kept out of Southern Indiana, where the teachings of Republicanism were especially needed, and Richard W. Thompson, then the professed champion of Fillmore, but in reality the stipendiary of the Democrats, traversed that region on the stump, denounced the Republicans as " Abolitionists," " disunionists," and " incendiaries," and was everywhere unchallenged in his course. Similar tactics, though not so deplorably despicable, prevailed in several of the other States, giving unmistakable evidence of the need of a still further and more thorough enlightenment of the people as to the spirit and aims of slavery.   In the light of these facts, I was not at all cast down by the defeat of Fremont. He was known as an explorer, and not as a statesman. If he had succeeded, with mere politicians in his cabinet, a Congress against him, and only a partially developed anti-slavery sentiment behind him, the cause of freedom would have been in fearful peril. The revolution so hopefully begun might have been arrested by half-way measures, promoting the slumber rather than the agitation of the truth, while the irritating nostrums of Buchanan Democracy, so necessary to display the abominations of slavery, would have been lost to us.   The moral power of the canvass for Fremont was itself a great gain, notwithstanding the cowardice of some of its leaders. The Republican movement could not now go backward, and with a probation of four years to prepare for the next conflict, unembarrassed by the responsibilities of power, and free to profit by the blunders and misdeeds of its foe, it was pretty sure of a triumph in 1860.   Fremont had received a popular vote of one million three hundred and forty-one thousand two hundred and sixty-four, carrying eleven States and one hundred and fourteen electoral votes; while only four years before, John P. Hale, standing on substantially the same platform, had received only a little more than one hundred and fifty-seven thousand, and not a single electoral vote. This showed a marvelous anti-slavery progress, considering the age of the movement, the elements it forced into combination, and the difficulties under which it struggled into life; and no one could misinterpret its significance.

CHAPTER VIII.

PROGRESS OF REPUBLICANISM.

The Dred Scott decision—The struggle for freedom in Kansas—
Instructive debates in Congress—Republican gains in the
Thirty-fifth Congress—The English bill—Its defeat and the
effect—Defection of Douglas—Its advantages and its perils
—Strange course of the New York Tribune and other Repub-
lican papers—Republican retreat in Indiana—Illinois Re-
publicans stand firm, and hold the party to its position—
Gains in the Thirty-sixth Congress—Southern barbarism and
extravagance—John Brown's raid—Cuba and the slave
trade—Oregon and Kansas—Aids to anti-slavery progress—
The Speakership and Helper's book—Southern insolence and
extravagance—Degradation of Douglas—Slave code for the
Territories—Outrages in the South—Campaign of 1860—
Charleston convention and division of the Democrats—
Madness of the factions—Bell and Everett—Republican
National Convention and its platform—Lincoln and Seward
—Canvass of Douglas—The campaign for Lincoln—Con-
duct of Seward—Republican concessions and slave-holding
madness.

THE Republicans, however, were sorely disappointed by their defeat; but this second great victory of slavery did not at all check the progress of
the anti-slavery cause. It had constantly gathered
strength from the audacity and recklessness of
slave-holding fanaticism, and it continued to do so.
On the 6th of March, 1857, the Supreme Court of

(158)

the United States harnessed itself to the car of
slavery by its memorable decision in the case of
Dred Scott, affirming that Congress had no power
to prohibit slavery in the Territories, and, inferen-
tially, that the Constitution carried with it the right
to hold slaves there, even against the will of their
people. The point was not before the court, and
the opinion of Chief Justice Taney was therefore
purely extra-judicial. It was simply a political
harangue in defense of slavery. It created a profound impression throughout the free States, and
became a powerful weapon in the hands of Republicans. It was against the whole current of ad-
judications on the subject, and they denounced it
as a vile caricature of American jurisprudence.
They characterized it as the distilled diabolism of
two hundred years of slavery, stealthily aiming
at the overthrow of our Republican institutions,
while seeking to hide its nakedness under the fig-
leaves of judicial fairness and dignity. They branded it as the desperate attempt of slave-breeding
Democracy to crown itself king, by debauching the
Federal judiciary and waging war against the advance of civilization. Their denunciations of the
Chief Justice were unsparing and remorseless; and
they described him as "pouring out the hoarded
villainies of a life-time into a political opinion
which he tried to coin into law." When Senator
Douglas sought to ridicule their clamor by inquiring whether they would take an appeal from

the Supreme Court of the United States to a town meeting, they answered: "Yes, we appeal from the court to the people, who made the Constitution, and have the right, as the tribunal of last resort, to define its meaning." Nothing could more clearly have marked the degradation to which the power of slavery had reduced the country than this decision, and no other single event could have so prepared the people for resistance to its aggressions. It was thoroughly cold-blooded in its letter and spirit, and no Spanish Inquisitor ever showed less sympathy for his victim than did the Chief Justice for the slave.

But the Dred Scott iniquity did not stand alone. It had been procured for the purpose of fastening slavery upon all the Territories, and it had, of course, a special meaning when applied to the desperate struggle then in progress to make Kansas a slave State. The conduct of the Administration during this year, in its treatment of the free State men of that Territory, forms one of the blackest pages in the history of slavery. The facts respecting their labors, trials, and sufferings, and the methods employed to force upon them the Lecompton Constitution, including wholesale ballot-stuffing and every form of ruffianism, pillage, and murder, need not be recited; but all these were but the outcroppings and counterpart of the Dred Scott decision, and the horrid travesty of the principle of popular sovereignty in the Territories.

The whole power of the Administration, acting as the hired man of slavery, was ruthlessly employed for the purpose of spreading the curse over Kansas, and establishing it there as an irreversible fact; and all the departments of the Government now stood as a unit on the side of this devilish conspiracy. Everybody knew that the Lecompton Constitution was the work of outside ruffians, and not of the people of the Territory, whose Legislature in February, 1858, solemnly protested against their admission under that Constitution, and whose protest was totally unheeded. The Congressional debates during this period greatly contributed to the anti-slavery education of the people, by more clearly unmasking the real spirit and designs of the slaveholders. We were treated to the kind of talk then becoming current about " Northern mud-sills," " filthy operatives," the " ownership of labor by capital," and the beauties and beatitudes of slavery. Such maddened extremists as Hammond and Keitt of South Carolina, and such blatant doughfaces as Petit of Indiana, became capital missionaries in the cause of freedom. Their words were caught up by the press of the free States, and added their beneficent help to the work so splendidly going forward through the providential agency of " Uncle Tom's Cabin."

In the meantime, freedom had made large gains in the composition of the Thirty-fifth Congress, which now had charge of the Lecompton swin-

11

dle. The Senate contained twenty Republican
members and the House ninety-two. Kansas had
not been forced into the Union as a slave State,
but she was helpless at the feet of the Executive.
In the midst of the angry debate a new proposition
was brought forward, on the twenty-third of April,
which was even more detestable than the Lecompton bill itself. This was known as the " English
bill," which offered Kansas a very large and tempting land grant, if she would come into the Union
under the Lecompton Constitution, but provided
that if she voted to reject the land grant she should
neither receive the land nor be admitted as a State
until the Territory acquired a population sufficient
to elect a representative to the House. The in-
famy of this proposition was heightened by the fact
that these long-suffering pioneers, weary and har-
assed by their protracted struggle and longing for
peace, were naturally tempted to purchase it at any
price. It was a proposition of gigantic bribery,
after bluster and bullying had been exhausted. It
was, in fact, both a bribe and a menace, and measured at once the political morality of the men who
favored it, and the extremity to which the slave-
holders were driven in the prosecution of their
desperate enterprise. After a protracted debate in
both Houses, and at the end of a struggle of five
months, the bill was passed and received the Executive approval ; but the rejoicing of the slave-
holders and their allies was short-lived. The peo-

ple of Kansas were not in the market. They had
suffered too much and too long in the battle for
freedom to make merchandise of their convictions
and sacrifice the future of a great commonwealth.
They spurned the bribe, and took the chances of
triumph through an indefinitely prolonged conflict,
while recruits to the ranks of freedom were naturally falling into line throughout the Northern
States.

In December of this year I attended another
fugitive slave case at Indianapolis. . The claimant
was one Vallandingham, of Kentucky, whose agent
caught the alleged fugitive in Illinois, and was
passing through Indianapolis on his way home.
The counsel for the negro, Elsworth, Coburn,
Colley, and myself, brought the case before Judge
Wallace, on *habeas corpus*, and had him discharged.
The claimant immediately had him arrested and
taken before Commissioner Rea, for trial. We
asked for the continuance of the case on the affi-
davit of the negro that he was free, and could prove
it if allowed three weeks' time in which to procure
his witnesses; but the Commissioner ruled that the
proceeding was a summary *ex-parte* one, and that
the defendant had no right to any testimony. Of
course we were forced into trial, and after allowing
secondary proof where the highest was attainable,
and permitting hearsay evidence and mere rumor,
the Commissioner granted his certificate for the removal of the adjudged fugitive. We again brought

the case before Judge Wallace, on *habeas corpus,*
when the negro denied all the material facts of the
marshal's return, under oath, and asked to be allowed to prove his denial; but the Judge refused
this, and he was handed over to the marshal for
transportation South.   On the trial he was shown
to have been free by the act of his master in sending him into a free State; but under cover of an
infamous law, and by the help of truculent officials,
he was remanded into slavery.   The counsel for
the negro, with a dozen or more who joined them,
resolved upon one further effort to save him.   The
project was that two or three men selected for the
purpose were to ask of the jailer the privilege of
seeing him the next morning and giving him good-
bye; and while one of the party engaged the jailer
in conversation, the negro was to make for the
door, mount a horse hitched near by, and effect
his escape.   The enterprise had a favorable beginning.   The negro got out, mounted a horse, and
might have escaped if he had been a good horse-
man; but he was awkward and clumsy, and unfortunately mounted the wrong horse, and a very poor
traveler; and when he saw the jailer in pursuit,
and heard the report of his revolver, he surrendered,
and was at once escorted South.   Walpole and his
brother were for the claimant.   This is the only
felony in which I was ever involved, but none of
the parties to it had any disposition whatever to
confess it at the time.

The Republican party gathered fresh courage and strength in the year 1858 from the defection of Douglas. His unmistakable ability and hitherto unquestioned devotion to slavery had singled him out as the great leader and coming man of his party. He was ambitious, and by no means scrupulous in his political methods. The moral character of slavery gave him not the slightest concern, ostentatiously declaring that he did not care whether it was "voted up or voted down" in the Territories, and always lavishing his contempt upon the negro. He was the great champion of popular sovereignty, but at the same time fully committed himself to the decision of the Supreme Court of the United States, whatever it might be ; and after that decision had been given, and, in effect, against his particular hobby, he defended it, while vainly striving to vindicate his consistency. But the Lecompton swindle was so revolting a mockery of the right of the people of Kansas, that his own Democratic constituents would not endorse it, and he was obliged, contrary to his strong party inclinations, to take his stand against it. It was an event of very great significance, both North and South, and gave great comfort to anti-slavery men of all shades of opinion ; but it brought with it, at the same time, a serious peril to the Republican party.

His accession to the Anti-Lecompton ranks was deemed so important that many leading Republicans, of different States, thought he should be welcomed and honored by the withdrawal of all party opposition to his re-election to the Senate. They argued that in no other way could the despotic power of the Democratic party be so effectually broken, and the real interests of re-publicanism advanced. This feeling, for a time, prevailed extensively, and threatened to put in abeyance or completely supersede the principles so broadly laid down in the national platform of 1856. The "New York Tribune" took the lead in beating this retreat. It sympathised with Douglas to the end of his canvass, and in connection with kindred agencies probably saved him from defeat. It urged the disbanding of the Republican party, and the formation of a new combination against the Democrats, composed of Republicans, Doug-las Democrats, Know-Nothings, and old Whigs, but without the avowal of any principles. It pro-posed that by the common consent of these parties the Republicans should be allowed to name the next candidate for the Presidency, and the other parties the candidate for the Vice Presidency; or that this proposition should be reversed, if found advisable, with a view to harmony. The different wings of this combination were to call themselves by such names and proclaim such principles in different States and localities as might seem to them most conducive to local success and united ascendancy. This abandonment of republicanism was likewise favored by such papers as the "Cin-

cinnati Gazette," which pronounced the policy of
Congressional prohibition worthless as a means of
excluding slavery from the Territories, and openly
committed itself to the admission of more slave
States, whenever demanded by a popular majority
in any Territory. "The Indianapolis Journal" and
other leading Republican organs spoke of Congressional prohibition as "murdered by Dred
Scott," and as having no longer any practical value.
In the spring of this year the Republicans of Indiana, in their State convention, not only surrendered the policy of Congressional prohibition, and
adopted the principle of popular sovereignty, but
made opposition to the Lecompton Constitution
the sole issue of the canvass. Under such leaders
as Oliver P. Morton and his Whig and Know-
Nothing associates, Republicanism simply meant
opposition to the latest outrage of slavery, and
acquiescence in all preceding ones; but this
shameful surrender of the cause to its enemies was
deservedly condemned in the election which followed. The Legislature of the State, however,
at its ensuing session, overwhelmingly endorsed
the Douglas dogma, and even the better class of
Republican papers urged the abandonment of the
Republican creed. But, very fortunately for the
cause, the Republicans of Illinois could not be
persuaded to take Mr. Douglas into their embrace
on the score of a single worthy act, and forget, if
not forgive, his long career of effective and un-

tiring hostility to the principles they cherished ; and his nomination by the Democrats, on a platform very offensive to Republicans, fully justified their course. The result was the nomination of Mr. Lincoln as a candidate for the succession to Mr. Douglas, and the great joint debate which did so much to educate the mind of the free States and prepare the way for Mr. Lincoln's nomination the following year, while revealing the moral unworthiness of his great rival, and justifying the policy which made necessary this memorable contest in Illinois.

The steady march of the Republican party toward ascendancy was shown in the Thirty-sixth Congress, which met in December, 1859. There were now twenty-four Republican senators, and one hundred and nine representatives. Early in the first session of this Congress an interesting debate occurred in the Senate on a proposition to provide for the education of the colored children of the District of Columbia. Mr. Mason condemned the proposition, and said it was wise to prohibit the education of the colored race. Jefferson Davis declared that the Government was not made for them, and that " we have no right to tax our people to educate the barbarians of Africa." These and kindred utterances were well calculated to aid the work of anti-slavery progress. John Brown's raid into Virginia kindled the ire of the slaveholders to a degree as yet unprecedented, and

although his act found few defenders in the Northern States, the heroism with which he met his
fate, the pithy correspondence between Gov. Wise
and Mrs. Child, the language of Southern senators
in dealing with the subject, and the efforts made
to ferret out Brown's associates, all tended to
strengthen the growing hostility to slavery and
prepare the way for the final conflict. The designs
of the slaveholders upon Cuba, which were avowed
in this Congress, and their purpose to acquire it for
the extension of slavery, by purchase if they could,
but if not by war, served the same purpose. The
growing demand for the revival of the African
slave trade, as shown by the avowals of leading
men in both houses of Congress, and their cold-
blooded. utterances on the subject, produced a profound impression on the country, and called forth
the startling fact that the city of New York was
then one of the greatest slave-trading marts in the
world, and that from thirty to sixty thousand
persons a year were taken from Africa to Cuba by
vessels from that single port. Such facts as these,
and that the laws of the Union for the suppression
of the traffic were not only a dead letter but that
the slave masters and their allies sullenly refused
to take any steps whatever for the remedy of this
organized inhumanity, were capital arguments for
the Republicans, which they employed with telling
effect. The refusal to admit Oregon as a State
without a constitutional provision excluding people

of color, the rejection of Kansas on her application
with a Constitution fairly adopted by her people, and
the great speech of Sumner on " The Barbarism of
Slavery," which this last application called forth,
all served their purpose in the growth of anti-
slavery opinion.   So did the attempt to divide California for the purpose of introducing slavery into
the southern portion; the veto of an Act of the
Territorial Legislature of Kansas abolishing slavery, and of a similar act in Nebraska; the acts of
several Southern States permitting free colored
persons to sell themselves as slaves if they chose
to do so in preference to expulsion from the land
of their birth and their homes; the decision of the
courts of Virginia that slaves had no social or civil
rights, and no legal capacity to choose between
being emancipated or sold as slaves; the refusal of
the Government to give a passport to a colored
physician of Massachusetts, for the reason that such
privileges were never conferred upon persons of
color ; and the revolutionary sentiments uttered by
governors and legislatures of various Southern
States, some of which declared that the election of
a Republican President would be sufficient cause for
withdrawal from the Union.   That these were important aids to the progress of freedom was shown
by the passage of laws in various Northern States
for the protection of personal liberty, forbidding the
use of local jails for the detention of persons claime.
as fugitive slaves, and securing for them the righ.

of trial by jury and the benefit of the writ of *habeas corpus.* This healthy reaction was still further shown in wholesome judicial decisions in several Northern States affirming the citizenship of negroes, and denying the right of transit of slave-holders with their slaves over their soil.

The struggle for the Speakership in this Congress, which lasted eight weeks, was also a first-rate training school for Republicanism. Helper's famous book, "The Impending Crisis," had made a decided sensation throughout the country, and John Sherman, the principal candidate of the Republicans for Speaker, had endorsed it, though he now denied the fact. Mr. Millson of Virginia, declared that the man who "consciously, deliberately, and of purpose, lends his name and influence to the propagation of such writings, is not only not fit to be Speaker, but he is not fit to live." De Jarnette, of the same State, said that Mr. Seward was "a perjured traitor, whom no Southerner could consistently support or even obey, should the nation elect him President." Mr. Pryor said that eight million Southern freemen could not be subjugated by any combination whatever, "least of all by a miscellaneous mob of crazy fanatics and conscience-stricken traitors." Mr. Kiett said that "should the Republican party succeed in the next Presidential election, my advice to the South is to snap the cords of the Union at once and forever." Mr. Crawford of Georgia said, " we will never submit to

the inauguration of a black Republican President ";
and these and like utterances were applauded by
the galleries. The growing madness and desperation in the Senate were equally noteworthy. This
was shown by the removal of Mr. Douglas from
the chairmanship of the Committee on Territories,
and the determined purpose to read him out of the
party for refusing to violate the principle of popular
sovereignty in the Territory of Kansas. The
attempt to hunt down a man who had done the
South such signal service in dragooning the Northern Democracy into its support could not fail to
divide the party, and at the same time completely
unmask the extreme and startling designs which
the slave power had been stealthily maturing. But
that power was now absolutely bent upon its purpose, and morally incapable of pausing in its work.
Its demand was a slave code for the Territories,
and it would accept nothing less. Jefferson Davis
was the champion of this policy, which he embodied in a series of resolutions and made them the
text of an elaborate argument ; and Mr. Douglas
replied in a speech which at once vindicated himself
and overwhelmingly condemned the party with
which he had so long acted. The resolutions, however, were adopted by the Senate, which thus pro-
claimed its purpose to nationalize slavery.

In the meantime these remarkable legislative proceedings had their counterpart in increasing lawlessness and violence throughout the South. This

was illustrated in such facts as the expulsion of members of the Methodist Church North from Texas, the imprisonment of Rev. Daniel Worth, in North Carolina, for circulating Helper's " Impending Crisis "; the exile from Kentucky of the Rev. John G. Fee and his colony of peaceable and law-abiding people, on account of their anti-slavery opinions ; and the espionage of the mails by every Southern postmaster, who under local laws had the power to condemn and "burn publicly" whatever he deemed unfit for circulation, which laws had been pronounced constitutional by Caleb Cushing, while Attorney General of the United States under Mr. Pierce, and were "cheerfully acquiesced in " by Judge Holt, Postmaster General under Buchanan. In Virginia the spirit of lawlessness became such a rage that one of her leading newspapers offered a reward of fifty thousand dollars for the head of Wm. H. Seward, while another paper offered ten thousand dollars for the kidnapping and delivery in Richmond of Joshua R. Giddings, or five thousand dollars for his head. In short, the reign of barbarism was at last fully ushered in, and the whole nation was beginning to realize the truth of Mr. Lincoln's declaration, which he borrowed from St. Mark, that "a house divided against itself can not stand." The people of the free States were at school, with the slaveholders as their masters ; and the dullest scholars were now beginning to get their lessons. Even the Know-Nothings and Silver-

Grey Whigs were coming up to the anxious seat, under the enlightening influence and saving-grace of slaveholding madness and crime. The hour was ripe for action, and the dawn of freedom in the South was seen in the coming emancipation of the North.

The Presidential Campaign of 1860 was a very singular commentary on the Compromise measures of 1850 and the "finality" platforms of 1852. The sectional agitation which now stirred the country outstripped all precedent, and completely demonstrated the folly of all schemes of compromise. The Democratic National Convention met in the city of Charleston on the twenty-third day of May. Its action now seems astounding, although it was the inevitable result of antecedent facts. The Democratic party had the control of every department of the Government, and a formidable popular majority behind it. It had the complete command of its own fortunes, and there was no cause or even excuse for the division which threatened its life. The difference between the Southern Democrats and the followers of Douglas was purely metaphysical, eluding entirely the practical common sense of the people. Both wings of the party now stood committed to the Dred Scott decision, and that surrendered everything which the extreme men of the South demanded. It was "a quarrel about goats' wool," and yet the Southern Democrats were maddened at the thought of submitting to

the nomination of Douglas for the Presidency.
His sin in the Lecompton matter was counted unpardonable, and they seemed to hate him even more
intensely than they hated the Abolitionists. A
committee on resolutions was appointed, which submitted majority and minority, or Douglas and
anti-Douglas, reports. These were hotly debated,
but the Douglas platform was adopted, which led
to the secession of the Southern delegates. On
the fifty-seventh ballot Mr. Douglas received a
clear majority of the Electoral College, but the
Convention then adjourned till the eighteenth of
June, in the hope that harmony might in some way
be restored. On reassembling this was found impossible, and the balloting was resumed, which
finally gave Mr. Douglas all the votes cast but
thirteen, and he was declared the Democratic nominee. The Convention then nominated for the
Vice Presidency Herschel V. Johnson, of Georgia,
a disciple of Calhoun, whose extreme opinions
were well known. He was unequivocally committed to the doctrine that neither the General
Government nor a Territorial Government can
impair the right of slave property in the common
Territories. This illustration of the political profligacy of the Douglas managers, and burlesque
upon popular sovereignty, was as remarkable as
the madness of the seceders in fighting him for his
supposed anti-slavery proclivities. The bolters
from this convention afterward nominated John C.

Breckenridge as their candidate for President and
Joseph Lane for Vice President. The Democratic
canvass was thus inaugurated, and the overthrow
of the party provided for in the mere wantonness
of political folly.

On the ninth of May what was called the Constitutional Union Party held its convention at Baltimore, and nominated John Bell for President and
Edward Everett for Vice President. It adopted no
platform, and owing to its neutrality of tint, its
action had no significance aside from its possible
effect on the result of the struggle between the
Democrats and Republicans.

The Republican National Convention met at
Chicago on the sixteenth of May. It was attended
by immense numbers, and its action was regarded
with profound and universal solicitude. The platform of the Convention affirmed the devotion of
the party to the union of the States and the rights
of the States; denounced the new dogma that the
Constitution carried slavery into the Territories;
declared freedom to be their normal condition;
denied the power of Congress or of a Territorial
Legislature to give legal existence to slavery in
any territory; branded as a crime the reopening of
the African slave trade; condemned the heresy of
Know-Nothingism, and demanded the passage of a
Homestead law. The principles of the party were
thus broadly stated and fully re-affirmed, and the
issues of the canvass very clearly presented.

The leading candidates were Seward and Lincoln, who pretty evenly divided the Convention, and thus created the liveliest interest in the result. The friends of Mr. Seward had unbounded confidence in his nomination, and their devotion to his fortunes was intense and absolute. The radical anti-slavery element in the party idolized him, and longed for his success as for a great and coveted national blessing. The delegates from New Jersey, Pennsylvania, Indiana, and Illinois, representing a superficial and only half-developed Republicanism, labored with untiring and exhaustless zeal for the nomination of Mr. Lincoln, fervently pleading for "Success rather than Seward." Henry S. Lane and Andrew G. Curtin, then candidates for Governor in the States of Indiana and Pennsylvania, respectively, were especially active and persistent, and their appeals were undoubtedly effective. When Seward was defeated many an anti-slavery man poured out his tears over the result, while deploring or denouncing the conservatism of old fossil Whiggery, which thus sacrificed the ablest man in the party, and the real hero of its principles. Time, however, led these men to reconsider their estimate both of Seward and Lincoln, and convinced them that the action of the convention, after all, was for the best. On the second ballot Hamlin was nominated for Vice President over Clay, Banks, Hickman, and others, and the Republican campaign thus auspiciously inaugurated.

The canvass for Douglas was prosecuted with remarkable energy and zeal. He was himself the great leader of his party on the stump, and his efforts evinced singular courage, audacity, and will. It soon became evident, however, that his election was impossible; but this did not cool his ardor or relax his efforts. He kept up the fight to the end ; and after his defeat, and when he saw the power that had destroyed him organizing its forces for the destruction of the Union, he espoused the side of his country, and never faltered in his course. But as to slavery he seemed to have no conscience, regarding it as a matter of total moral indifference, and thus completely confounding the distinction between right and wrong. During the closing hours of his life he probably saw and lamented this strange infatuation ; and he must, at all events, have deplored the obsequious and studied devotion of a life-time to the service of a power which at last demanded both the sacrifice of his country and himself. The canvass for Lincoln was conducted by the ablest men in the party, and was marked by great earnestness and enthusiasm. It was a repetition of the Fremont campaign, with the added difference of a little more contrivance and spectacular display in its demonstrations, as witnessed in the famous organization known as the " Wide-Awakes." The doctrines of the Chicago platform were very thoroughly discussed, and powerfully contributed to the further political education of the

people. The speeches of Mr. Seward were singularly able, effective and inspiring, and he was
the acknowledged leader of his party and the idol
of the Republican masses everywhere. This was
the day of his glory, and nothing yet foreshadowed
the political eclipse which awaited him in the near
future. The triumph of the Republicans in this
struggle was not, however, final. A great work
yet remained to be done. A powerful anti-slavery
party had at last appeared, as the slow creation of
events and the fruit of patient toil and endeavor;
but it had against it a popular majority of nearly
a million. Both Houses of Congress and the
Supreme Court of the United States disputed its
authority and opposed its advance. The President-
elect could not form his cabinet without the leave
of the Senate, which was controlled by slavery, nor
could he set the machinery of his Administration
in motion, at home or abroad, through the exercise
of his appointing power, without the consent of his
political opponents. As Mr. Seward declared in
the Senate, " he could not appoint a minister or
even a police agent, negotiate a treaty or procure
the passage of a law, and could hardly draw a
musket from the public arsenal to defend his own
person." The champions of slavery had no dream
of surrender, and no excuse whatever for extreme
measures ; and with moderate counsels and the
prudent economy of their advantages, they were
the undoubted masters of their own fortunes for

indefinite years to come. But their extravagant and exasperating demands, and the splendid madness of their latter day tactics as illustrated in their warfare against Douglas, were the sure presages of their overthrow. There was method in their madness, but it was the method of self-destruction. This was made still more strikingly manifest during the months immediately preceding the inauguration of Mr. Lincoln. The Republicans, notwithstanding their great victory, so recoiled from the thought of sectional strife that for the sake of peace they were ready to forego their demand for the Congressional prohibition of slavery in the Territories. They were willing to abide by the Dred Scott decision and the enforcement of the Fugitive Slave law. They even proposed a Constitutional amendment which would have made slavery perpetual in the Republic; but the pampered frenzy of the slave oligarchy defied all remedies, and hurried it headlong into the bloody conspiracy which was to close forever its career of besotted lawlessness and crime.

CHAPTER IX.

THE NEW ADMINISTRATION AND THE WAR.

EARLY in January, 1861, I paid a visit to Mr. Lincoln at his home in Springfield. I had a curiosity to see the famous " rail splitter," as he was then familiarly called, and as a member-elect of the Thirty-seventh Congress I desired to form some acquaintance with the man who was to play so conspicuous a part in the impending national crisis. Although I had zealously supported him in the canvass, and was strongly impressed by the grasp of thought and aptness of expression which marked his great debate with Douglas, yet as a thorough-going Free Soiler and a member of the radical wing of Republicanism, my prepossessions

(181)

were against him. He was a Kentuckian, and a
conservative Whig, who had supported General
Taylor in 1848, and General Scott four years later,
when the Whig party finally sacrificed both its
character and its life on the altar of slavery. His
nomination, moreover, had been secured through
the diplomacy of conservative Republicans, whose
morbid dread of "abolitionism" unfitted them, as I
believed, for leadership in the battle with slavery
which had now become inevitable, while the defeat of Mr. Seward had been to me a severe disappointment and a real personal grief. The rumor
was also current, and generally credited, that
Simon Cameron and Caleb B. Smith were to be
made Cabinet Ministers, in recognition of the important services rendered by the friends of these
gentlemen in the Chicago Convention. Still, I did
not wish to do Mr. Lincoln the slightest injustice,
while I hoped and believed his courage and firmness would prove equal to the emergency.

On meeting him I found him far better looking
than the campaign pictures had represented. His
face, when lighted up in conversation, was not un-
handsome, and the kindly and winning tones of his
voice pleaded for him like the smile which played
about his rugged features. He was full of anecdote and humor, and readily found his way to the
hearts of those who enjoyed a welcome to his fire-
side. His face, however, was sometimes marked
by that touching expression of sadness which be-

came so generally noticeable in the following years.
On the subject of slavery I was gratified to find
him less reserved and more emphatic than I expected. The Cabinet rumor referred to was true.
He felt bound by the pledges which his leading
friends had made in his name pending the National
Convention ; and the policy on which he acted in
these and many other appointments was forcibly
illustrated on a subsequent occasion, when I earnestly protested against the appointment of an incompetent and unworthy man as Commissioner of
Patents. "There is much force in what you say,"
said he, "but, in the balancing of matters, I guess
I shall have to appoint him." This "balancing
of matters" was a source of infinite vexation during his administration, as it has been to every one
of his successors ; and its most deplorable results
have been witnessed in the assassination of a president. Upon the whole, however, I was much
pleased with our first Republican Executive, and
I returned home more fully inspired than ever with
the purpose to sustain him to the utmost in facing
the duties of his great office.

The closing months of Mr. Buchanan's Administration were dismal and full of apprehension.
One by one the slaveholding States were seceding
from the Union. The President, in repeated mes-
sages, denied their right to secede, but denied also
the right of the Government to coerce them into
obedience. It should be remembered, to his credit,

that he did insist upon the right to enforce the
execution of the laws in all the States, and earnestly urged upon Congress the duty of arming
him with the power to do this; but Congress, much
to its discredit, paid no attention to his wishes,
leaving the new Administration wholly unprepared
for the impending emergency, while strangely up-
braiding the retiring President for his non-action.
For this there could be no valid excuse.   The people of the Northern States, now that the movement
in the South was seen to be something more than
mere bluster, were equally alarmed and bewildered.
The "New York Herald" declared that "coercion,
if it were possible, is out of the question." The
"Albany Argus" condemned it as "madness."
The "Albany Evening Journal" and many other
leading organs of Republicanism, East and West,
disowned it, and counseled conciliation and further
concessions to the demands of slavery.   The "New
York Tribune" emphatically condemned the policy of coercion, and even after the cotton States
had formed their Confederacy and adopted a provisional Government, it declared that "whenever
it shall be clear that the great body of the Southern people have become conclusively alienated
from the Union and anxious to escape from it, we
will do our best to forward their views." The
"Tribune" had before declared that "whenever a
considerable section of our Union shall deliberately
resolve to go out, we shall resist all coercive

measures designed to keep it in. We hope never
to live in a Republic whereof one section is
pinned to the other by bayonets." It is true,
that it justified the secession of the Southern
States as a revolutionary right; but although
these States defended it as a constitutional one,
the broader and higher ground of Mr. Greeley
necessarily gave powerful aid and comfort to their
movement. In the meantime, great meetings
in Philadelphia and New York strongly condemned the Abolitionists, and urged the most extravagant additional concessions to slavery for the
sake of peace. On the 12th of January Mr. Seward made his great speech in the Senate, declaring that he could "afford to meet prejudice with
conciliation, exaction with concession which sur-
renders no principle, and violence with the right
hand of peace." He was willing to give up Congressional prohibition of slavery in the Territories,
enforce the Fugitive Slave law, and perpetuate
slavery in the Republic by amending the Constitution for that purpose. The Crittenden compromise,
which practically surrendered everything to slavery, only failed in the Senate by one vote, and this
failure resulted from the non-voting of six rebel
senators, who were so perfectly devil-bent upon
the work of national dismemberment that they
would not listen to any terms of compromise, or
permit their adoption. The Peace Congress, assembled for the purpose of devising some means

of national pacification, agreed upon a series of measures covering substantially the same ground as the Crittenden compromise, while both Houses of Congress agreed to a constitutional amendment denying any power to interfere with slavery " until every State in the Union, by its individual State action, shall consent to its exercise." The feverish dread of war which prevailed throughout the Northern States was constantly aggravated by multiplying evidences of slaveholding desperation. The general direction of public opinion pointed to the Abolitionists as the authors of these national troubles, while the innocent and greatly-abused slaveholders were to be petted and placated by any measures which could possibly serve the purpose. Indeed, the spirit of Northern submission had never, in the entire history of the anti-slavery conflict, been more strikingly exhibited than during the last days of the Thirty-sixth Congress, when the Capital of the Republic was threatened by armed treason, and the President-elect reached Washington in a disguise which baffled the assassins who had conspired against his life. To the very last the old medicine of compromise and conciliation seemed to be the sovereign hope of the people of the free States; and although it had failed utterly, and every offer of friendship and peace had been promptly spurned as the evidence of weakness or cowardice, they clung to it till the guns of Fort Sumter roused them from their perilous dream.

The inauguration of the President was awaited with great anxiety and alarm. The capture of Washington by the rebels was seriously apprehended, and had undoubtedly been meditated. The air was filled with rumors respecting the assassination of the President, and the stories told of the various methods of his taking off would have been amusing if the crisis had not been so serious. General Scott took all the precautions for the preservation of the peace which the small force at his command, and the District militia, enabled him to do. The day was beautiful, and the procession to the Capitol quite imposing. Mr. Lincoln and ex-President Buchanan entered the Senate chamber arm in arm; and the latter was so withered and bowed with age that in contrast with the towering form of Mr. Lincoln he seemed little more than half a man. The crowd which greeted the President in front of the east portico of the Capitol was immense, and has never been equaled on any similar occasion with the single exception of General Garfield's inauguration. Mr. Lincoln's voice, though not very strong or full-toned, rang out over the acres of people before him with surprising distinctness, and was heard in the remotest parts of his audience. The tone of moderation, tenderness, and good-will, which marked his address, made an evident impression, and the most heartfelt plaudits were called forth by the closing passage :

"We are not enemies, but friends. We must not be enemies. Though passion may have strained, it must not break, our bonds of affection. The mystic cords of memory, stretching from every battle-field and patriot grave to every living heart and hearthstone all over this broad land, will yet swell the chorus of union, when again touched, as they surely will be, by the better angels of their nature."

But as an offering of friendship and fair dealing to the South, this speech failed of its purpose as signally as all kindred endeavors had done from the beginning. The "Richmond Enquirer" and "Whig," the "Charleston Mercury," and other leading organs of secession, denounced the inaugural, and seemed to be maddened by the very kindliness of its tone and the moderation of its demands. Their purpose was disunion and war, and every passing day multiplied the proofs that no honorable escape from this fearful alternative was possible.

The policy of the new Administration prior to the attack upon Sumter forms perhaps the most remarkable chapter in the history of the war. All the troubles of the previous Administration were now turned over to Mr. Lincoln, and while no measures had been provided to aid him in their settlement the crisis was constantly becoming more imminent. The country was perfectly at sea; and while all hope of reconciliation was fading from day to day, Mr. Seward insisted that peace would come within "sixty days." His optimism would have been most amusing, if the salvation of the country had not been at stake. The President himself not only still hoped, but believed, that there would be no war; and notwithstanding all the abuse that had been heaped upon Mr. Buchanan by the Republicans for his feeble and vacillating course, and especially his denial of the right of the government to coerce the recusant States, the policy of the new Administration, up to the attack upon Sumter, was identical with that of his predecessor. In Mr. Seward's official letter to Mr. Adams, dated April 10, 1861, he says the President "would not be disposed to reject a cardinal dogma of theirs (the secessionists), namely, that the Federal Government could not reduce the seceding States to obedience by conquest, even though he were disposed to question that proposition. But in fact the President willingly accepts it as true. Only an imperial and despotic Government could subjugate thoroughly disaffected and insurrectionary members of the State. * * * The President, on the one hand, will not suffer the Federal authority to fall into abeyance, nor will he, on the other hand, aggravate existing evils by attempts at coercion, which must assume the direct form of war against any of the revolutionary States." These are very remarkable avowals, in the light of the absolute unavoidableness of the conflict at the time they

were made; and they naturally tended to precipi-
tate rather than to avert the threatened catastrophe.
It will not do to say that Secretary Seward spoke
only for himself, and not for the Administration;
for the fact has since been established by the evidence of other members of the Cabinet that Mr.
Lincoln, while he had great faith in Mr. Seward at
first, was always himself the President.   No member of it was his dictator.   I do not say that he endorsed all Mr. Seward's peculiar views, for the
latter went still further, as the country has since
learned, and favored the abandonment of Fort
Sumter and other Southern forts, as a part of a
scheme of pacification looking to an amendment
of the Constitution in the interest of slavery.
During this early period Mr. Chase himself, with
all his anti-slavery radicalism and devotion to the
Union, became so far the child of the hour as to
deprecate the policy of coercion and express his
belief that if the rebel States were allowed to go in
peace they would soon return.   But "war legis-
lates," and the time had now come when nothing else could break the spell of irresolution and
blindness which threatened the Union even more
seriously than armed treason itself.

Notwithstanding this strange epoch of Republican feebleness and indecision, the warfare against
Mr. Buchanan was never intermitted.   It had been
prosecuted with constantly increasing vigor since
the year 1856, and had now become so perfectly

relentless and overwhelming that he was totally
submerged by the waves of popular wrath ; and for
twenty odd years no political resurrection has been
thought possible. Although his personal integrity
was as unquestionable as that of John C. Calhoun
or George III, and his private life as stainless,
yet his public character has received no quarter
from his enemies and but little defense from his
friends. One of his most formidable critics, writing long years after the war, describes him as
" hungry for regard, influence and honor, but too
diminutive in intellect and character to feel the
glow of true ambition—a man made, so to speak,
to be neither loved nor hated, esteemed nor despised, slighted nor admired ; intended to play an
influential part in the agitation of parties, and by
history to be silently numbered with the dead, because in all his doings there was not a single deed ;
a man to whom fate could do nothing worse than
place him at the helm in an eventful period."
While there is a measure of truth in this picture, I
believe any fair-minded man will pronounce it over-
drawn, one-sided, and unjust, after reading the recently published life of Mr. Buchanan by George
Ticknor Curtis, dealing fully with his entire public
career in the clear, cold light of historic facts.
The most pronounced political foe of Mr. Buchanan can not go over the pages of this elaborate
and long-delayed defense without modifying some
of his most decided opinions ; but one thing remains

obviously true, and that is that in dealing with the question of slavery Mr. Buchanan was wholly without a conscience. The thought seems never to have dawned upon him that the slave was a man, and therefore entitled to his natural rights. In a public speech on the ninth of July, 1860, defining his position, and referring to the Dred Scott decision, he says: "It is to me the most extraordinary thing in the world that this country should now be distracted and divided because certain persons at the North will not agree that their brethren at the South should have the same rights in the Territories which they enjoy. What would I, as a Pennsylvanian, say or do, supposing any one was to contend that the Legislature of any Territory could outlaw iron or coal within the Territory? The principle is precisely the same. The Supreme Court of the United States has decided, what was known to us all to have been the existing state of affairs for fifty years, that slaves are property. Admit that fact, and you admit everything."

In this passage, as in all that he has written on the subject of slavery, humanity is totally ignored. The right of property in man is just as sacred to him, "as a Pennsylvanian," as the right of property in iron or coal. He unhesitatingly accepts the Dred Scott decision as law, which the moral sense of the nation and its ablest jurists pronounced a nullity. Mr. Jefferson, in speaking of slavery, said he trembled for his country, and declared that

one hour of bondage is fraught with more misery
·than whole ages of our colonial oppression.   Such
a sentiment in the mouth of Mr. Buchanan would
have been as unnatural as a voice from the dead.
He saw nothing morally offensive in slavery, or
repugnant to the principles of Democracy.   He
reverenced the Constitution, but always forgot that
its compromises were agreed to in the belief that
the institution was in a state of decay, and would
soon wear out its life under the pressure of public
opinion and private interest.   Throughout his
public life he never faltered in his devotion to the
South, joining hands with alacrity in every measure which sought to nationalize her sectional interest.   The growing anti-slavery opinion of the
free States, which no power could prevent, and the
great moral currents of the times, which were as
resistless as the tides of the sea, had no meaning
for him, because the Democracy he believed in had
no foundation in the sacredness of human rights.

   Mr. Lincoln, in spite of the troubled state of
the country, was obliged to encounter an army of
place-seekers at the very beginning of his administration.   I think there has been nothing like it in
the history of the Government.   A Republican
member of Congress could form some idea of the
President's troubles from his own experience.   I
fled from my home in the latter part of February,
in the hope of finding some relief from these im-
portunities; but on reaching Washington I found
   13

the business greatly aggravated. The pressure was so great and constant that I could scarcely find time for my meals, or to cross the street, and I was obliged to give my days and nights wholly to the business, hoping in this way I should be able in a little while to finish it; but it constantly increased. I met at every turn a swarm of miscellaneous people, many of them looking as hungry and fierce as wolves, and ready to pounce upon members as they passed, begging for personal intercession, letters of recommendation, etc. During my stay in Washington through the months of March and April, there was no pause in this business. After Fort Sumter had been taken and the armory at Harper's Ferry had been burned; after a Massachusetts regiment had been fired on in passing through Baltimore, and thirty thousand men were in Washington for defensive purposes; after the President had called for seventy-five thousand volunteers, and the whole land was in a blaze of excitement, the scuffle for place was unabated, and the pressure upon the strength and patience of the President unrelieved. This was not very remarkable, considering the long-continued monopoly of the offices by the Democrats; but it jarred upon the sentiment of patriotism in such a crisis, and to those who were constantly brought face to face with it, it sometimes appeared as if the love of office alone constituted the animating principle of the party.

When Congress assembled in special session on the Fourth of July, the atmosphere of the Northern States had been greatly purified by the attack on Fort Sumter. The unavoidableness of war was now absolute, and the tone of the President's message was far bolder and better than that of his inaugural. The policy of tenderness towards slavery, however, still revealed itself, and called forth the criticism of the more radical Republicans. They began to distrust Mr. Seward, who no longer seemed to them the hero of principle they had so long idolized, while his growing indifference to the virtue of temperance was offensive to many. He impressed his old anti-slavery friends as a deeply disappointed man, who was in danger of being morally lost. Their faith was even a *little* shaken in Secretary Chase. Of course, they did not believe him false to his long-cherished anti-slavery convictions, but he was amazingly ambitious, and in the dispensation of his patronage he seemed anxious to make fair weather with some of his old conservative foes, while apparently forgetting the faithful friends who had stood by him from the very beginning of his career, and were considered eminently fit for the positions they sought. The rumor was afloat that even Charles Sumner was urging the claims of Mr. Crittenden to a place on the Supreme Bench, as a means of conciliating the State of Kentucky. Washington was largely a city of secessionists, and the departments of the

Government were plentifully supplied by sympathizers with treason, while the effort put forth at this session to dislodge them was not responded to by the Administration. What became known as the Border State policy was beginning to assert itself everywhere, and was strikingly illustrated in the capture of fugitive slaves and their return to their rebel masters by our commanding generals, and by reiterated and gratuitous disavowals of "abolitionism" by prominent Republicans.

But the war spirit was fully aroused, and active preparations were on foot for an advance upon the enemy. The confidence in General Scott seemed to be unbounded, and I found everybody taking it for granted that when the fight began our forces would prove triumphantly victorious. On the day before the battle of Bull Run I obtained a pass from General Scott, intending to witness the engagement, believing I could do so, of course, with perfect safety, as our army would undoubtedly triumph. I had a very strong curiosity to see a great battle, and was now gratified with the prospect of doing so; but a lucky accident detained me. The battle was on Sunday, and about eleven o'clock at night I was roused from my slumber by Col. Forney, who resided on Capital Hill near my lodgings, and who told me our army had been routed, and that the rebels were marching upon the capital and would in all probability capture it before morning. No unmiraculous event could have

been more startling. I was perfectly stunned and
dumbfounded by the news; but I hastened down
to the Avenue as rapidly as possible, and found the
space between the Capitol and the Treasury Building a moving mass of humanity. Every man
seemed to be asking every man he met for the
latest news, while all sorts of rumors filled the air.
A feeling of mingled horror and despair appeared to
possess everybody. The event was so totally un-
looked for, and the disappointment so terrible, that
people grew suddenly sick at heart, and felt as if
life itself, with all its interests and charms, had been
snatched from their grasp. The excitement, turmoil and consternation continued during the night
and through the following day; but no one could
adequately picture or describe it. Our soldiers
came straggling into the city, covered with dirt
and many of them wounded, while the panic
which led to the disaster spread like a contagion
through all classes.

On the day following this battle Congress met
as usual, and undoubtedly shared largely in the
general feeling. A little before the battle General
Mansfield had issued an order declaring that fugitive slaves would under no circumstances whatever
be permitted to reside or be harbored in the quarters and camps of the troops serving in his department; and now, both Houses of Congress promptly and with great unanimity and studious emphasis
declared that the purpose of the war was not the

"conquest" or "subjugation" of the conspirators
who were striking at the Nation's life, or the overthrow of their "established institutions," but to defend "the supremacy of the Constitution," and to
"preserve the Union"; and that "as soon as these
objects are accomplished the war ought to cease."
To thorough-going anti-slavery men this seemed
like an apology for the war, and a most ill-timed
revival of the policy of conciliation, which had
been so uniformly and contemptuously spurned
by the enemy.   It failed utterly of its purpose, and
this historic resolve of Congress was only useful
to the rebels, who never failed to wield it as a
weapon against us, after the teaching of events had
compelled us to make slavery the point of attack.
The Confiscation Act of the 6th of August was regarded as a child of the same sickly ancestry.
The section of the Act making free the slaves employed against us by the rebels in their military
operations was criticised as a bribe to them to fight
us, rather than a temptation to espouse our cause.
If they engaged in the war at all, they were obliged
to do so as our enemies; but if they remained
at home on their plantations in the business of
feeding the rebel armies, they would have the protection of both the loyal and Confederate Governments.   The policy of both parties to the struggle
was thus subordinated to the protection of slavery.
· But on the 31st of August a new war policy was
inaugurated by the proclamation of General Fre-

mont, giving freedom to the slaves of rebels in his
department. It was greeted by the people of the
Northern States with inexpressible gladness and
thanksgiving. The Republican press everywhere
applauded it, and even such Democratic and conservative papers as the "Boston Post," the "Detroit
Free Press," the "Chicago Times," and the "New
York Herald" approved it. During the ten days
of its life all party lines seemed to be obliterated
in the fires of popular enthusiasm which it kindled,
and which was wholly unprecedented in my experience. I was then on the stump in my own
State, and I found the masses everywhere so wild
with joy, that I could scarcely be heard for their
shouts. As often as I mentioned the name of "Fremont," the prolonged hurrahs of the multitude followed, and the feeling seemed to be universal that
the policy of "a war on peace principles" was
abandoned, and that slavery, the real cause of the
war, was no longer to be the chief obstacle to its
prosecution.

But in the midst of this general exultation and
joy the President annulled the proclamation because it went beyond the Confiscation Act of the
6th of August, and was offensive to the Border
States. It was a terrible disappointment to the
Republican masses, who could not understand
why loyal slaveholders in Kentucky should be offended because the slaves of rebels in Missouri were
declared free. From this revocation of the new

war policy, dated the pro-slavery reaction which at once followed. It balked the popular enthusiasm which was drawing along with it multitudes of conservative men. It caused timid and halting men to become cowards outright. It gave new life to slavery, and encouraged fiercer assaults upon "abolitionism." It revived and stimulated Democratic sympathy for treason wherever it had existed, and necessarily prolonged the conflict and aggravated its sorrows; while it repeated the ineffable folly of still relying upon a policy of moderation and conciliation in dealing with men who had defiantly taken their stand outside of the Constitution and laws, and could only be reached by the power of war.

When Congress met in December, the policy of deference to slavery still continued. The message of the President was singularly dispassionate, deprecating "radical and extreme measures," and recommending some plan of colonization for the slaves made free by the Confiscation Act. Secretary Cameron, however, surprised the country by the avowal of a decidedly anti-slavery war policy in his report; but in a discussion in the House early in December, on General Halleck's "Order No. Three," I took occasion to expose his insincerity by referring to his action a little while before in restoring to her master a slave girl who had fled to the camp of Colonel Brown, of the Twentieth Indiana regiment, who had refused to give her up. On the nineteenth of December, a joint select Committee on the Conduct of the War was appointed, composed of three members of the Senate and four members of the House. The Senators were B. F. Wade, of Ohio; Z. Chandler, of Michigan, and Andrew Johnson, of Tennessee; and the House members were John Covode, of Pennsylvania; M. F. Odell, of New York; D. W. Gooch, of Massachusetts, and myself. The committee had its birth in the popular demand for a more vigorous prosecution of the war, and less tenderness toward slavery; and I was gratified with my position on it because it afforded a very desirable opportunity to learn something of the movements of our armies and the secrets of our policy.

On the sixth of January, by special request of the President, the committee met him and his Cabinet at the Executive Mansion, to confer about the military situation. The most striking fact revealed by the discussion which took place was that neither the President nor his advisers seemed to have any definite information respecting the management of the war, or the failure of our forces to make any forward movement. Not a man of them pretended to know anything of General McClellan's plans. We were greatly surprised to learn that Mr. Lincoln himself did not think he had any *right* to know, but that, as he was not a military man, it was his duty to defer to General McClellan. Our grand

armies were ready and eager to march, and the
whole country was anxiously waiting some decisive
movement; but during the delightful months of
October, November and December, they had been
kept idle for some reason which no man could explain, but which the President thought could be
perfectly accounted for by the General-in-Chief.
Secretary Cameron said he knew nothing of any
plan for a forward movement. Secretary Seward
had entire confidence in General McClellan, and
thought the demand of the committee for a more
vigorous policy uncalled for. The Postmaster-
General made no definite avowals, while the other
members of the Cabinet said nothing, except Secretary Chase, who very decidedly sympathized with
the committee in its desire for some early and decisive movement of our forces. The spectacle seemed
to us very disheartening. The testimony of all the
commanding generals we had examined showed
that our armies had been ready to march for months;
that the weather and roads had been most favorable since October ; and that the Army of the Potomac was in a fine state of discipline, and nearly two
hundred thousand strong, while only about forty
thousand men were needed to make Washington
perfectly safe. Not a general examined could tell
why this vast force had so long been kept idle, or
what General McClellan intended to do. The fate
of the nation seemed committed to one man called
a " General-in-Chief," who communicated his

secrets to no human being, and who had neither age nor military experience to justify the extraordinary deference of the President to his wishes. He had repeatedly appeared before the committee, though not yet as a witness, and we could see no evidence of his pre-eminence over other prominent commanders; and it seemed like a betrayal of the country itself to allow him to hold our grand armies for weeks and months in unexplained idleness, on the naked assumption of his superior wisdom. Mr. Wade, as Chairman of the committee, echoed its views in a remarkably bold and vigorous speech, in which he gave a summary of the principal facts which had come to the knowledge of the committee, arraigned General McClellan for the unaccountable tardiness of his movements, and urged upon the Administration, in the most undiplomatic plainness of speech, an immediate and radical change in the policy of the war. But the President and his advisers could not yet be disenchanted, and the conference ended without results.

When General McClellan was placed at the head of our armies the country accepted him as its idol and hero. The people longed for a great captain, and on very inadequate grounds they assumed that they had found him, and that the business of war was to be carried on in earnest. But they were doomed to disappointment, and the popular feeling was at length completely reversed. The pendulum vibrated to the other extreme, and it is not easy to realize the wide-spread popular discontent which finally revealed itself respecting the dilatory movements of our forces. The people became inexpressibly weary of the reiterated bulletins that "all is quiet on the Potomac"; and the fact that General McClellan was in full sympathy with the Border State policy of the President aggravated their unfriendly mood. A majority of the members of the committee became morbidly sensitive, and were practically incapable of doing General McClellan justice. They were thoroughly discouraged and disgusted; but when Secretary Cameron left the Cabinet and Stanton took his place, their despondency gave place to hope. He had faith in the usefulness of the committee, and co-operated with it to the utmost. · He agreed with us fully in our estimate of General McClellan, and as to the necessity of an early forward movement. We were delighted with him, and had perfect confidence in his integrity, sagacity and strong will. We worked from five to six hours per day, including the holiday season, and not excepting the Sabbath, going pretty thoroughly into the Bull Run disaster, the battle of Ball's Bluff, and the management of the Western Department.

During the months of January and February, the committee made repeated visits to the President for the purpose of urging the division of the Army of the Potomac and its organization into army corps. We insisted upon this on the strength

of the earnest recommendations of our chief commanders, and with a view to greater military effi-
ciency; but the President said General McClellan
was opposed to it, and would, he believed, resign
his command in the alternative of being required
to do it. Mr. Lincoln said he dreaded "the moral
effect of this"; but in the latter part of February,
he began to lose his faith in the General, and
finally, after nearly two months of perseverance by
the committee, he gave his order early in March,
which General McClellan obeyed with evident hesitation and very great reluctance. A few days later
the long-tried patience of the President became
perfectly exhausted. He surprised and delighted
the committee by completely losing his temper,
and on the 11th relieved General McClellan from
the command of all our forces except the Army of
the Potomac. The rebels, in the meantime, had
evacuated their works at Centreville and Manassas,
and retreated with their munitions in safety. A
majority of the committee at this time strongly
suspected that General McClellan was a traitor,
and they felt strengthened in this suspicion by
what they afterward saw for themselves at Centreville and Manassas, which they visited on the
thirteenth of March. They were certain, at all
events, that his heart was not in the work. He
had disregarded the President's general order of
the nineteenth of January, for a movement of all
our armies, which resulted in the series of vic-

tories of Fort Henry, Fort Donelson, etc., which
so electrified the country. He had protested
against the President's order of the thirty-first of
January, directing an expedition for the purpose
of seizing a point upon the railroad southwest of
Manassas Junction. He had opposed all forward
movements of the Army of the Potomac, and resolutely set his face against the division of our forces
into army corps, as urged by all our chief commanders. And he had again and again refused to
co-operate with the navy in breaking up the
blockade of the Potomac, while his order to move
in the direction of the enemy at Centreville and
Manassas was given after the evacuation of these
points.

Our journey to Manassas was full of interest and
excitement. About ten miles from Washington
we came in sight of a large division of the Grand
Army of the Potomac, which had started toward
the enemy in obedience to the order of General
McClellan. The forest on either side of the road
was alive with soldiers, and their white tents were
to be seen in all directions through the pine forests,
while in the adjacent fields vast bodies of soldiers
in their uniforms were marching and counter-
marching, their bayonets glittering in the sun-
light. Large bodies of cavalry were also in motion, and the air was filled with the sound of mar-
tial music and the blasts of the bugle. Soldiers
not on drill were running races, playing ball, and

enjoying themselves generally in every sort of sport. The spectacle was delightfully exhilarating, and especially so to men just released from the dreary confinement and drudgery of their committee rooms.

CHAPTER X.

THE NEW ADMINISTRATION AND THE WAR (CONTINUED).

The wooden guns—Conference with Secretary Stanton—His relations to Lincoln—Strife between Radicalism and Conservatism—Passage of the Homestead Law—Visit to the President—The Confiscation Act and rebel landowners—Greeley's "prayer of twenty millions," and Lincoln's reply—Effort to disband the Republican party—The battle of Fredericksburg and General Burnside—The Proclamation of Emancipation—Visit to Mr. Lincoln—General Fremont—Report of the War Committee—Visit to Philadelphia and New York—Gerrit Smith—The Morgan Raid.

ON approaching Centreville the first object th at attracted our attention was one of the huge earthworks of the enemy, with large logs placed in the embrasures, the ends pointing toward us, and painted black, in imitation of cannon. The earthworks seemed very imperfectly constructed, and from this fact, and the counterfeit guns which surmounted them, it was evident that no fight had been seriously counted on by the absconding forces. The substantial character of their barracks, bake-ovens, stables, and other improvements, confirmed this view; and on reaching Manassas we found the same cheap defenses and the same

(208)

evidences of security, while the rebel forces were much less than half as great as ours, and within a day's march from us. What was the explanation of all this? Why had we not, long before, driven in the rebel pickets, and given battle to the enemy, or at least ascertained the facts as to the weakness of his position? Could the commander be loyal who had opposed all the previous forward movements of our forces, and only made this advance after the enemy had evacuated? These were the questions canvassed by the members of the committee in their passionate impatience for decisive measures, and which they afterward earnestly pressed upon the President as a reason for relieving General McClellan of his command. They were also greatly moved by the fact already referred to, that General McClellan had neglected and repeatedly refused to co-operate with the navy in breaking up the blockade of the Potomac, which could have been done long before according to the testimony of our commanders, while he had disobeyed the positive order of the President respecting the defenses of Washington by reserving only nineteen thousand imperfectly disciplined men for that service, through which the capital had been placed at the mercy of the enemy. Meanwhile the flame of popular discontent had found further fuel in the threats of McClellan to put down slave insurrections " with an iron hand," and his order expelling the Hutchinson from the Army

14

of the Potomac for singing Whittier's songs of liberty. Of course I am not dealing with the character and capacity of General McClellan as a commander, but simply depicting the feeling which extensively prevailed at this time, and which justified itself by hastily accepting merely apparent facts as conclusive evidence against him.

On the 24th day of March, Secretary Stanton sent for the committee for the purpose of having a confidential conference as to military affairs. He was thoroughly discouraged. He told us the President had gone back to his first love as to General McClellan, and that it was needless for him or for us to labor with him, although he had finally been prevailed on to restrict McClellan's command to the Army of the Potomac. The Secretary arraigned the General's conduct in the severest terms, particularizing his blunders, and branding them. He told us the President was so completely in the power of McClellan that he had recently gone to Alexandria in person to ask him for some troops from the Army of the Potomac for General Fremont, which were refused. He said he believed there were traitors among the commanders surrounding General McClellan, and if he had had the power he would have dismissed eight commanders when the wooden-gun discovery was made ; and he fully agreed with us as to the disgraceful fact that our generals had not long before discovered, as they could have done, the real facts as to the rebel forces and their defenses.

It was quite evident from these facts that Stanton, with all his force of will, did not rule the President, as the public has generally supposed. He would frequently overawe and sometimes browbeat others, but he was never imperious in dealing with Mr. Lincoln. This I have from Mr. Watson, for some time Assistant Secretary of War, and Mr. Whiting while Solicitor of the War Department. Lincoln, however, had the highest opinion of Stanton, and their relations were always most kindly, as the following anecdote bears witness: A committee of Western men, headed by Lovejoy, procured from the President an important order looking to the exchange and transfer of Eastern and Western soldiers with a view to more effective work. Repairing to the office of the Secretary, Mr. Lovejoy explained the scheme, as he had before done to the President, but was met with a flat refusal.

"But we have the President's order, sir," said Lovejoy.

"Did Lincoln give you an order of that kind?" said Stanton.

"He did, sir."

"Then he is a d——d fool," said the irate secretary.

"Do you mean to say the President is a d——d fool?" asked Lovejoy, in amazement.

"Yes, sir, if he gave you such an order as that."

The bewildered Illinoisan betook himself at once to the President, and related the result of his conference.

" Did Stanton say I was a d——d fool ? " asked Lincoln at the close of the recital.

" He did, sir, and repeated it."

After a moment's pause, and looking up, the President said, " If Stanton said I was a d——d fool, then I must be one, for he is nearly always right, and generally says what he means. I will step over and see him."

Whether this anecdote is literally true or not, it illustrates the character of the two men.

On Sunday, the thirteenth of April, we were again summoned to meet Secretary Stanton, and he had also invited Thaddeus Stevens, of the House Ways and Means Committee, Mr. Fessenden, of the Senate Finance Committee, and Mr. Wilson and Colonel Blair, of the Senate and House Military Committees. The business of this conference was to consider the necessity of immediate measures for raising thirty million dollars to pay the troops un-wisely accepted by the President in excess of the number called for by Congress, and the proper action to be taken relative to the sale of Austrian guns by a house in New York for shipment to the enemy. The Secretary was this time in fine spirits, and I was much interested in the free talk which occurred. Mr. Stevens indulged in his customary bluntness of speech, including a little spice of profanity by way of emphasis and embellishment. He declared that not a man in the Cabinet, the present com-pany excepted, was fit for his business. Mr. Fes-

senden said he fully endorsed this, while sly glances
were made at Colonel Blair, whose brother was
thus palpably hit. Mr. Stevens said he was tired
of hearing d——d Republican cowards talk about
the Constitution; that there *was* no Constitution
any longer so far as the prosecution of the war was
concerned; and that we should strip the rebels of
all their rights, and give them a reconstruction on
such terms as would end treason forever. Secretary Stanton agreed to every word of this, and said
it had been his policy from the beginning. Fessenden denounced slave-catching in our army, and
referred to a recent case in which fugitives came
to our lines with the most valuable information as
to rebel movements, and were ordered out of camp
into the clutches of their hunters. Stanton said
that ten days before McClellan marched toward
Manassas, contrabands had come to him with the
information that the rebels were preparing to retreat, but that McClellan said he could not trust
them. Wade was now roused, and declared that
he had heard McClellan say he had uniformly
found the statements of these people reliable, and
had got valuable information from them. But
McClellan was still king, and the country was a.
long way yet from that vigorous war policy which
alone could save it.

In the meantime the strife between the radical and
conservative elements in the Republican party found
expression in other directions. Secretary Seward, in

his letter to Mr. Dayton, of the 22d of April, declared that "the rights of the States and the condition of every human being in them will remain subject to exactly the same laws and forms of administration, whether the revolution shall succeed or whether it shall fail." Secretary Smith had previously declared, in a public speech, that "this is not a war upon the institution of slavery, but a war for the restoration of the Union," and that "there could not be found in South Carolina a man more anxious, religiously and scrupulously, to observe all the features of the Constitution, than Abraham Lincoln." He also opposed the arming of the negroes, declaring that "it would be a disgrace to the people of the free States to call on four millions of blacks to aid in putting down eight millions of whites." Similar avowals were made by other members of the Cabinet. This persistent purpose of the Administration to save the Union and save slavery with it, naturally provoked criticism, and angered the anti-slavery feeling of the loyal States. The business of slave-catching in the army continued the order of the day, till the pressure of public opinion finally compelled Congress to prohibit it by a new article of war, which was approved by the President on the 13th of March. The repressive power of the Administration, however, was very formidable, and although the House of Representatives, as early as the 20th of December, 1861, had adopted a resolution offered by myself, instructing the Judiciary Committee to

report a bill so amending the Fugitive Slave Act
of 1850 as to forbid the return of fugitives without
proof first made of the loyalty of the claimant, yet
on the 26th of May, 1862, the House, then overwhelmingly Republican, voted down a bill declaring free the slaves of armed rebels, and making
proof of loyalty by the claimant of a fugitive necessary to his recovery. This vote sorely disappointed
the anti-slavery sentiment of the country. On this
measure I addressed the House in a brief speech,
the spirit of which was heartily responded to by my
constituents and the people of the loyal States generally. They believed in a vigorous prosecution of
the war, and were sick of "the never-ending gabble
about the sacredness of the Constitution." " It will
not be forgotten," I said, " that the red-handed mur-
derers and thieves who set this rebellion on foot
went out of the Union yelping for the Constitution
which they had conspired to overthrow by the
blackest perjury and treason that ever confronted
the Almighty." This speech was the key-note of
my approaching Congressional canvass, and I was
one of the very few men of decided anti-slavery convictions who were able to stem the conservative
tide which swept over the Northern States during
this dark and dismal year. I had against me the
general drift of events; the intense hostility of Governor Morton and his friends throughout the State;
nearly all the politicians in the District, and nine of
its twelve Republican newspapers, and the des-

perate energy and cunning of trained leaders in both
political parties, who had pursued me like vultures
for a dozen years. My triumph had no taint of
compromise in it, and nothing saved me but perfect
courage and absolute defiance of my foes.

One of the great compensations of the war was
the passage of the Homestead Act of the 20th of
May. It finally passed the House and Senate by
overwhelming majorities. Among the last acts of
Mr. Buchanan's administration was the veto of a
similar measure, at the bidding of his Southern
masters; and the friends of the policy had learned
in the struggle of a dozen years that its success was
not possible while slavery ruled the government.
The beneficent operation of this great and far-
reaching measure, however, was seriously crippled
by some unfortunate facts. In the first place, it provided no safeguards against speculation in the public domain, which had so long scourged the Western States and Territories, and was still extending
its ravages. Our pioneer settlers were offered homes
of one hundred and sixty acres each on condition
of occupancy and improvement, but the speculator
could throw himself across their track by buying
up large bodies of choice land to be held back from
settlement and tillage for a rise in price, and thus
force them further into the frontier, and on to less
desirable lands.

In the next place, under the new and unguarded
land-grant policy, which was simultaneously in-

augurated, millions of acres fell into the clutches of
monopolists, and are held by them to-day, which
would have gone to actual settlers under the Homestead law, and the moderate land-grant policy orig-
inated by Senator Douglas in 1850. This was not
foreseen or intended. The nation was then engaged
in a struggle for its existence. and thus exposed to
the evils of hasty legislation. The value of the lands
given away was not then understood as it has been
since, while the belief was universal that the lands
granted would be restored to the public domain on
failure to comply with the conditions of the grants.
The need of great highways to the Pacific was then
regarded as imperative, and unattainable without
large grants of the public lands. These are exten-
uating facts; but the mischiefs of this ill-starred legislation are none the less to be deplored.

In the third place, under our new Indian treaty
policy, invented about the same time, large bodies
of land, when released by our Indian tribes, were
sold at low rates to individual speculators and monopolists, or to railway corporations, instead of being
conveyed, as before, to the United States, and thus
subjected to general disposition, as other public
land. These evils are now remedied, but for nearly
ten years they were unchecked. The title to Indian lands was secured through treaties concocted
by a ring of speculators and monopolists outside of
the Senate, and frequently ratified by that body
near the close of a long session, when less than half

a dozen members were in their seats, and the entire business was supervised by a single Western senator acting as the agent of his employers and the sharer in their plunder.   These fatal mistakes in our legislation have made the Homestead law a half-way measure, instead of that complete reform in our land policy which was demanded, and they furnish a remarkable commentary upon the boasted friendship of the Republican party for the landless poor.

The conservative war-policy of the Administration continued to assert itself. The action of the President in promptly revoking the order of General Hunter, of the ninth of May, declaring free the slaves of the States of Georgia, Florida, and South Carolina, aggravated the growing impatience of the people. On the ninth day of June I submitted a resolution instructing the judiciary committee to report a bill repealing the Fugitive Slave Act, which was laid on the table by a vote of sixty-six to fifty-one, sixteen Republicans voting in the affirmative. On the second of July I called to see the President, and had a familiar talk about the war. He looked thin and haggard, but seemed cheerful. Although our forces were then engaged in a terrific conflict with the enemy near Richmond, and everybody was anxious as to the result, he was quite as placid as usual, and could not resist his "ruling passion" for anecdotes. If I had judged him by appearances I should have pronounced him incapable of any deep earnestness of feeling; but his manner was so kindly, and so free from the ordinary crookedness of the politician and the vanity and self-importance of official position, that nothing but good-will was inspired by his presence. He was still holding fast his faith in General McClellan, and this was steadily widening the breach between him and Congress, and periling the success of the war. The general gloom in Washington increased till the adjournment, but Mr. Sumner still had faith in the President, and prophesied good things as to his final action.

The Confiscation Act of this session, which was approved by the President on the seventeenth day of July, providing that slaves of rebels coming into our lines should be made free, and that the property of their owners, both real and personal, should be confiscated, would have given great and wide-spread satisfaction; but the President refused to sign the bill without a modification first made exempting the fee of rebel land-owners from its operation, thus powerfully aiding them in their deadly struggle against us. This action was inexpressibly provoking; but Congress was obliged to make the modification required, as the only means of securing the important advantages of other features of the measure. This anti-republican discrimination between real and personal property when the nation was struggling for its life against a rebellious aristocracy founded on the monopoly of land and the ownership of negroes, roused a popular opposition which thus far was altogether unprecedented. The feeling in Congress, however, was far more intense than throughout the country. No one at a distance could have formed any adequate conception of the hostility of Republican members toward Mr. Lincoln at the final adjournment, while it was the belief of many that our last session of Congress had been held in Washington. Mr. Wade said the country was going to hell, and that the scenes witnessed in the French Revolution were nothing in comparison with what we should see here.

Just before leaving Washington I called on the President again, and told him I was going to take the stump, and to tell the people that he would co-operate with Congress in vigorously carrying out the measures we had inaugurated for the purpose of crushing the rebellion, and that now the quickest and hardest blows were to be dealt. He told me I was authorized to say so, but said that more than half the popular clamor against the management of the war was unwarranted; and when I referred to the movements of General McClellan he made no committal in any way.

On the nineteenth of August Horace Greeley wrote his famous anti-slavery letter to the President, entitled "The Prayer of Twenty Millions." It was one of the most powerful appeals ever made in

behalf of justice and the rights of man. In his
reply Mr. Lincoln said: "If I could save the Union
without freeing any slave, I would do it; if I could
save it by freeing all the slaves, I would do it; and
if I could save it by freeing some and leaving others alone, I would do that." These words served
as fresh fuel to the fires of popular discontent, and
they were responded to by Mr. Greeley with admirable vigor and earnestness. The anti-slavery
critics of the President insisted that in thus dealing
with slavery as a matter of total indifference he
likened himself to Douglas, who had declared
that he didn't care whether slavery was voted up or
voted down in the Territories. They argued that
as slavery was the cause of the war and the
obstacle to peace, it was the duty of the Government to lay hold of the conscience of the
quarrel, and strike at slavery as the grand rebel.
Not to do so, they contended, now that the opportunity was offered, was to make the contest a mere
struggle for power, and thus to degrade it to the
level of the wars of the Old World, which bring
with them nothing for freedom or the race. They
insisted that the failure of the Government to give
freedom to our millions in bondage would be a
crime only to be measured by that of putting them
in chains if they were free. They reminded the President of his declaration that a house divided against
itself can not stand, and that the Republic can
not permanently exist half slave and half free; and

they urged that this baptism of fire and blood would be impious if the cause which produced it should be spared to canker the heart of the nation anew, and repeat its diabolical deeds. A Union with slavery spared and reinstated would not be worth the cost of saving it. To argue that we were fighting for a political abstraction called the Union, and not for the destruction of slavery, was to affront common sense, since nothing but slavery had brought the Union into peril, and nothing could make sure the fruits of the war but the removal of its cause. It was to delude ourselves with mere phrases, and conduct the war on false pretenses. It was to rival the folly of the rebels, who always asseverated that they were not fighting for slavery, but only for the right of local self government, when the whole world knew the contrary. These ideas, variously presented and illustrated, found manifold expression in innumerable Congressional speeches and in the newspapers of the Northern States, and a month later brought forth the President's proclamation of the twenty-second of September, giving the insurgents notice that on the first day of January following he would issue his proclamation of general emancipation, if they did not in the meantime lay down their arms. The course of events and the pressure of opinion were at last forcing him to see that the nation was wrestling with slavery in arms; that its destruction was not a debatable and distant alternative, but a pressing and absolute necessity; and that his Border State policy, through which he had so long tried to pet and please the power that held the nation by the throat, was a cruel and fatal mistake. This power, however, had so completely woven itself into the whole fabric of American society and institutions, and had so long fed upon the virtue of our public men, that the Administration was not yet prepared to divorce itself entirely from the madness that still enthralled the conservative element of the Republican party.

It was during this year that a formidable effort was made by the old Whig element in the Republican party to disband the organization and form a new one, called the "Union party." They were disposed to blame the Abolitionists for the halting march of events, and to run away from the real issues of the conflict. They were believers in the Border State policy, and favored the colonization of the negroes, while deprecating "radical and extreme measures." They forgot that the Republican principle was as true in the midst of war as in seasons of peace, and that instead of putting it in abeyance when the storm came, we should cling to it with redoubled energy and purpose. They forgot that the contest of 1860 was not only a struggle between slavery and freedom, but a struggle of life and death, inasmuch as the exclusion of slavery from all federal territory would not only put the nation's brand upon it in the States of the South,

and condemn it as a public enemy, but virtually
sentence it to death.   They forgot that the charge
of "abolitionism," which was incessantly hurled at
the Republican party, was thus by no means wanting
in essential truth, and that when the slaveholders
were vanquished in the election of Mr. Lincoln,
their appeal from the ballot to the bullet was the
logical result of their insane devotion to slavery,
and their conviction that nothing could save it but
the dismemberment of the Republic.   They forgot
that the Rebellion was simply an advanced stage of
slaveholding rapacity, and that instead of tempting us
to cower before it and surrender our principles, it
furnished an overwhelming argument for standing
by them to the death.   This movement was fruitful of
great mischief throughout the loyal States, and on
my return to Washington in the fall of this year
I was glad to find this fact generally admitted, and
my earnest opposition to it fully justified by the
judgment of Republican members of Congress.

Immediately after the battle of Fredricksburg, on
the 13th of December, the Committee on the Conduct of the War visited that place for the purpose
of inquiring into the facts respecting that fearful
disaster.   The country was greatly shocked and excited, and eager to know who was to blame.   We
examined Burnside, Hooker, Sumner, and Wood-
bury; but prior to this, in a personal interview with
General Burnside, he frankly told me that *he* was
responsible for the attack.   He seemed to be loaded

down with a mountain of trouble and anxiety, and I could see that he felt just as a patriotic man naturally would, after sacrificing thousands of men by a mistaken movement.   He said he had no military ambition, and frankly confessed his incapacity to command a large army, as he had done to the President and Secretary of War, when they urged him to assume this great responsibility; and that he was very sorry he had ever consented to accept it. His conversation disarmed all criticism, while his evident honesty decidedly pleased me.   It was a sad thought, while standing on the banks of the Rappahannock, that here were more than a hundred thousand men on either side of a narrow river, brethren and kindred, and naturally owing each other nothing but good will, who were driven by negro slavery into the wholesale slaughter of each other.   But General Burnside told me our men did not feel toward the rebels as they felt toward us, and he assured me that this was the grand obstacle to our success.   Our soldiers, he said, were not sufficiently fired by resentment, and he exhorted me, if I could, to breathe into our people at home the same spirit toward our enemies which inspired them toward us.   As I approached one of the principal hospitals here, I was startled by a pile of arms and legs of wounded soldiers, and on entering the building I found scores of men in the last stages of life, stretched on the floor with nothing under them but a thin covering of hay, and nothing over them

15

but a coarse blanket or quilt, and without a spark
of fire to warm them, though the weather was extremely cold and they were literally freezing to
death.   Some of them were too far gone to speak,
and looked at me so pleadingly that I can never
forget the impression it made.   Arrangements were
made for their comfort as soon as it was possible.

On New Year's day I joined the immense throng
of callers at the White House, but did not enjoy
the delay of the President in issuing his Proclamation of Emancipation.   It came late in the day, and
brought relief to multitudes of anxious people.
Perhaps no subject has ever been more widely
misunderstood than the legal effect of this famous
document, and the circumstances under which it
was issued.   Mr. Lincoln was himself opposed to
the measure, and when he very reluctantly issued his
preliminary proclamation in September, he wished
it distinctly understood that the deportation of
the slaves was, in his mind, inseparably connected
with the policy.   Like Mr. Clay and other prominent leaders of the old Whig party, he believed in
colonization, and that the separation of the two
races was necessary to the welfare of both.   He
was at that time pressing upon the attention of
Congress a scheme of colonization in Chiriqui in
Central America, which Senator Pomeroy espoused
with great zeal, and in which he had the favor of a
majority of the Cabinet, including Secretary Smith,
who warmly endorsed the project.   Subsequent

developments, however, proved that it was simply
an organization for land-stealing and plunder, and
it was abandoned ; but it is by no means certain that
if the President had foreseen this fact, his preliminary notice to the rebels would have been given.
There are strong reasons for saying that he doubted his right to emancipate under the war power,
and that he meant what he said when he compared
an executive order to that effect to the "Pope's
Bull against the Comet."

But he saw no way of escape. The demand for
such an edict was wide-spread and rapidly extending in the Republican party. The power to issue
it was taken for granted. All doubts on the subject were consumed in the burning desire of the
people, or forgotten in the travail of war. The
anti-slavery element was becoming more and more
impatient and impetuous. Opposition to that
element now involved more serious consequences
than offending the Border States. Mr. Lincoln
feared that enlistments would cease, and that Congress would even refuse the necessary supplies to
carry on the war, if he declined any longer to place
it on a clearly defined anti-slavery basis. It was in
yielding to this pressure that he finally became the
liberator of the slaves through the triumph of our
arms which it ensured.

The authority to emancipate under the war
power is well settled, but it could only be asserted
over territory occupied by our armies. Each Commanding General, as fast as our flag advanced,

could have offered freedom to the slaves, as could
the President himself. This was the view of Secretary Chase. A paper proclamation of freedom, as
to States in the power of the enemy, could have no
more validity than a paper blockade of their coast.
Mr. Lincoln's proclamation did not apply to the
Border States, which were loyal, and in which
slavery was of course untouched. It did not pretend to operate upon the slaves in other large districts, in which it would have been effective at once,
but studiously excluded them, while it applied mainly to States and parts of States within the military
occupation of the enemy, where it was necessarily
void. But even if the proclamation could have
given freedom to the slaves according to its scope,
their permanent enfranchisement would not have
been secured, because the *status* of slavery, as it existed under the local laws of the States prior to the
war, would have remained after the re-establishment
of peace. All emancipated slaves found in those
States, or returning to them, would have been subject to slavery as before, for the simple reason that
no military proclamation could operate to abolish
their municipal laws. Nothing short of a Constitutional amendment could at once give freedom to
our black millions and make their re-enslavement
impossible ; and " this," as Mr. Lincoln declared
in earnestly urging its adoption, " is a king's cure
for all evils. It winds the whole thing up." All
this is now attested by very high authorities on

International and Constitutional law; and while it takes nothing from the honor so universally accorded to Mr. Lincoln as the great Emancipator, it shows how wisely he employed a grand popular delusion in the salvation of his country. His proclamation had no present legal effect within territory not under the control of our arms; but as an expression of the spirit of the people and the policy of the Administration, it had become both a moral and a military necessity.

During this month I called with the Indiana delegation to see the President respecting the appointment of Judge Otto, of Indiana, as Assistant Secretary of the Interior. He was afterward appointed, but Mr. Lincoln then only responded to our application by treating us to four anecdotes. Senator Lane told me that when the President heard a story that pleased him he took a memorandum of it and filed it away among his papers. This was probably true. At any rate, by some method or other, his supply seemed inexhaustible, and always aptly available. Early in February General Burnside came before the War Committee, and gave the most startling testimony as to the demoralization of the Army of the Potomac, the bickerings and jealousies of the commanding generals, and the vexations of the President in dealing with the situation. On the 18th of March I called on Mr. Lincoln respecting the appointments I had recommended under the conscription law, and took occasion to refer to the failure of

General Fremont to obtain a command. He said
he did not know where to place him, and that it
reminded him of the old man who advised his son
to take a wife, to which the young man responded,
" Whose wife shall I take ?" The President proceeded to point out the practical difficulties in the
way by referring to a number of important com-
mands which might suit Fremont, but which
could only be reached by removals he did not wish
to make. I remarked that I was very sorry if
this was true, and that it was unfortunate for our
cause, as I believed his restoration to duty would
stir the country as no other appointment could.
He said, " it would stir the country on one side,
and stir it the other way on the other. It would
please Fremont's friends, and displease the conservatives ; and that is all I can see in the *stirring*
argument." " My proclamation," he added, " was
to stir the country ; but it has done about as much
harm as good." These observations were characteristic, and showed how reluctant he was to turn
away from the conservative counsels he had so
long heeded.

On the 3d day of April the final report of the
Committee on the Conduct of the War was completed, and the portion of it relating to the Army
of the Potomac was in the hands of the Associated
Press, and awaited by the public with a curiosity
which it is not easy now to realize. The formation of the committee, as already stated, grew out

of the popular demand for a more vigorous war policy, and its action was thus exposed to the danger of hasty conclusions; but the press and public opinion of the loyal States, with remarkable unanimity, credited it with great usefulness to the country, through its labors to rescue the control of the war from incompetent and unworthy hands.

I returned home by way of Philadelphia and New York, and had a delightful visit in the former place with James and Lucretia Mott, whom I had not seen since 1850. In New York I attended the great "Sumter meeting" of the 13th, and spoke at one of the stands with General Fremont and Roscoe Conkling. While in the city I met Mr. Bryant, Phebe Carey, Mr. Beecher and other notables, and on my way home tarried two days with Gerrit Smith, at his hospitable home in Peterboro. According to his custom he invited a number of his neighbors and friends to breakfast, and by special invitation I addressed the people in the evening, at the "free church" of the town, on topics connected with the war. I could see that Mr. Smith did not approve the severity of my language, and that this was a source of amusement to some of his neighbors, but the course of events afterward radically changed his views, and he admitted that in his public addresses he was greatly aided by the imprecatory psalms. I had several delightful rambles with him, our conversation turning chiefly upon reformatory and theological topics, and I found myself more than ever in love with this venerable philanthropist whom I had only met once before, on his visit to Washington the previous year.

On the night of the 8th of July the fire-bells of the town of Centreville, in which I resided, roused the people, who rushed into the streets to learn that General John Morgan, with six thousand cavalry and four pieces of artillery, had crossed the Ohio, and was moving upon the town of Corydon. The Governor had issued a call for minute men for the defense of the State, and within forty-eight hours sixty five thousand men tendered their services. Messengers were at once dispatched to all parts of Wayne County conveying the news of the invasion, and the next morning the people came pouring in from all directions, while the greatest excitement prevailed. The town had eighty muskets, belonging to its Home Guard, and I took one of them, which I afterward exchanged for a good French rifle; and having put on the military equipments, and supplied myself with a blanket and canteen, I was ready for marching orders. The volunteers who rallied at Centreville were shipped to Indianapolis, and were about seven hours on the way. I was a member of Company C, and the regiment to which I belonged was the One Hundred and Sixth, and was commanded by Colonel Isaac P. Gray. Of the force which responded to the call of the Governor, thirteen regiments and one battalion were organized specially for the emergency, and

sent into the field in different directions, except the
One Hundred and Tenth and the One Hundred and
Eleventh, which remained at Indianapolis. The
One Hundred and Sixth was shipped by rail to
Cincinnati, and but for a detention of several hours
at Indianapolis, caused by the drunkenness of an
officer high in command, it might possibly have
encountered Morgan near Hamilton, the next
morning, on the way South. Our reception in Cincinnati was not very flattering. The people there
seemed to feel that Ohio was able to take care of
herself; and, in fact, nothing could have been more
unreasonable than sending a body of infantry one
hundred miles in pursuit of a cavalry force in that
vicinity, where an ample body of cavalry was in
readiness, and the river well guarded by gun-boats.

We were re-shipped to Indianapolis by rail,
where we were mustered out of service and returned
to our homes after a campaign of eight days. This
was the sum of my military experience, but it afforded me some glimpses of the life of a soldier,
and supplied me with some startling facts respecting the curse of intemperance in our armies.

CHAPTER XI.

INCIDENTS AND END OF THE WAR.

Campaigning in Ohio—Attempted repeal · of the Fugitive Slave Law—Organized movement in favor of Chase for the Presidency—Confiscation of rebel lands—Fort Pillow and the treatment of Union soldiers at Richmond—Mr. Lincoln's letter to Hodges—Southern Homestead Bill and controversy with Mr. Mallory—Nomination of Andrew Johnson—Enforcement of party discipline—Mr. Lincoln's change of opinion as to confiscation of rebel lands—Opposition to him in Congress—General Fremont and Montgomery Blair—Visit to City Point—Adoption of the XIII Constitutional Amendment—Trip to Richmond and incidents—Assassination of the President—Inauguration of Johnson and announcement of his policy—Feeling toward Mr. Lincoln — Capitulation with Gen. Johnson.

In the latter part of July of this year I addressed several meetings in Ohio, in company with Gov. Brough, beginning at Toledo. His speeches were too conservative for the times, as he soon discovered by their effect upon the people; but I found him singularly genial and companionable, and full of reminiscences of his early intimacy with Jackson, Van Buren and Silas Wright. Early in September I returned to Ohio to join Hon. John A. Bingham in canvassing Mr. Ashley's district under the employment of the State Republican Commit-

(234)

tee. Mr. Vallandingham, then temporarily colo-
nized in Canada, was the Democratic candidate for
Governor, and the canvass was "red-hot." At no
time during the war did the *spirit* of war more
completely sway the loyal masses. It was no
time to mince the truth, or "nullify damnation
with a phrase," and I fully entered into the spirit
of General Burnside's advice already referred to, to
breathe into the hearts of the people a feeling of
animosity against the rebels akin to that which inspired their warfare against us. I remember that
at one of the mass-meetings I attended, where Col.
Gibson was one of the speakers, a Cincinnati
reporter who had prepared himself for his work
dropped his pencil soon after the oratorical fireworks began, and listened with open mouth and
the most rapt attention till the close of the speech ;
and he afterward wrote to his employer an account
of the meeting, in which he said that reporting
was simply impossible, and he could only say the
speaking was "beautifully terrible." As a stump-
speaker Col. Gibson was then without a rival in
the West. His oratory was an irresistible fascination, and no audience could ever grow tired of him.
The speeches of Mr. Bingham were always admirable. His rhetoric was singularly charming. He
was an artist in his work, but seldom repeated himself, while gathering fresh inspiration, and following
some new line of thought at every meeting. After
our work was done in the Toledo district I accom-

panied Mr. Ashley to Jefferson, where he and others were to address a mass-meeting, which we found assembled in front of the court house. The day was rainy and dismal, and the meeting had already been in session for hours; but after additional speeches by Ashley and Hutchins I was so loudly called for a little while before sunset, that I responded for about three-quarters of an hour, when I proposed to conclude, the people having been detained already over four hours while standing in a cold drizzling rain; but the cry of "go on" was very emphatic, and seemed to be unanimous. "Go ahead," said a farmer, "we'll hear you; it's past milking time anyhow!" It seemed to me I had never met such listeners. I was afterward informed that the test of effective speaking on the Reserve is the ability to hold an audience from their milking when the time for it comes, and I thought I passed this test splendidly. After my return from Ohio I made a brief canvass in Iowa, along with Senator Harlan and Governor Stone, and spent the remainder of the fall on the stump in my own State.

In the 38th Congress, Speaker Colfax made me Chairman of the Committee on Public Lands, which gratified me much. It opened a coveted field of labor on which I entered with zeal. On the 14th of December I introduced a bill for the repeal of the Fugitive Slave Law, and in order to test the sense of the House on the question, I offered a reso-

lution instructing the Judiciary Committee to report such a bill. Greatly to my astonishment it
was laid on the table by a vote of yeas eighty-two,
nays seventy-four. Many Republicans declined to
vote, and we were evidently still under the lingering spell of slavery. Early in January an organized
movement was set on foot in the interest of Mr.
Chase for the Presidency, and I was made a member of a Central Committee which was appointed
for the purpose of aiding the enterprise. I was a
decided friend of Mr. Chase, and as decidedly dis-
pleased with the hesitating military policy of the
Administration; but on reflection I determined to
withdraw from the committee and let the presidential matter drift. I had no time to devote to the
business, and I found the committee inharmonious,
and composed, in part, of men utterly unfit and unworthy to lead in such a movement. It was fearfully mismanaged. A confidential document known
as the "Pomeroy circular," assailing Mr. Lincoln
and urging the claims of Mr. Chase, was sent to
numerous parties, and of course fell into the hands
of Mr. Lincoln's friends. They became greatly excited, and by vigorous counter measures created a
strong reaction. A serious estrangement between
the President and his Secretary was the result,
which lasted for several months. The Chase movement collapsed, and when the Republican members
of the Ohio Legislature indorsed the re-nomination
of Mr. Lincoln, Mr. Chase withdrew from the con-

test.   The opposition to Mr. Lincoln, however, continued, and was secretly cherished by many of the
ablest and most patriotic men in the party.   The
extent of their opposition in Congress can never be
known, and it was greatly aggravated by successive
military failures; but it lacked both courage and
leadership, and culminated in the nomination of
General Fremont in the latter part of May.

In this Congress a new joint select committee
on the "conduct of the war" was organized,
armed with new powers, and authorized to sit in
vacation; and in common with most of the members of the former committee I was re-appointed.
During the latter part of January I reported from
the Committee on Public Lands a proposition to
extend the Homestead Law of 1862 to the forfeited
and confiscated lands of Rebels.   It was a very
radical proposition, proposing to deal with these
lands as *public* lands, and parcel them out into
small homesteads among the poor of the South,
black and white.   The subject was a large one, involving many important questions, and I devoted
much time and thought to the preparation of a
speech in support of the measure.   In the month
of April a portion of the Committee on the Conduct
of the War visited Fort Pillow, for the purpose of
taking testimony respecting the rebel atrocities at
that place; and this testimony and that taken at
Annapolis, early in May, respecting the treatment
of our soldiers in the prisons at Richmond was

published, as a special instalment of our proceedings, for popular use, accompanied by photographs
of a number of the prisoners in their wasted and
disfigured condition. The report produced a
powerful effect on the public mind, and caused
unspeakable trouble and vexation to the enemy.
I assisted in the examination of our prisoners at
Annapolis, and never before had been so touched
by any spectacle of human suffering. They were
in the last stages of life, and could only answer
our questions in a whisper. They were living
skeletons, and it seemed utterly incredible that
life could be supported in such wasted and attenu-
ated shadows of themselves. They looked at us,
in attempting to tell their story, with an expression
of beseeching tenderness and submission which no
words could describe. Not one of them expressed
any regret that he had entered into the service of
the country, and each declared that he would do
so again, if his life should be spared and the opportunity should be offered. In examining one of
these men I was perfectly unmanned by my tears;
and on retiring from the tent to give them vent I
encountered Senator Wade, who had fled from the
work, and was sobbing like a child. It was an altogether unprecedented experience, and the impression it produced followed me night and day for
weeks.

The conservative policy of the Administration
found a new and careful expression in Mr. Lin-

coln's letter to A. G. Hodges, of the 4th of April. It showed great progress as compared with previous utterances, but his declaration that " I claim not to have controlled events, but confess plainly that events have controlled me," was displeasing to the more anti-slavery Republicans. They insisted that the Administration had no right to become the foot-ball of events. It had no right, they said, at such a time, to make itself a negative expression or an unknown quantity in the Algebra which was to work out the grand problem. It had no right, they insisted, to take shelter beneath a debauched and sickly public sentiment, and plead it in bar of the great duty imposed upon it by the crisis. It had no right, certainly, to lag behind that sentiment, to magnify its extent and potency, and thus to become its virtual ally, instead of endeavoring to control it, and to indoctrinate the country with ideas suited to the emergency. It was the duty of the President, like John Bright and the English Liberals, to lead, not follow public opinion. These criticisms found every variety of utterance through Congressional speeches and the press, and met with a cordial response from the people; and they undoubtedly played their part in preparing the country and the Administration for the more vigorous policy which was to follow.

On the 12th of May the House passed my Southern Homestead Bill by the strictly party vote of seventy-five to sixty-four. In my closing speech on the subject I was frequently interrupted by Wood of New York, and Mallory of Kentucky, and the debate ran into very sharp personalities; but the opposition of these members only tended to strengthen the measure. On the 19th I was drawn into an exceedingly angry altercation with Mr. Mallory, who charged me with forging some very personal remarks about himself, and interpolating them into the "Congressional Globe" as a part of my speech of the 12th. He was exceedingly insolent and overbearing in his manner, growing more and more so as he proceeded, and strikingly recalling the old days of slavery. He summoned a number of his friends as witnesses, who testified that they did not *hear* me use the language in question, and several of them, like Kernan of New York, declared that they had occupied positions very near me, had given particular attention to my words, and would certainly have remembered them if they had been uttered. I kept cool, but asserted very positively that I did use the exact words reported, and in proof of my statement I appealed to a number of my friends, who sustained me by their distinct and positive recollection. Here was a conflict of testimony in which every witness recollected the facts according to his politics; but pending the proceedings I was fortunate enough to find the notes of the "Globe" reporter, which perfectly vindicated me from Mr. Mallory's charges, and suddenly put his bluster and billingsgate to flight. He uncondition-

16

ally retracted his charges, while his swift witnesses
were sufficiently rebuked and humiliated by this unexpected catastrophe. I was heartily complimented
on my triumph, and my dialogue with Mr. Mallory
was put in pamphlet as a campaign document by
his opponents and liberally scattered over his district, where it did much service in defeating his
re-election to the House.

The passage of the Southern Homestead Bill,
however, could only prove a very partial measure
without an enactment reaching the fee of rebel land
owners, and I confidently anticipated the endorse-
ment of such a measure by the Republican National Convention, which was to meet in Baltimore,
on the seventh of June. I was much gratified
when the National Union League approved it, in its
Convention in that city the day before ; and a resolution embodying it was also reported favorably
by the sub-committee on resolutions of the National Republican Convention the next day. But
the General Committee, on the motion of McKee
Dunn of Indiana, always an incorrigible conservative, struck it out, much to the disappointment of
the Republican masses. To me it was particularly
vexatious, as the measure was a pet one of mine,
having labored for it with much zeal, and in the
confidence that the National Convention would approve it. Mr. Dunn was a Kentuckian of the
Border State School, and although a friend of mine,
and an upright and very gentlemanly man, he had

a genius for being on the wrong side of vital questions during the war. Speaker Colfax used to say,
laughingly, that in determining his own course he
first made it a point to find out where McKee Dunn
stood; and then, having ascertained Julian's position, he always took a middle ground, feeling perfectly sure he was right.

But to me the nomination of Andrew Johnson
for Vice President was a still greater disappointment. I knew he did not believe in the principles
embodied in the platform. I had become intimately acquainted with him while we were fellow-
members of the Committee on the Conduct of the
War, and he always scouted the idea that slavery
was the cause of our trouble, or that emancipation
could ever be tolerated without immediate colonization. In my early acquaintance with him I had
formed a different opinion; but he was, at heart, as
decided a hater of the negro and of everything
savoring of abolitionism, as the rebels from whom he
had separated. His nomination, however, like that
of Mr. Lincoln, seemed to have been preordained
by the people, while the intelligent, sober men, in
Congress and out of Congress, who lamented the
fact, were not prepared to oppose the popular will.
Mr. Lincoln's nomination was nearly unanimous,
only the State of Missouri opposing him; but of the
more earnest and thorough-going Republicans in
both Houses of Congress, probably not one in ten
really favored it. It was not only very distasteful

to a large majority of Congress but to many of the most prominent men of the party throughout the country. During the month of June the feeling against Mr. Lincoln became more and more bitter and intense, but its expression never found its way to the people.

Notwithstanding the divisions which existed in the Republican ranks, party discipline was vigorous and absolute. "Civil Service Reform" was in the distant future, and the attempt to inaugurate it would have been counted next to treasonable. Loyalty to Republicanism was not only accepted as the best evidence of loyalty to the country, but of fitness for civil position. After my nomination for re-election this year, Mr. Holloway, who was still holding the position of Commissioner of Patents, and one of the editors of a Republican newspaper in my district, refused to recognize me as the party candidate, and kept the name of my defeated competitor standing in his paper. It threatened discord and mischief, and I went to the President with these facts, and on the strength of them demanded his removal from office. He replied, "If I remove Mr. Holloway I shall have a quarrel with Senator Lane on my hands." I replied that Senator Lane would certainly not quarrel with him for turning a man out of office who was fighting the Republican party and the friends of the Administration. "Your nomination," said he, "is as binding on Republicans as mine, and you

can rest assured that Mr. Holloway shall support
you, openly and unconditionally, or lose his head."
This was entirely satisfactory, but after waiting a
week or two for the announcement of my name I returned to Mr. Lincoln with the information that Mr.
Holloway was still keeping up his fight, and that I
had come to ask of him decisive measures. I saw in
an instant that the President now meant business.
He dispatched a messenger at once, asking Mr.
Holloway to report to him forthwith, in person,
and in a few days my name was announced in his
paper as the Republican candidate, and that of my
competitor withdrawn.

Having understood that Mr. Lincoln had
changed his opinion respecting the power of Congress to confiscate the landed estates of rebels, I
called to see him on the subject on the 2d of July,
and asked him if I might say to the people that
what I had learned on this subject was true, assuring him that I could make a far better fight for our
cause if he would permit me to do so. He replied
that when he prepared his veto of our law on the
subject two years before, he had not examined the
matter thoroughly, but that on further reflection,
and on reading Solicitor Whiting's law argument,
he had changed his opinion, and thought he would
now sign a bill striking at the fee, if we would
send it to him. I was much gratified by this statement, which was of service to the cause in the
canvass ; but, unfortunately, constitutional scruples

respecting such legislation gained ground, and although both Houses of Congress at different times endorsed the principle, it never became a law, owing to unavoidable differences between the President and Congress on the question of reconstruction. The action of the President in dealing with rebel land owners was of the most serious character. It paralyzed one of the most potent means of putting down the Rebellion, prolonging the conflict and aggravating its cost, and at the same time left the owners of large estates in full possession of their lands at the end of the struggle, who naturally excluded from the ownership of the soil the freedmen and poor whites who had been friendly to the Union; while the confiscation of life estates as a war measure was of no practical advantage to the Government or disadvantage to the enemy.

The refusal of the President to sign the Reconstruction Act which passed near the close of the session, and his proclamation and message giving his reasons therefor, still further exasperated a formidable body of earnest and impatient Republicans. A scathing criticism of the President's position by Henry Winter Davis, which was signed by himself and Senator Wade, fitly echoed their feelings. Mr. Davis was a man of genius. Among the famous men in the Thirty-eighth Congress he had no superior as a writer, debater and orator· He was a brilliant man, whose devotion to his country in this crisis was a passion, while his hos-

tility to the President's policy was as sincere as it
was intense; but the passage of the somewhat incongruous bill vetoed by the President, would probably have proved a stumbling-block in the way of
the more radical measures which afterward prevailed. This could not then be foreseen, and as
the measure was an advanced one, the feeling
against Mr. Lincoln waxed stronger and stronger
among his opposers. They had so completely lost
their faith in him that when Congress adjourned
they seriously feared his veto of the bill just
enacted, repealing the Fugitive Slave law; while
the independent movement in favor of General Fremont threatened a serious division in the Republican ranks, and the triumph of General McClellan.
"These," as Mr. Lincoln said on another occasion, "were dark and dismal days," and they were
made still more so by the course of military events.
The capture of Richmond, which General Grant
had promised, had not been accomplished, although
he had been furnished with all the troops he wanted.
Our Grand Army of the Potomac made advances
in that direction, but with great slaughter and
no actual results; while the Administration was
blamed for his failures. General Grant finally
reached the position occupied by McClellan in
1862, but with terrific losses, and Richmond still
in possession of the rebels. His delay and inaction
at this point created great popular discontent in the
North; but while Lincoln supplied him with ample

reinforcements, and he now had an army twice as large as that of General Lee, which was costing the nation over a million dollars per day, he continued idle during the summer. It was evident that nothing could save us but military success; and most fortunately for the Republican cause it came in due season, rallied and reunited its supporters, and thus secured their triumph at the polls.

Near the close of the canvass, while on a visit to Washington, I learned how it happened that Montgomery Blair had finally been got out of the Cabinet, and General Fremont induced to leave the track as the candidate of the Cleveland Convention. The radical pressure upon Mr. Lincoln for the removal of Blair was very formidable, and the emergency seemed so critical that it finally resulted in a compromise, by which Fremont agreed to retire from the race, if Blair should be required to leave the Cabinet. This was carried out, and thus, at last, the President was obliged to make terms with the " Pathfinder," who achieved a long-coveted victory over an old foe. The election of Mr. Lincoln was followed by a remarkable measure of party union and harmony, and the tone of his message in December was encouraging. The appointment and confirmation of Mr. Chase as Chief Justice of the Supreme Court met the most cordial approval of Republicans everywhere. As a healing measure, following his retirement from the treasury for valid reasons, it was most timely.

During the month of December, the Committee on the Conduct of the War visited City Point, for the purpose of taking testimony respecting the explosion of the mine at Petersburg. General Grant spent several hours with the Committee, speaking very freely and familiarly of the faults and virtues of our various commanders, and impressing every one by his strong common-sense. While at dinner with us on our steamer, he drank freely, and its effect became quite manifest. It was a painful surprise to the Committee, and was spoken of with bated breath; for he was the Lieutenant-General of all our forces, and the great movements which finally strangled the Rebellion were then in progress, and, for aught we knew, might possibly be deflected from their purpose by his condition.

In January, 1865, the Committee on the Conduct of the War investigated the famous Fort Fisher expedition, in which three hundred tons of powder were to be exploded in the vicinity of the Fort as a means of demolishing it, or paralyzing the enemy. The testimony of General Butler in explanation and defense of the enterprise was interesting and spicy, and he was subsequently contradicted by General Grant on material points. On the last day of this month one of the grandest events of the century was witnessed in the House of Representatives in the final passage of the Constitutional Amendment forever prohibiting slavery. Numerous propositions on the subject had been

submitted, but the honor of drafting the one
adopted belongs to Lyman Trumbull, who had introduced it early in the first session of this Congress.   It passed the Senate on the 8th of April,
1864, only six members voting against it, namely,
Davis, Hendricks, McDougall, Powell, Riddle and
Saulsbury, but failed in the House on the 15th of
June following.   It now came up on the motion
of Mr. Ashley to reconsider this vote.   Congress
had abolished slavery in the District of Columbia,
and prohibited it in all the Territories.   It had repealed the Fugitive Slave law, and declared free all
negro soldiers in the Union armies and their families; and the President had played his grand part
in the Proclamation of Emancipation.   But the
question now to be decided completely overshad-
owed all others.   The debate on the subject had
been protracted and very spirited, the opposition
being led by Pendleton, Fernando Wood, Voor-
hies, Mallory and Eldridge, who all denied that
the power to amend the Constitution conferred the
right to abolish slavery, as Garret Davis and
Saulsbury had done in the Senate.   The time for
the momentous vote had now come, and no language could describe the solemnity and impress-
iveness of the spectacle pending the roll-call.   The
success of the measure had been considered very
doubtful, and depended upon certain negotiations,
the result of which was not fully assured, and the
particulars of which never reached the public.

The anxiety and suspense during the balloting produced a deathly stillness, but when it became certainly known that the measure had prevailed the cheering in the densely-packed hall and galleries surpassed all precedent and beggared all description. Members joined in the general shouting, which was kept up for several minutes, many embracing each other, and others completely surrendering themselves to their tears of joy. It seemed to me I had been born into a new life, and that the world was overflowing with beauty and joy, while I was inexpressibly thankful for the privilege of recording my name on so glorious a page of the nation's history, and in testimony of an event so long only dreamed of as possible in the distant future. The champions of negro emancipation had merely hoped to speed their grand cause a little by their faithful labors, and hand over to coming generations the glory of crowning it with success; but they now saw it triumphant, and they had abundant and unbounded cause to rejoice. It has been aptly said that the greatest advantage of a long life is the opportunity it gives of seeing moral experiments worked out, of being present at the fructification of social causes, and of thus gaining a kind of wisdom which in ordinary cases seems reserved for a future life; but that an equivalent for this advantage is possessed by such as live in those critical periods of society when retribution is hastened, or displayed in clear connection with the origin of events. It strengthens faith to observe the sure operation of moral causes in ripening into great and beneficent results. To be permitted to witness the final success of the grandest movement of ancient or modern times was a blessed opportunity. To have labored for it in the goodly fellowship of its confessors and martyrs was cause for devout thanksgiving and joy. To be accredited to share in the great historic act of its formal consummation was a priceless privilege. A few days after the ratification of this Amendment, on the motion of Mr. Sumner, Dr. Rock, a colored lawyer of Boston, was admitted to practice in the Supreme Court of the United States, which had pronounced the Dred Scott decision only a few years before; and this was followed a few days later by a sermon in the hall of the House by Rev. Mr. Garnett, being the first ever preached in the Capitol by a colored man. Evidently, the negro was coming to the front.

In the latter part of March I visited New York, where I witnessed the immense throngs of shouting people on Wall Street, called together by the news of the fall of Richmond. Broadway, robed in its innumerable banners, was one of the finest sights I had ever beheld. On the tenth of April the Committee on the Conduct of the War left Washington for South Carolina, for the purpose of taking further testimony, and intending to be present at the great anniversary of the thirteenth at Charles-

ton.   We reached Fortress Monroe the next evening, where we learned that the "Alabama," which
the Navy Department had furnished us, would
be detained twenty-four hours to coal, by reason
of which we proceeded directly to Richmond on
the "Baltimore."   At City Point, Admiral Porter
furnished us with a pilot, as there was some
danger of torpedoes up the James River.   Our
steamer reached the city about bedtime, but we
remained on board till morning, lulled into a
sweet sleep by the music of the guitar and the
singing of the negroes below.   At eight o'clock
in the morning our party went out sight-seeing,
some in carriages, but most of us on horseback,
with an orderly for each to show him the way.
The first notable place we visited was General
Weitzel's headquarters, just vacated by Jefferson
Davis.   The building was a spacious three-story
residence, with a large double parlor, a ladies' parlor, and a small secluded library attached, in which
all sorts of treason were said to have been hatched.
We next visited the capitol, an ancient-looking
edifice, which would bear no comparison with our
modern State Capitols in size or style of architect-
ure.   The library made a respectable appearance,
but I think it contained few modern publications,
especially of our own authors.   I noticed, however, a liberal supply of theological works of the
most approved orthodoxy.   The view of the city
from the top of the building was admirable.   We

could see Libby Prison, Castle Thunder and Bell Isle, the former of which we afterward visited. After seeing the rebel fortifications we were glad to get back to our steamer. Before starting the next morning we saw the " Richmond Whig," containing an order signed by General Weitzel, inviting Hunter, McMullen and other noted rebel leaders, including members of the rebel legislature, to meet in Richmond on the twenty-fifth to confer with our authorities on the restoration of peace, transportation and safe conduct being ordered for the purpose. We were all thunderstruck, and fully sympathized with the hot indignation and wrathful words of the chairman of our committee. We soon afterward learned that the order had been directed by the President, and while we were thoroughly disgusted by this display of misguided magnanimity we saw rebel officers strutting around the streets in full uniform, looking as independent as if they had been the masters of the city. We left on the afternoon of the twelfth, and were interested in seeing Drury's Landing, Dutch-Gap Canal, Malvern Hills and other points of historic interest. Before reaching Fortress Monroe the next day, Senators Wade and Chandler changed their minds respecting our journey to Charleston, which was abandoned, and after spending a few hours very pleasantly at that place and Point Lookout, we reached Washington on the evening of the fourteenth.

Soon after retiring I was roused from a deep sleep by loud raps at my door. W. L. Woods, clerk of my committee, entered in the greatest excitement, and told me that Lincoln had just been assassinated, and Seward and son probably, and that rebel assassins were about to take the town. Supposing all this to be true I grew suddenly cold, heart-sick and almost helpless. It was a repetition of my experience when the exaggerated stories about the Bull Run disaster first reached me in the summer of 1861. I soon rallied, however, and joined the throng on the street. The city was at once in a tempest of excitement, consternation and rage. About seven and a half o'clock in the morning the church bells tolled the President's death. The weather was as gloomy as the mood of the people, while all sorts of rumors filled the air as to the particulars of the assassination and the fate of Booth. Johnson was inaugurated at eleven o'clock on the morning of the 15th, and was at once surrounded by radical and conservative politicians, who were alike anxious about the situation. I spent most of the afternoon in a political caucus, held for the purpose of considering the necessity for a new Cabinet and a line of policy less conciliatory than that of Mr. Lincoln; and while everybody was shocked at his murder, the feeling was nearly universal that the accession of Johnson to the Presidency would prove a godsend to the country. Aside from Mr. Lincoln's known policy of tenderness to the Rebels, which

now so jarred upon the feelings of the hour, his well-
known views on the subject of reconstruction were
as distasteful as possible to radical Republicans.
In his last public utterance, only three days before
his death, he had declared his adherence to the plan
of reconstruction announced by him in December,
1863, which in the following year so stirred the ire
of Wade and Winter Davis as an attempt of the
Executive to usurp the powers of Congress.. According to this plan the work of reconstruction in
the rebel States was to be inaugurated and carried
on by those only who were qualified to vote under
the Constitution and laws of these States as they existed prior to the Rebellion.   Of course the negroes
of the South could have no voice in framing the institutions under which they were to live, and the
question of negro suffrage would thus have been
settled by the President, if he had lived and been
able to maintain this policy, while no doubt was
felt that this calamity had now been averted and the
way opened for the radical policy which afterward
involved the impeachment of Johnson, but finally
prevailed.   It was forgotten in the fever and turbu-
lence of the moment, that Mr. Lincoln, who was
never an obstinate man, and who in the matter of
his Proclamation of Emancipation had surrendered
his own judgment under the pressure of public
opinion, would not have been likely to wrestle with
Congress and the country in a mad struggle for his
own way.

On the following day, in pursuance of a previous engagement, the Committee on the Conduct of the War met the President at his quarters in the Treasury Department. He received us with decided cordiality, and Mr. Wade said to him: "Johnson, we have faith in you. By the gods, there will be no trouble now in running the government!" The President thanked him, and went on to define his well-remembered policy at that time. "I hold," said he, "that robbery is a crime; rape is a crime; murder is a crime; *treason* is a crime, and *crime* must be punished. Treason must be made infamous, and traitors must be impoverished." We were all cheered and encouraged by this brave talk, and while we were rejoiced that the leading conservatives of the country were not in Washington, we felt that the presence and influence of the committee, of which Johnson had been a member, would aid the Administration in getting on the right track. We met him again the next day and found the symptoms of a vigorous policy still favorable, and although I had some misgivings, the general feeling was one of unbounded confidence in his sincerity and firmness, and that he would act upon the advice of General Butler by inaugurating a policy of his own, instead of administering on the political estate of his predecessor.

In the meantime the prevailing excitement was greatly aggravated by the news of the capitulation between General Sherman and General Johnson

17

of the 16th of April.   Its practical surrender of all
the fruits of the national triumph so soon after the
murder of the President, produced an effect on the
public mind which can not be described.   General
Sherman had heard of the assassination when the
capitulation was made, and could not have been
ignorant of the feeling it had aroused.   On the face
of the proceeding his action seemed a wanton betrayal of the country to its enemies ; but when this
betrayal followed so swiftly the frightful tragedy
which was then believed to have been instigated by
the Confederate authorities, the patience of the people became perfectly exhausted.   For the time being,
all the glory of his great achievements in the war
seemed to be forgotten in the anathemas which
were showered upon him from every quarter of the
land ; but the prompt repudiation of his stipulations
by the Administration soon assuaged the popular
discontent, while it provoked an estrangement between Secretary Stanton and himself which was
never healed.

The outpouring of the people at Mr. Lincoln's
funeral was wholly unprecedented, and every possible arrangement was made by which they could
manifest their grief for their murdered President ;
but their solicitude for the state of the country was
too profound to be intermitted.   What policy was
now to be pursued ?   Mr. Lincoln's latest utterances
had been far from assuring or satisfactory.   The
question of reconstruction had found no logical

solution, and all was confusion respecting it. The question of negro suffrage was slowly coming to the front, and could not be much longer evaded. The adequate punishment of the rebel leaders was the demand of the hour. What would the new President do? He had suddenly become the central figure of American politics, and both radicals and conservatives were as curious to know what line of policy he would follow as they were anxious to point his way. His demeanor, at first, seemed modest and commendable, but his egotism soon began to assert itself, while his passion for stump-speaking was pampered by the delegations which began to pour into the city from various States and flatter him by formal addresses, to which he replied at length. This business was kept up till the people became weary of the din and clatter of words, and impatient for action.

CHAPTER XII.

RECONSTRUCTION AND SUFFRAGE—THE LAND QUESTION.

Visit of Indianians to the President—Gov. Morton and reconstruction—Report of Committee on the Conduct of the War—Discussion of negro suffrage and incidents—Personal matters—Suffrage in the District of Columbia—The Fourteenth Constitutional Amendment—Breach between the President and Congress—Blaine and Conkling—Land bounties and the Homestead Law.

ON the twenty-first of April I joined a large crowd of Indianians in one of the calls on the President referred to at the close of the last chapter. Gov. Morton headed the movement, which I now found had a decidedly political significance. He read a lengthy and labored address on " The Whole Duty of Man " respecting the question of Reconstruction. He told the President that a State could " neither secede nor by any possible means be taken out of the Union "; and he supported and illustrated this proposition by some very remarkable statements. He elaborated the proposition that the loyal people of a State have the right to govern it ; but he did not explain what would become of the State if the people were all disloyal, or the loyal so few as

to be utterly helpless. The lawful governments of
the South were overthrown by treason; and the
Governor declared there was " no power in the
Federal Government to punish the people of a State
collectively, by reducing it to a territorial condition, since the crime of treason is individual, and .
can only be treated individually." According
to this doctrine a rebellious State becomes independent. If the people could rightfully be over-
powered by the national authority, that very fact
would at once re-clothe them in all their rights,
just as if they had never rebelled. In framing
their new governments Congress would have no
right to prescribe any conditions, or to govern
them in any way pending the work of State reconstruction, since this would be to recognize the
States as Territories, and violate the principle of
State rights. The Governor's theory of reconstruction, in fact, made our war for the Union
flagrantly unconstitutional. The crime of treason
being " individual," and only to " be treated individually," we had no right to hold prisoners of
war, seize property, and capture and confiscate
vessels, without a regular indictment and trial;
and this being so, every Rebel in arms was in the
full legal possession of his political rights, and no
power could prevent him from exercising them except through judicial conviction of treason in the
district in which the overt act was committed.
Singularly enough, he seemed entirely unaware of

the well-settled principle which made our war for
the Union a territorial conflict, like that of a war
with Mexico or England; that the Rebels, while
still liable to be hung or otherwise dealt with for
treason, had taken upon themselves the further
character of public enemies; and that being now
conquered they were conquered enemies, having
simply the rights of a conquered people. The
Governor further informed the President that if the
revolted districts should be dealt with as mere
Territories, or conquered provinces, the nation
would be obliged to pay the debts contracted by
them prior to the war. These remarkable utterances, which he repudiated in less than a year
afterward, were emphatically endorsed by the President, who entered upon the same theme at a dismal length, freely indulging in his habit of bad
English and incoherence of thought. I was disgusted, and sorry that the confidence of so many
of my radical friends had been entirely misplaced.

During the latter part of April and early part of
May the Committee on the Conduct of the War
completed its final report, making eight considerable volumes, and containing valuable material for
any trustworthy history of the great conflict. Its
opinions were sometimes colored by the passions
of the hour, and this was especially true in the case
of General McClellan; but subsequent events have
justified its conclusions generally as to nearly every
officer and occurrence investigated, while its use-

fulness in exposing military blunders and incompetence, and in finally inaugurating the vigorous war
policy which saved the country, will scarcely be
questioned by any man sufficiently well-informed
and fair-minded to give an opinion.

On the 12th of May, a caucus of Republicans
was held at the National Hotel to consider the
necessity of taking decisive measures for saving
the new Administration from the conservative control which then threatened it. Senators Wade and
Sumner both insisted that the President was in no
danger, and declared, furthermore, that he was in
favor of negro suffrage; and no action was taken
because of the general confidence in him which I
was surprised to find still prevailed. In the meantime, pending the general drift of events, the suffrage question was constantly gaining in significance, and demanding a settlement. It was neither
morally nor logically possible to escape it; and on
my return to my constituents I prepared for a thorough canvass of my district. The Republicans
were everywhere divided on the question, while the
current of opinion was strongly against the introduction of the issue as premature. The politicians
all opposed it on the plea that it would divide
the Republicans and restore the Democrats to
power, and that we must wait for the growth
of a public opinion that would justify its agitation. Governor Morton opposed the policy
with inexpressible bitterness, declaring, with an

oath, that "negro suffrage must be put down," while every possible effort was made to array the soldiers against it. His hostility to the suffrage wing of his party seemed to be quite as relentless as to the Rebels, while the great body of the Republicans of the district deferred strongly to his views. In the beginning of the canvass I even found a considerable portion of my old anti-slavery friends unprepared to follow me; but feeling perfectly sure I was right, and that I could revolutionize the general opinion, I entered upon the work, and prosecuted it with all my might for nearly four months. My task was an arduous one, but I found the people steadily yielding up their prejudices, and ready to lay hold of the truth when fairly and dispassionately presented, while the soldiers were among the first to accept my teachings. The tide was at length so evidently turning in my favor that on the 28th of September Governor Morton was induced to make his elaborate speech at Richmond, denouncing the whole theory of Republican reconstruction as subsequently carried out, and opposing the policy of negro suffrage by arguments which he seemed to regard as overwhelming. He made a dismal picture of the ignorance and degradation of the plantation negroes of the South, and scouted the policy of arming them with political power. But their fitness for the ballot was a subordinate question. A great national emergency pleaded for their right to it on other and far more imperative grounds. The question involved the welfare of both races, and the issues of the war. It involved not merely the fate of the negro, but the safety of society. It was, moreover, a question of national honor and gratitude, from which no escape was morally possible. To leave the ballot in the hands of the ex-rebels, and withhold it from these helpless millions, would be to turn them over to the unhindered tyranny and misrule of their enemies, who were then smarting under the humiliation of their failure, and making the condition of the freedmen more intolerable than slavery itself, through local laws and police regulations.

The Governor referred to the Constitution and laws of Indiana, denying the ballot to her intelligent negroes, and subjecting colored men to prosecution and fine for coming into the State; and asked with what face her people could insist upon conferring the suffrage upon the negroes of the Southern States? But this was an evasion of the question. The people of Indiana had no right to take advantage of their own wrong, or to sacrifice the welfare of four million blacks on the altar of Northern consistency. He should have preached the duty of practical repentance in Indiana, instead of making the sins of her people an excuse for a far greater inhumanity to the negroes of the South.

He urged that the policy of negro suffrage would give the lie to all the arguments that had ever been employed against slavery as degrading and

brutalizing to its victims. He said it was " to pay
the highest compliment to the institution of slavery," and " stultify ourselves."   But this was be-
littling a great national question, by the side of
which all considerations of party consistency were
utterly trivial and contemptible. The ballot for
the negro was a logical necessity, and it was a
matter of the least possible consequence whether
the granting of it would " stultify ourselves " or
not.

He insisted that the true policy was to give the
Southern negroes a probation of fifteen or twenty
years to prepare for the ballot. He would give
them " time to acquire a little property ; time to
get a little education ; time to learn something
about the simplest forms of business, and to prepare themselves for the exercise of political power."
But he did not explain how all this was to be done,
under the circumstances of their condition. He
declared that not one of them in five hundred
could read, or was worth five dollars in property
of any kind, owning nothing but their bodies, and
living on the plantations of white men upon whom
they were dependent for employment and subsist-
ence.   How could such men acquire " education,"
and " property," under the absolute sway of a people who regarded them with loathing and contempt ?
Who would grant them this " probation," and help
them turn it to good account ? Was some miracle
to be wrought through which the slave-masters

were to be transfigured into negro apostles and devotees? Besides, under Governor Morton's theory of reconstruction and State rights, neither Congress nor the people of the loyal States had anything to do with the question. It was no more their concern in South Carolina than in Massachusetts. His suggestion of a probation for Southern negroes was therefore an impertinence. If not, why did he not recommend a " probation " for the hordes of " white trash " that were as unfit for political power as the negroes?

He was very earnest and eloquent in his condemnation of Mr. Sumner for proposing to give the ballot to the negroes and disfranchise the white Rebels, but his moral vision failed to discern anything amiss in his own ghastly policy of arming the white Rebels with the ballot and denying it to the loyal negroes.

He argued that the right to vote carried with it the right to hold office, and that negro suffrage would lead to the election of negro Governors, negro judges, negro members of Congress, a negro balance of power in our politics, and a war of races. He seemed to have no faith at all in the beneficent measures designed to guard the black race from outrage and wrong, while full of apprehension that the heavens would fall if such measures were adopted.

This speech was published in a large pamphlet edition and extensively scattered throughout the country; but it proved a help rather than a hindrance to my enterprise. I replied to it in several incisive newspaper articles, and made its arguments a text for a still more thorough discussion of the issue on the stump, and at the close of my canvass the Republicans of the district were as nearly a unit in my favor as a party can be made respecting any controverted doctrine.

I now extended my labors briefly outside of my district, and by special invitation from citizens of Indianapolis and members of the Legislature, then in session, I spoke in that city on the 17th of November. Every possible effort was made by the Johnsonized Republicans to prevent me from having an audience, but they failed utterly; and I analyzed the positions of Governor Morton in a speech of two hours, which was reported for the "Cincinnati Gazette" and subsequently published in a large pamphlet edition. The political rage and exasperation which now prevailed in the ranks of the Anti-Suffrage faction can be more readily imagined than described. Their organ, the "Indianapolis Journal," poured out upon me an incredible deliverance of vituperation and venom for scattering my heresies outside of my Congressional district, declaring that I had "the temper of a hedgehog, the adhesiveness of a barnacle, the vanity of a peacock, the vindictiveness of a Corsican, the hypocrisy of Aminadab Sleek and the duplicity of the devil." I rather enjoyed these paroxysms of malignity, which broke out all over the State among the Governor's conservative satellites, since my only offense was fidelity to my political opinions, the soundness of which I was finding fully justified by events ; for the friends of the Governor, in a few short months, gathered together and cremated all the copies of his famous speech which could be found. But the disowned document was printed as a campaign tract by the Democrats for a dozen successive years afterward, and circulated largely in several of the Northern States, while the Governor himself, by a sudden and splendid somersault, became the champion and exemplar of the very heresies which had so furiously kindled his ire against me. These performances are sufficiently remarkable to deserve notice. They did much to make Indiana politics spicy and picturesque, and showed how earnestly the radical and conservative wings of the Republican party could wage war against the common enemy without in the least impairing their ability or disposition to fight each other.

I have referred to these facts because they form a necessary part of the story I am telling. The question of Negro Suffrage was a very grave one, and the circumstances connected with its introduction as a political issue are worthy of record ; while Governor Morton was a sort of phenomenal figure in American politics during the war period, and played a very remarkable part in the affairs of Indiana. It has been aptly said of him, and not by an enemy, that his inconsistencies, in a study of his character, form the most charming part of it, and that no man in public life ever brought such magnificent resources to the support of both sides of a question. His force of will was as matchless as his ambition for power was boundless and unappeasable. He was made for revolutionary times, and his singular energy of character was pre-eminently destructive; but it can not be denied that his services to the country in this crisis were great. Mr. Von Holst, in his "Constitutional and Political History of the United States," has a chapter on " The Reign of Andrew Jackson." When the history of Indiana shall be written, it might fitly contain a chapter on " The Reign of Oliver P. Morton." He made himself not merely the master of the Democratic party of the State, and of its Rebel element, but of his own party as well. His will, to a surprising extent, had the force of law in matters of both civil and military administration. His vigor in action and great personal magnetism so rallied the people to his support, that with the rarest exceptions the prominent leaders of his party quietly succumbed to his ambition, and recoiled from the thought of confronting him, even when they believed him in the wrong.

His hostility to me began with my election to Congress in 1849, in which, as a Free Soiler, I had the united support of the Democratic party of my district, of which he was then a member. I never obtained his forgiveness for my success in that contest, and his unfriendliness was afterward aggra-

vated by his failure as a Republican leader to sup-
plant me in the district, and it continued to the
end.   I knew him from his boyhood.   We resided
in the same village nearly twenty years, and began
our acquaintance as members of the same debating
club.   For years we were intimate and attached
friends, and I believe no man was before me in ap-
preciating his talents and predicting for him a career of political distinction and usefulness.   During
the war, earnest efforts were made by his friends
and mine looking to a reconciliation, and the restoration of that harmony in the party which good
men on both sides greatly coveted; but all such
efforts necessarily failed.   If I had been willing to
subordinate my political convictions and sense of
duty to his ambition, peace could at once have
been restored; but as this was impossible, I was
obliged to accept the warfare which continued and
increased, and which I always regretted and deplored.   I only make these statements in justice
to the truth.

The bill providing for negro suffrage in the District of Columbia was among the first important
measures of the Thirty-ninth Congress.   The debate upon it in January, 1866, was singularly able
and thorough, and gave strong evidence of political progress.   All efforts to postpone the measure,
or to make suffrage restrictive, were voted down,
and on the announcement of its passage the cheering was tremendous.   Beginning on the floor, it

was quickly caught up by the galleries, and the scene resembled that which followed the passage of the Constitutional Amendment already referred to. The majority was over two to one, thus clearly foreshadowing the enfranchisement of the negro in the insurrectionary districts. I believe only two of my colleagues voted with me for its passage.

The question of reconstruction was brought directly before Congress by the report of the joint select committee on that subject, submitting the Fourteenth Constitutional Amendment. The second section of the Amendment was a measure of compromise, and attempted to unite the radical and conservative wings of the party by restricting the right of representation in the South to the basis of suffrage, instead of extending that basis in conformity to the right of representation. It was a proposition to the Rebels that if they would agree that the negroes should not be counted in the basis of representation, we would hand them over, unconditionally, to the tender mercies of their old masters. It sanctioned the barbarism of the Rebel State Governments in denying the right of representation to their freedmen, simply because of their race and color, and thus struck at the very principle of Democracy. It was a scheme of cold-blooded treachery and ingratitude to a people who had contributed nearly two hundred thousand soldiers to the armies of the Union,

and among whom no traitor had ever been found; and it was urged as a means of securing equality of white representation in the Government
. when that object could have been perfectly attained by a constitutional amendment arming the negroes of the South with the ballot, instead of leaving them in the absolute power of their enemies. Of course, no man could afford to vote against the proposition to cut down rebel representation to the basis of suffrage; but to recognize the authority of these States to make political outlaws of their colored citizens and incorporate this principle into the Constitution of the United States, was a wanton betrayal of justice and humanity. Congress, however, was unprepared for more thorough work. The conservative policy which had so long sought to spare slavery was obliged, as usual, to feel its way cautiously, and wait on the logic of events; while the negro, as I shall show, was finally indebted for the franchise to the desperate madness of his enemies in rejecting the dishonorable proposition of his friends.

As the question of reconstruction became more and more engrossing, the signs of a breach between the President and Congress revealed themselves. He had disappointed the hopes of his radical friends, and begun to show his partiality for conservative and Democratic ideas. His estrangement from his party probably had its genesis in the unfortunate exhibition of himself at the inauguration of Mr. Lin-

18

coln, and the condemnation of it by leading Republicans, which he could not forget.   Instead of keeping his promise to be the " Moses " of the colored people he turned his back upon them in a very offensive public speech.   His veto of the Freedmen's Bureau bill finally stripped him of all disguises, and placed him squarely against Congress and the people, while the House met his defiance by a concurrent resolution emphatically condemning his reconstruction policy, and thus opening the way for the coming struggle between Executive usurpation and the power of Congress.   His maudlin speech on the 22d of February to the political mob which called on him, branding as traitors the leaders of the party which had elected him, completely dishonored him in the opinion of all Republicans, and awakened general alarm.   Everybody could now see the mistake of his nomination at Baltimore, and that he was simply a narrow-minded dogmatist and a bulldog in disposition, who would do anything in his power to thwart the wishes of his former friends.

During the month of March of this year, at the request of intelligent working men in the employ of the Government, I introduced a bill making eight hours a day's work in the navy yards of the United States.   This was the beginning of the eight hour agitation in Congress.   I had not given much thought to the necessity for such legislation in this country, but the proposed measure seemed to me an augury of good to the working classes, as the

Ten Hour movement had proved itself to be twenty years before. It could plead the time laws of England as a precedent, enacted to protect humanity against the " Lords of the Loom." These laws recognized labor as capital endowed with human needs, and entitled to the special guardianship of the State, and not as merchandise merely, to be governed solely by the law of supply and demand. While I was a believer in Free Trade, I was not willing to follow its logic in all cases of conflict between capital and labor. My warfare against chattel slavery and the monopoly of the soil had assumed the duty of the Government to secure fair play and equal opportunities to the laboring masses, and I was willing to embody that idea in a specific legislative proposition, and thus invite its discussion and the settlement of it upon its merits.

In April of this year a notable passage at arms occurred in the House between Mr. Conkling and Mr. Blaine, which has been made historic by the subsequent career of these great Republican chiefs. The altercation between them was protracted and very personal, and grew out of the official conduct of Provost Marshal General Fry. The animosity engendered between these rivals at this early day seems never to have been intermitted, and it can best be appreciated by referring to the closing passages of their remarkable war of words on the 30th of this month. Mr. Conkling's language was very contemptuous, and in concluding he said :

" If the member from Maine had the least idea how profoundly indifferent I am to his opinion upon the subject which he has been discussing, or upon any other subject personal to me, I think he would hardly take the trouble to rise here and express his opinion. And as it is a matter of entire indifference to me what that opinion may be, I certainly will not detain the House by discussing the question whether it is well or ill founded, or by noticing what he says. I submit the whole matter to the members of the House, making, as I do, an apology (for I feel that it is due to the House) for the length of time which I have occupied in consequence of being drawn into explanations, originally by an interruption which I pronounced the other day ungentlemanly and impertinent, and having nothing whatever to do with the question."

Mr. Blaine, in reply, referred to Mr. Conkling's " grandiloquent swell " and his " turkey gobbler strut," and concluded:

" I know that within the last five weeks, as members of the House will recollect, an extra strut has characterized the gentleman's bearing. It is not his fault. It is the fault of another. That gifted and satirical writer, Theodore Tilton, of the "New York Independent," spent some weeks recently in this city. His letters published in that paper, embraced, with many serious statements, a little jocose satire, a part of which was the statement that the mantle of the late Winter Davis had fallen upon the member from New York. The gentleman took it seriously, and it has given his strut additional pomposity. The resemblance is great. It is striking. Hyperion to a satyr, Thersites to Hercules, mud to marble, dung-hill to diamond, a singed cat to a Bengal tiger, a whining puppy to a roaring lion. Shade of the mighty Davis, forgive the almost profanation of that jocose satire!"

This uncomely sparring match seemed. to have no significance at the time beyond the amusement it afforded and the personal discredit it attached to the combatants; but in its later consequences it has not only seriously involved the political fortunes of both these ambitious men, but rent the Republican party itself into warring factions. Still more, it has connected itself in the same way, and not very remotely, with the nomination of General Garfield in 1880, and his subsequent assassination. Such are the strange political revenges of a personal quarrel.

During this session of Congress the policy of Military Land Bounties was very earnestly agitated, and threatened the most alarming consequences. Probably no great question has been so imperfectly understood by our public men as the land question, and the truth of this is attested by the multiplied schemes of pillage and plunder to which the public domain has been exposed within the past thirty or forty years. Among these the project of Land Bounties to soldiers has been con-

spicuous. Of the millions of acres disposed of
by the Government through assignable land-war-
rants in the pretended interest of the soldiers of the
Mexican War a very small fraction was appropriated to their use. The great body of the land fell into
the hands of monopolists, who thus hindered the
settlement and productive wealth of the country,
while the sum received by the soldier for his war-
rant was in very many cases a mere mockery of
his just claims, and in no instance an adequate
bounty. The policy, however, had become traditional, and now, at the close of the grandest of all
our wars, it was quite natural for the country's
defenders to claim its supposed benefits. Congress was flooded with their petitions, and it
required uncommon political courage to oppose
their wishes. It was very plausibly urged that the
Nation, with its heavy load of debt, could not pay
a bounty in money, and that it should be done by
drawing liberally upon the thousand million acres
of the public domain. Some of the advocates of
this policy openly favored the repeal of the Homestead law for this purpose, just as Thurlow Weed,
earlier in the war, had demanded its repeal so that
our public lands could be mortgaged to European
capitalists in security for the money we needed to
carry on the struggle. The situation became critical. Everybody was eager to reward the soldier,
and especially the politicians ; and there seemed to
be no other way to do it than by bounties in land,

for which all our previous wars furnished precedents. The House Committee on Public Lands considered the question with great care and anxiety, and in the hope of check-mating the project made a report in response to one of the many petitions for land bounty which had been referred to it, embodying some very significant facts. It showed that more than two millions and a quarter of soldiers would be entitled to a bounty in land, and that it would require more than one third of the public domain remaining undisposed of, and cover nearly all of it that was really fit for agriculture; that the warrants would undoubtedly be made assignable, as in the case of previous bounties, and that land speculation would thus find its new birth and have free course in its dreadful ravages; and that it would prove the practical overthrow of the policy of our pre-emption and homestead laws and turn back the current of American civilization and progress. The report further insisted that the Nation could not honorably plead poverty in bar of the great debt it owed its defenders, and it was accompanied by a bill providing a bounty in money at the rate of eight and one third dollars per month for the time of their service, which was drawn after conferring with intelligent men among them who fully appreciated the facts and arguments of the committee. This report and its accompanying bill had an almost magical effect. They not only perfectly satisfied the soldiers everywhere, but revolutionized

the opinion of both Houses of Congress, and thus
saved the public domain from the wholesale spoliation that had threatened it.   The bill was referred
to the Military Committee, and afterward became
well known by the title of "General Schenck's bill."
It passed the House, but failed in the Senate.   It
passed the House repeatedly at different sessions of
Congress afterward, although it never became a
law ; but it was the timely and fortunate instrument
through which the public domain was saved from
the wreck which menaced it in the hasty adoption
of a scheme which would have proved as worthless
to our soldiers as disastrous to the country.

CHAPTER XIII.

MINERAL LANDS AND THE RIGHT OF PRE-EMPTION.

The lead and copper lands of the Northwest—The gold-bearing regions of the Pacific, and their disposition—A legislative reminiscence—Mining Act of 1866, and how it was passed—Its deplorable failure, and its lesson—Report of the Land Commission—The Right of Pre-emption, and the "Dred Scott decision" of the settlers.

THE action of the Government in dealing with the mineral lands of the United States forms one of the most curious chapters in the history of legislation. It had its beginning in the famous Congressional Ordinance of May 20, 1785, which reserved one third part of all gold, silver, lead and copper mines to be sold or otherwise disposed of as Congress might direct. From this time till the discovery of gold in California in 1848, the legislation of Congress respecting mineral lands related exclusively to those containing the base or merely useful metals, and applied only to the regions now embraced by the States of Michigan, Wisconsin, Iowa, Illinois and Missouri. The policy of reserving mineral lands from sale was obviously of feudal origin, and naturally led to the leasing of such lands by the Government, which was inau-

gurated by the Act of Congress of March 3, 1807.
The Act of Congress of March 3, 1829, provided
for the sale of the reserved lead mines and contiguous lands in Missouri, on six months' notice, but
mineral lands elsewhere remained reserved, and
continued to be leased by the Government. This
policy was thoroughly and perseveringly tried,
and proved utterly unprofitable and ruinous.
President Polk, in his message of December 2,
1845, declared that the income derived from the
leasing system for the years 1841, 1842, 1843 and
1844 was less than one fourth of its expense, and
he recommended its abolition, and that these lands
be brought into market. The leasing policy
drew into the mining regions a population of va-
grants, idlers and gamblers, who resisted the pay-
ment of taxes on the product of the mines, and
defied the agents of the Government. It excluded
sober and intelligent citizens, and hindered the establishment of organized communities and the development of the mines. The miners were violently
opposed to the policy of sale, but the evils incident
to the leasing policy became so intolerable that
the Government was at length obliged to provide
for the sale of the lands in fee, which it did by Acts
of Congress of July 11, 1846, and March 1 and 3,
1847. The tracts occupied and worked by the
miners under their leases possessed every variety
of shape and boundary, but there were no difficulties which were not readily adjusted under the

rectangular system of surveys and the regulations
of the Land Department. A new class of men at
once took possession of these regions as owners of
the soil, brought their families with them, laid the
foundations of social order, expelled the semi-bar-
barians who had secured a temporary occupancy,
and thus, at once promoted their own welfare, the
prosperity of the country, and the financial interests of the Government. Under this reformed policy the lead and copper lands of the regions named
were disposed of in fee.

But the gold-bearing regions covered by our
Mexican acquisitions created a new dispensation
in mining, and invited the attention of Congress to
the consideration of a new and exceedingly important question. How should these mineral lands be
disposed of? They covered an area of a million
square miles, and their exploration and development
became a matter of the most vital moment, not only
in a financial point of view, but as a means of promoting the settlement and tillage of the agricultural
lands contiguous to the mineral deposits. President
Fillmore, in his message of December 2, 1849, recommended the sale of these lands in small par-
cels, and Mr. Ewing, his Secretary of the Interior,
urged upon Congress the consideration of the subject, and recommended the policy of leasing them;
but no attention seems to have been given to these
recommendations. By Act of Congress of September 27, 1850, mineral lands in Oregon were re-

served from sale; and by Acts of March 3, 1853, and of July 22, 1854, they were reserved in California and New Mexico. This was the extent of Congressional action. Early in the late war, the Secretary of the Interior, Hon. Caleb B. Smith, referred to the question, and the Commissioner of the General Land Office afterward repeatedly recommended the policy of leasing, but Congress took no notice of the subject. My interest in the question was first awakened in the fall of 1864, in carefully overhauling our land policy. Our mineral lands for more than sixteen years had been open to all comers from whatever quarter of the globe, during which time more than a thousand million dollars had been extracted, from which not a dollar of revenue reached the National Treasury save the comparatively trifling amount derived from the Internal Revenue tax on bullion. This fact was so remarkable that it was difficult to accept it as true. The Government had no policy whatever in dealing with these immense repositories of national wealth, and declined to have any; for a policy implies that something is to be done, and points out the method of doing it. It had prohibited the sale of mineral lands, and then come to a dead halt. The Constitution expressly provides that Congress shall have power " to make all needful rules and regulations respecting the territory or other property belonging to the United States "; but Congress, in reserving these lands from sale and taking no

measures whatever respecting their products, simply abandoned them, and, as the trustee of the
Nation, became as recreant as the father who aban-
dons his minor child.

The case was a very curious one, and the more
I considered it, the more astonished I became at
the strange indifference of the Government, and
that no public man of any party had ever given the
subject the slightest attention. The Nation had
been selling its lands containing iron, copper and
lead, and the policy of vesting an absolute fee in individual proprietors had been accepted on actual
trial, and after the leasing policy had signally failed,
and I could see nothing in the distinction between
the useful and precious metals which required a
different policy for the latter. Some policy was
absolutely demanded. The country, loaded down
by a great and constantly increasing war debt,
could not afford to turn away from so tempting a
source of revenue. To sleep over its grand opportunity was as stupid as it was criminal. It was ob-
vious that if the Government continued to reserve
these lands from sale, some form of tax or royalty
on their products must be resorted to as a measure
of financial policy ; but this would have involved the
same political anomaly as the policy of leasing, and
the same failure. In principle it was the same. To
retain the fee of the lands in the Government and im-
pose a rent upon their occupants, would make the
Government a great landlord, and the miners its ten-

ants.   Such a policy would not be American, but
European.   It would not be Democratic, but Feudal.
It would be to follow the Governments of the Old
World, which reserve their mineral lands for the
Crown, because they are esteemed too precious for
the people.   It was at war with our theory of
Democracy, which has respect chiefly to the individual, and seeks to strengthen the Government
by guarding his rights and promoting his well-
being.   These considerations convinced me that
the time had come to abandon the non-action course
of the Government, and adopt a policy in harmony
with our general legislation ; and that the survey
and sale of these lands in fee was the best and only
method of promoting security of titles, permanent
settlements, and thorough development.   As early
as December, 1864, I therefore introduced a bill
embodying this policy, which was followed by a
similar measure, early in the Thirty-ninth Congress,
accompanied by an elaborate report, arguing the
question pretty fully, and combating all the objections to the principle and policy of sale.   My views
were commended by Secretary McCullough, as
they had been by Mr. Chase, while I was glad to
find them supported by intelligent men from California, who spoke from actual observation and ex-
tensive experience in mining.

But although this measure fully protected all
miners in the right of exploration and discovery,
and carefully guarded against any interference with

vested rights, the idea was in some way rapidly and extensively propagated that it contemplated a sweeping confiscation of all their claims, and the less informed among them became wild with excitement. The politicians of California and Nevada, instead of endeavoring to enlighten them and quiet this excitement, yielded to it absolutely. They became as completely its instruments as they have since been of the Anti-Mongolian feeling. They argued, at first, that no Congressional legislation was necessary, and that while the Government should retain the fee of these lands, the miners should have the entire control of them under regulations prescribed by themselves. This, it was believed, would placate the miners and settle the question; but the introduction of the measure referred to, and the agitation of the question, had made some form of legislation inevitable, and the question now was to determine what that legislation should be. Senators Conness of California, and Stewart of Nevada, who were exceedingly hostile to the bill I had introduced, and feared its passage, sought to avert it by carrying through the Senate "a bill to regulate the occupation of mineral lands and to extend the right of pre-emption thereto," which they hoped would satisfy their constituents and prevent further legislation. They supported it as the next best thing to total non-action by Congress. It provided for giving title to the miners, but it did this by practi-

cally abdicating the jurisdiction of the National
Government over these lands, with its recognized
and well-settled machinery for determining all
questions of title and boundary, and handing them
over to "the local custom or rules of the miners."
These "local rules" were to govern the miner in
the location, extension and boundary of his claim,
the manner of developing it, and the survey also,
which was not to be executed with any reference
to base lines as in the case of other public lands,
but in utter disregard of the same.   The Surveyor
General was to make a plat or diagram of the
claim, and transmit it to the Commissioner of the
General Land Office, who, as the mere agent and
clerk of the miner, with no judicial authority
whatever, was required to issue the patent.   In
case of any conflict between claimants it was to be
determined by the "local courts," without any
right of appeal to the local land offices, the General Land Office, or to the Federal courts.   The
Government was thus required to part with its
lands by proceedings executed by officials wholly
outside of its jurisdiction, and irresponsible to its
authority.   The act not only abolished our rectangular system of surveys, but still further insulted
the principles of mathematics and the dictates of
common sense by providing that the claimant
should have the right to follow his vein or lode,
"with its dips, angles and variations to any depth,
although it may enter the land adjoining, which

land adjoining shall be sold subject to this condition "; a right unknown to the mining codes of England, France or Prussia, and not sanctioned by those of Spain or Mexico. Subject to this novel principle the crudely extemporized rules of the miners were to be recognized as law, and this system of instability and uncertainty made the basis of title and the arbiter of all disputes, instead of sweeping it away and ushering in a system of permanence and peace through the well-appointed agency of the Land Department. It was easy to see that this was an act to encourage litigation and for the benefit of lawyers, and not to promote the real interest of the miners or increase the product of the mines.

This was made perfectly clear at the time, by the report of a Senate committee of the Legislature of Nevada. In speaking of the local laws of the miners, it says, " There never was confusion worse confounded. More than two hundred districts within the limits of a single State, each with its self-approved code; these codes differing not alone each from the other, but presenting numberless instances of contradiction in themselves. The law of one point is not the law of another five miles distant, and a little further on will be a code which is the law of neither of the former, and so on, *ad infinitum;* with the further disturbing fact superadded, that the written laws themselves may be overrun by some peculiar custom which can be

19

found nowhere recorded, and the proof of which will vary with the volume of interested affidavits which may be brought on either side to establish it. Again, in one district the work to be done to hold a claim is nominal, in another exorbitant, in another abolished, in another adjourned from year to year. A stranger, seeking to ascertain the law, is surprised to learn that there is no satisfactory public record to which he can refer; no public officer to whom he may apply, who is under any bond or obligation to furnish him information, or guarantee its authenticity. Often, in the new districts, he finds there is not even the semblance of a code, but a simple resolution adopting the code of some other district, which may be a hundred miles distant. What guarantee has he for the investment of either capital or labor under such a system?" The report proceeds to show that these regulations can have no permanency. "A miner's meeting," it declares, "adopts a code; it stands apparently as the law. Some time after, on a few days' notice, a corporal's guard assembles, and, on simple motion, radically changes the whole system by which claims may be held in a district. Before a man may traverse the State, the laws of a district, which by examination and study he may have mastered, may be swept away, and no longer stand as the laws which govern the interest he may have acquired; and the change has been one which by no reasonable diligence could he be expected

to have knowledge of." Of course these facts thus
officially stated in the interest of the miners of
Nevada, were applicable to California, and all the
mining States and Territories, and they fitly and
very forcibly rebuked the attempt to enact the Senate bill.

When this bill reached the House it was properly referred to the Committee on Public Lands,
which then had under consideration the bill I had
reported providing for the survey and sale of mineral
lands through the regular machinery of the Land
Department. The House Committee subsequently
reported it favorably, and could not be persuaded
by the delegations from California and Nevada to
adopt the Senate bill as a substitute. Senators
Stewart and Conness, finding their project thus baffled, and becoming impatient of delay as the session
neared its close, called up a House bill entitled
"An Act granting the right of way to ditch and
canal owners over the Public Lands in the States
of California, Oregon and Nevada," and succeeded,
by sharp practice, in carrying a motion to strike
out the whole of the bill except the enacting
clause, and insert the bill which the Senate had
already enacted and was then before the House
Committee. This maneuver succeeded, and the
bill, thus enacted by the Senate a second time, and
now under a false title, was sent to the House,
where it found its place on the Speaker's table,
and was lying in wait for the sudden and unlooked-

for movement which was to follow.   The title was
misleading, and thus enabled Mr. Ashley of Nevada, to obtain the floor when it was reached, and
under the gag, which of course would cut off all
amendment and debate, he attempted to force
through a measure revolutionizing the whole land
policy of the Government so far as relates to the
Western side of the continent, and surrendering the
national authority over its vast magazines of mineral wealth to the legalized jargon and bewilderment I have depicted.   I succeeded in preventing
a vote by carrying an adjournment, but the question came up the next day, and the Senators referred to, with their allies in the House, had used
such marvelous industry in organizing and drilling
their forces, and the majority of the members knew
so little about the question involved, that I found
the chances decidedly against me.   I was obliged,
also, to encounter a prevailing but perfectly unwarranted presumption that the representatives of
the mining States were the best judges of the
question in dispute, while it was foolishly regarded
as a local one, with which the old States had no
concern.   The clumsy and next to incomprehensi-
ble bill thus became a law, and by legislative
methods as indefensible as the measure itself.

Such is the history of this remarkable experiment
in legislation ; but it is an experiment no longer.
Its character has been perfectly established by time,
and the logic of actual facts.   It has been exten-

sively and thoroughly tried, and after repeated
attempts to amend it by supplementary legislation,
its failure stands recorded in the manifold evils it
has wrought. The Land Commission, appointed
under the administration of President Hayes in
pursuance of an Act of Congress to classify the Public Lands and codify the laws relating to their disposition, visited the mining States and Territories
in detail, and devoted ample time to the examination of witnesses and experts in every important
locality touching the policy and practical operation
of the laws in force relating to mineral lands. This
Commission condemned these laws on the strength
of overwhelming evidence, and recommended a
thorough and radical reform, including the reference
of all disputed questions as to title and boundary
to the regular officials of the United States; the
abolition of the " local custom or rules of miners,"
with the " local courts " provided for their adjudica-
tion ; and the adoption of the United States surveys as far as practicable, including the geodetical
principle of ownership in lieu of the policy of
allowing the miner to follow his vein, " with its
dips, angles and variations under the adjoining land
of his neighbor," which policy is declared to be the
source of incalculable litigation. The Commission,
in short, urged the adoption of the principles of the
Common Law and the employment of the appropriate machinery of the Land Department, as a
substitute for the frontier regulations which Con-

gress made haste to nationalize in 1866.   It declared that under these regulations "title after
title hangs on a local record which may be defective,
mutilated, stolen for blackmail, or destroyed to
accomplish fraud, and of which the grantor, the
Government, has neither knowledge nor control";
tnat in the evidence taken "it was repeatedly
shown that two or three prospectors, camped in
the wilderness, have organized a mining district,
prescribed regulations involving size of claims,
mode of location and nature of record, elected one
of their number recorder, and that officer, on the
back of an envelope, or on the ace of spades
grudgingly spared from his pack, can make with
the stump of a lead pencil an entry that the Government recognizes as the inception of a title which
may convey millions of dollars; that even when
the recorder is duly elected he is not responsible
to the United States, is neither bonded nor under
oath, may falsify or destroy his record, may vitiate
the title to millions of dollars, and snap his fingers
in the face of the Government; and that our present
mining law might fitly be entitled " An Act to cause
the Government to join, upon unknown terms, with
an unknown second party, to convey to a third
party an illusory title to an indefinite thing, and
encourage the subsequent robbery thereof."

These strong statements are made by a Government commission composed of able and impartial
men, who were guided in their patient search after

the truth by the evidence of "a cloud of witnesses," who spoke from personal knowledge and experience. The character of our mining laws is therefore not a matter of theory, but of demonstrated fact. They scourge the mining States and Territories with the unspeakable curse of uncertainty of land titles, as everywhere attested by incurable litigation and strife. They thus undermine the morals of the people, and pave the way for violence and crime. They cripple a great national industry and source of wealth, and insult the prin ciples of American jurisprudence. And the misfortune of this legislation is heightened by the probability of its continuance ; for it is not easy to uproot a body of laws once accepted by a people, however mischievous in their character. Custom, and the faculty of adaptation, have a very reconciling influence upon communities as well as individuals. Moreover, men absorbed .in a feverish and hazardous industry, and stimulated by the hope of sudden wealth, are not disposed to consider the advantages of permanent ownership and security of title. Their business is to make their locations according to local custom, and sell out to the capitalists ; while the men who feel the burden of litigation and the evil of uncertain titles, are not the men who control public opinion and influence the course of legislation. It may thus happen that a system of laws initiated by itinerant miners solely for the protection of their transient pos-

sessory interests, and carried through Congress
at their behest by parliamentary roguery, may be
permanently engrafted upon half the continent.
If California had been contiguous to the older
States, and her mining operations had only kept
pace with the progress of settlements, or if her
representatives had been less ready to sacrifice the
enduring interests of their constituents for temporary and selfish ends, the wretched travesty of law
which now afflicts the States and Territories of the
West would have been unknown, and the same
code and forms of administration would have pre
vailed from the lakes to the Pacific.

The lesson of this vital mistake is a pregnant one.
The laws regulating the ownership and disposition
of landed property not only affect the well-being
but frequently the destiny of a people. The system
of primogeniture and entail adopted by the Southern States of our Union favored the policy of great
estates, and the ruinous system of landlordism and
slavery which finally laid waste the fairest and most
fertile section of the Republic and threatened its
life ; while the New England States, in adopting a
different system, laid the foundations of their prosperity in the soil itself, and " took a bond of fate "
for the welfare of unborn generations. Their political institutions were the logical outcome of their
laws respecting landed property, which favored a
great subdivision of the land and great equality
among the people, thus promoting prosperous cul-

tivation, compact communities, general education, a healthy public opinion, democracy in managing the affairs of the church, and that system of local self-government which has since prevailed over so many States. So intimate and vital are the relations between a community and the soil it occupies that in the nomenclature of politics the word "people" and "land" are convertible terms; but no people can prosper under any system of land tenures which tolerates a vexatious uncertainty of title, and thus prompts every man to become the enemy of his neighbor in the scuffle for his rights. Such a state of affairs is worse than pestilence or famine; but the evil of uncertain titles puts on new and very aggravated forms in our gold-bearing regions. The business of mining naturally awakens the strongest passions. It sharpens the faculties and dulls the conscience. It gives to cupidity its keenest edge. Its prizes are often rich and suddenly gained, and when they are sought through the forms of a law which compels a man to choose between an expensive and hazardous litigation and robbery, human nature is severely tried. No situation could well be more deplorable than that which obliges a man to pay heavy black-mail as the only means of saving his property from legal confiscation by another; and the moral ravages of a code which allows this can not be computed. It tempts civilized men to become savages and savages to become devils. It is not a mistake merely, but a great misfortune, that our laws touching so delicate and vital a question as the ownership and transfer of mineral lands were not so framed as to avert these frightful evils. So far as the past is concerned they are without remedy, and there is no positive safeguard for the future but in a return to the time-honored principles which give to the owner of the surface all that may be found within his lines, extended downward vertically, and refer all disputes to the old-fashioned and familiar machinery of the General Land Office. This system gave order and peace to the great lead and copper regions of the Northwest, and it would bring with it the same inestimable blessings to the harrassed and sorely tried regions of the Pacific slope.

About the same time the action of Congress supplied another example of hasty and slip-shod legislation, which has been perhaps equally prolific of evil. The State of California, soon after her admission, had assumed the right to dispose of the public lands within her borders according to her own peculiar wishes, and in disregard of the authority of the United States. This led to such serious conflicts and complications, that a remedy was sought in a bill to quiet land titles in that State. It was a very questionable measure, inasmuch as the parties claiming title under the State could only be relieved by recognizing her illegal acts as valid, and at the expense of claimants under the laws of the United States. It necessarily involved the right of

pre-emption, and this was distinctly presented in connection with what was known as the Suscol Ranch
in that State. It contained about ninety thousand
acres, and was covered by an old Spanish grant
which the Supreme Court of the United States in the
year 1862 had pronounced void, soon after which
numerous settlers went upon the land as pre-emptors, as they had the right to do. Their claims as
such, being disputed by parties asserting title under
the void grant, the General Land Office, on the reference of the question to that department, decided in
favor of the pre-emptors, upon which the opposing
parties procured the submission of the question to
the Attorney General. That officer gave his opinion
to the effect that a settler under the pre-emption
laws acquires no vested interest in the land he
occupies by virtue of his settlement, and can acquire no such interest, till he has taken *all* the legal
steps necessary to perfect an entrance in the Land
Office, being, in the meantime, a mere tenant-at-will,
who may be ejected by the Government at any
moment in favor of another party. In pursuance
of this opinion scores of *bona fide* settlers were
driven from their pre-emptions, which the laws of
the United States had offered them, on certain prescribed conditions, with which they were willing
and anxious to comply, and their homes, with the
valuable improvements made upon them in good
faith, were handed over to speculators and monopolists. The proceeding was as outrageous as the

ruling which authorized it was surprising to the
whole country ; and it naturally awakened uneasiness and alarm among our pioneer settlers every
where. It seemed to me very proper, therefore,
that in a bill to quiet land titles in California, these
troubles on this Ranch should be settled by a fitting amendment, which should protect the rights of
these pre-emptors against the effect of the ruling
referred to. The opinion of the Attorney General
had completely overturned the whole policy of the
Government as popularly understood, and I simply
proposed to restore it by a proviso guarding the
rights of *bona fide* settlers who were claiming title
under the laws of the United States; but to my
perfect amazement I found the California delegation
bitterly opposed to this amendment. The reading
of it threw them into a spasm of rage, and showed
that they were less anxious to quiet titles in their
State than to serve the monopolies and rings which
had trampled on the laws of the United States, and
thus involved themselves in trouble. The zeal and
industry of the delegation in this opposition could
only be paralleled by their labors for the passage of
their mineral land bill ; and the same appeals were
made in both cases. They said this was a " local
measure," and that they understood the interests
of the Pacific coast better than men from the old
States, while they begged and button-holed members with a pertinacity very rarely witnessed in any
legislative body. They turned the business of log-

rolling to such account that the amendment was defeated by a strong majority, while it proved the entering wedge to other and greater outrages upon the rights of settlers which the country has since witnessed, and was followed by a decision of the Supreme Court of the United States, fully affirming the principle laid down in the opinion of the Attorney General. This ruling, which has been aptly styled "the Dred Scott decision of the American Pioneer," has been repeatedly re-affirmed, while the claim of pre-emption, once universally regarded as a substantial right, has faded away into a glamour or myth.

CHAPTER XIV.

RECONSTRUCTION AND IMPEACHMENT.

THE fall elections of this year were complicated
by the hostile influence of the Executive, but the
popular current was strongly on the side of Congress. A few prominent Republican members
followed the President, but the great body of them
stood firm. In my own Congressional district my
majority was over 6,200, notwithstanding the
formidable conservative opposition in my own
party, and its extraordinary efforts to divide the
Republicans through the patronage of the Administration. Nearly all of my old opponents in the
district and State were now Johnsonized, except
Gov. Morton, whose temporary desertion the year
before was atoned for by a prudent and timely repentance. He was not, however, thoroughly

(302)

reconstructed; for in the Philadelphia Loyal Convention which met in September of this year to consider the critical state of the country, he used his influence with the delegates from the South to prevent their espousal of Negro Suffrage, and begged Theodore Tilton to prevail on Frederick Douglass to take the first train of cars for home, in order to save the Republican party from detriment He was still under the shadow of his early · Democratic training; and he and his satellites, vividly remembering my campaign for Negro Suffrage the year before, and finding me thoroughly intrenched in my Congressional district, hit upon a new project for my political discomfiture. This was the re-districting of the State at the ensuing session of the Indiana Legislature, which they succeeded in accomplishing by disguising their real purpose. There was neither reason nor excuse for such a scheme at this time, apart from my political fortunes; and by the most shameless Gerrymandering three counties of my district, which gave me a majority of 5,000, were taken from me, and four others added in which I was personally but little acquainted, and which gave an aggregate Democratic majority of about 1,500. This was preliminary to the next Congressional race, and the success of the enterprise remained to be tested; but it furnished a curious illustration of the state of Indiana Republicanism at that time.

On the meeting of Congress in December the

signs of political progress since the adjournment
were quite noticeable. The subject of impeachment
began to be talked about, and both houses seemed
ready for all necessary measures. Since mingling
freely with their constituents, very few Republican
members insisted that the XIV Constitutional
Amendment should be accepted as a finality, or as
an adequate solution of the problem of reconstruction. The second section of that amendment, proposing to abandon the colored race in the South
on condition that they should not be counted in
the basis of representation, was now generally condemned, and if the question had been a new one it
could not have been adopted. This enlightenment
of Northern representatives was largely due to the
prompt and contemptuous rejection by the rebellious States of the XIV Amendment as a scheme of
reconstruction, and their enactment of black codes
which made the condition of the freedmen more deplorable than slavery itself. In this instance, as in
that of Mr. Lincoln's Proclamation of Emancipation, it was rebel desperation which saved the negro ;
for if the XIV Amendment had been at first accepted, the work of reconstruction would have ended
without conferring upon him the ballot. This will
scarcely be denied by any one, and has been frankly
admitted by some of the most distinguished leaders of the party.

The policy of treating these States as Territories
seemed now to be rapidly gaining ground, and com-

mended itself as the only logical way out of the political dilemma in which the Government was placed. But here again the old strife between radicalism and conservatism cropped out. The former opposed all haste in the work of reconstruction. It insisted that what the rebellious districts needed was not an easy and speedy return to the places they had lost by their treasonable conspiracy, but a probationary training, looking to their restoration when they should prove their fitness for civil government as independent States. It was insisted that they were not prepared for this, and that with their large population of ignorant negroes and equally ignorant whites, dominated by a formidable oligarchy of educated land-owners who despised the power that had conquered them, while they still had the sympathy of their old allies in the North, the withdrawal of Federal intervention and the unhindered operation of local supremacy would as fatally hedge up the way of justice and equality as the rebel despotisms then existing. The political and social forces of Southern society, if unchecked from without, were sure to assert themselves, and the more decided anti-slavery men in both houses of Congress so warned the country, and foretold that no theories of Democracy could avail unless adequately supported by a healthy and intelligent public opinion. They saw that States must grow, and could not be suddenly constructed where the materials were wanting, and that forms are

20

worthless in the hands of an ignorant mob. It was objected to the territorial theory that it was arbitrary, and would lead to corruption and tyranny like the pro-consular system of Rome; but it was simply the territorial system to which we had been accustomed from the beginning of the Government, and could not prove worse than the hasty re-admission of ten conquered districts to the dignity of States of the Union, involving, as it has done, the horrors of carpet-bag government, Ku Klux outrages, and a system of pro-consular tyranny as inconsistent with the rights of these States as it has been disgraceful to the very idea of free government and fatal to the best interests of the colored race.

But the strange chaos of opinion which now prevailed was unfavorable to sound thinking or wise acting. Great and far-reaching interests were at stake, but they were made the sport of politicians, and disposed of in the light of their supposed effect upon the ascendancy of the Republican party. Statesmanship was sacrificed to party management, and the final result was that the various territorial bills which had been introduced in both Houses, and the somewhat incongruous bills of Stevens and Ashley, were all superseded by the passage of the "Military bill," which was vetoed by the President, but re-enacted in the face of his objections. This bill was utterly indefensible on principle. It was completely at war with the genius and spirit of democratic government. Instead of furnishing the Rebel districts with civil governments, and providing for a military force adequate to sustain them, it abolished civil government entirely, and installed the army in its place. It was a confession of Congressional incompetence to deal with a problem which Congress alone had the right to solve. Its provisions perfectly exposed it to all the objections which could be urged to the plan of territorial reconstruction, while they inaugurated a centralized military despotism in the place of that system of well-understood local self-government which the territorial policy offered as a preparation for restoration. The measure was analyzed and exposed with great ability by Henry J. Raymond, whose arguments were unanswered and unanswerable; but nothing could stay the prevailing impatience of Congress for speedy legislation looking to the early return of the rebel districts to their places in the Union. The bill was a legislative solecism. It did not abrogate the existing Rebel State governments. It left the ballot in the hands of white Rebels, and did not confer it upon the black loyalists. It sought to conciliate the power it was endeavoring to coerce. It provided for negro suffrage as one of the fundamental conditions on which the rebellious States should be restored to their places in the Union, but left the negro to the mercy of their black codes, pending the decision of the question of their acceptance of the proposed conditions of restoration.

The freedmen were completely in the power of their old masters, so long as the latter might refuse the terms of reconstruction that were offered; and they had the option to refuse them entirely, if they saw fit to prefer their own mad ascendancy and its train of disorders to compulsory restoration. This perfectly inexcusable abandonment of negro suffrage was zealously defended by a small body of conservative Republicans who were still lingering in the sunshine of executive favor, and of whom Mr. Blaine was the chief; and it was through the timely action of Mr. Shellabarger, of Ohio, which these conservatives opposed, that the scheme of reconstruction was finally so amended as to make the Rebel State governments provisional only, and secure the ballot to the negro during the period, whether long or short, which might intervene prior to the work of re-admission. This provision was absolutely vital, because it took from the people of the insurrectionary districts every motive for refusing the acceptance of the terms proposed, and settled the work of reconstruction by this exercise of absolute power by their conquerors. It was this provision which secured the support of the Radical Republicans in Congress; but it did not meet their objections to this scheme of hasty military reconstruction, while these objections have been amply justified by time.

Thaddeus Stevens never appeared to such splendid advantage as a parliamentary leader as in this protracted debate on reconstruction. He was then nearly seventy-six, and was physically so feeble that he could scarcely stand; but his intellectual resources seemed to be perfectly unimpaired. Eloquence, irony, wit, and invective, were charmingly blended in the defense of his positions and his attacks upon his opponents. In dealing with the views of Bingham, Blaine, and Banks, he was by no means complimentary. He referred to them in his closing speech on the bill, on the thirteenth of February, when he said, in response to an interruption by Mr. Blaine, " What I am speaking of is this proposed step toward universal amnesty and universal Andy-Johnsonism. If this Congress so decides, it will give me great pleasure to join in the *io triumphe* of the gentleman from Ohio in leading this House, possibly by forbidden paths, into the sheep-fold or the goat-fold of the President." In speaking of the amendment to the bill offered by General Banks, he said, " It proposes to set up a contrivance at the mouth of the Mississippi, and by hydraulic action to control all the States that are washed by the waters of that great stream." He declared that, " The amendment of the gentleman from Maine lets in a vast number of Rebels, and shuts out nobody. All I ask is that when the House comes to vote upon that amendment, it shall understand that the adoption of it would be an entire surrender of those States into the hands of the Rebels. * * If, sir, I might presume upon my age, without claiming any of the wisdom of Nestor, I would suggest to the young gentlemen around me, that the deeds of this burning crisis, of this solemn day, of this thrilling moment, will cast their shadows far into the future, and will make their impress upon the annals of our history; and that we shall appear upon the bright pages of that history just in so far as we cordially, without guile, without bickering, without small criticisms, lend our aid to promote the great cause of humanity and universal liberty."

As a precautionary measure against executive usurpation, the Fortieth Congress was organized in March, 1867, immediately after the adjournment of the Thirty-ninth. After a brief session it adjourned till the third of July, to await the further progress of events. On re-assembling I found the feeling in favor of impeachment had considerably increased, but was not yet strong enough to prevail. All that could be done was the passage of a supplemental act on the subject of reconstruction, which naturally provoked another veto, in which the President re-affirmed the points of his message vetoing the original bill, and arraigned the action of Congress as high-handed and despotic. The message was construed by the Republicans as an open defiance, and many of them felt that a great duty had been slighted in failing to impeach him months before. The feeling against him became perfectly relentless, as I distinctly remember it, and shared in it myself; but on referring to the message now, I am astonished at the comparative moderation of its tone, and the strength of its positions. Its logic, in the main, is impregnable, if it be granted that the Rebel districts were not only States, but States *in the Union*, and the Congress which was now so enraged at the President had itself refused to deal with them as Territories or outlying provinces, and thereby invited the aggravating thrusts of the message at the consistency of his assailants.

Just before the adjournment of this brief session of Congress, an amusing incident occurred in connection with the introduction of the following resolution in the House:

"*Resolved*, That the doctrines avowed by the President of the United States, in his message to Congress of the fifteenth instant, to the effect that the abrogation of the governments of the Rebel States binds the Nation to pay the debts incurred prior to the late Rebellion, is at war with the principles of international law, a deliberate stab at the national credit, abhorrent to every sentiment of loyalty, and well-pleasing only to the vanquished traitors by whose agency alone the governments of said States were overthrown and destroyed."

The resolution was adopted by yeas one hundred, nays eighteen, and the announcement of the vote provoked the laughter of both sides of the House. It gratified the Republicans, because it was a thrust at Andrew Johnson, and perfectly accorded with their prevailing political mood, which was constantly becoming more embittered toward him. It equally gratified the Democrats, because they at once accepted it as a telling shot at Gov. Morton, who had fathered the condemned heresy nearly two years before in his famous Richmond speech, which he and his friends had been doing their best to forget. Party feeling had never before been more intense; but this resolution performed its mediatorial office with such magical effect in playing with two utterly diverse party animosities, that Republicans and Democrats were alike surprised to find themselves suddenly standing on common ground, and joyfully shaking hands in token of this remarkable display of their good fellowship.

Congress assembled again on the twenty-first of November, in consequence of the extraordinary conduct of the President. The popular feeling in favor of impeachment had now become formidable, and on the twenty-fifth the Judiciary Committee of the House finally reported in favor of the measure. The galleries were packed, and the scene was one of great interest, while all the indications seemed to point to success; but on the seventh of December, the proposition was voted down by yeas fifty-seven, nays one hundred and eight. The vote was a great surprise and disappointment to the friends of impeachment, and was construed by them as a wanton surrender by Congress, and the prelude to new acts of executive lawlessness. These acts continued to be multiplied, and the removal of Secretary Stanton finally so prepared the way that on the twenty-fourth of February, 1868, the House, by a vote of one hundred and twenty-six to forty-seven, declared in favor of impeachment. The crowds in the galleries, in the lobbies, and on the floor were unprecedented, and the excitement at high tide. The fifty-seven who had voted for impeachment in December, were now happy. They felt, at last, that the country was safe. The whole land seemed to be electrified, as they believed it would have been at any previous time if the House had had the nerve to go forward; and they rejoiced that the madness of Johnson had at last compelled Congress to face the great duty. A committee of seven was appointed by the Speaker to prepare articles of impeachment, of whom Thaddeus Stevens was chairman. He was now rapidly failing in strength, and every morning had to be carried up stairs to his seat in the House; but his humor never failed him, and on one of these occasions he said to the young men who had him in charge, "I wonder, boys, who will carry me when you are dead and gone." He was very thin, pale and haggard. His eye was bright, but his face was "scarred by the crooked autograph of pain." He was a constant sufferer, and during the sessions of the Committee kept himself stimulated by sipping a little wine or brandy; but he was its ruling spirit, and greatly speeded its work by the clearness of his perceptions and the strength of his will. His mental force seemed to defy the power of disease. The articles of impeachment were ready for submission in a few days, and adopted by the House, on the second of March, by a majority of considerably more than two thirds, when the case was transferred to the Senate.

The popular feeling against the President was now rapidly nearing its climax and becoming a sort of frenzy. Andrew Johnson was no longer merely a "wrong-headed and obstinate man," but a "genius in depravity," whose hoarded malignity and passion were unfathomable. He was not simply "an irresolute mule," as General Schenck had styled him, but was devil-bent upon the ruin of his country; and his trial connected itself with all the memories of the war, and involved the Nation in a new and final struggle for its life. Even so sober and unimaginative a man as Mr. Boutwell, one of the managers of the impeachment in the Senate, lost his wits and completely surrendered himself to the passions of the hour in the following passage of his speech in that body:

"Travelers and astronomers inform us that in the Southern heavens, near the Southern Cross, there is a vast space which the uneducated call the 'hole in the sky,' where the eye of man, with the aid of the powers of the telescope, has been unable to discover nebulæ, or asteroid, or comet, or planet, or star or sun. In that dreary, cold, dark region of space, which is only known to be less than infinite by the evidences of creation elsewhere, the great Author of celestial mechanism has left the chaos which was in the beginning. If this earth were capable of the sentiments and emotions of justice and virtue, which in human mortal beings are the evidences and the pledge of our divine origin and immortal destiny, it would heave and throe with the energy of the elemental forces of nature, and project this enemy of two races of men into that vast region, there forever to exist, in a solitude eternal as life, or as the absence of life, emblematical of, if not really, that 'outer darkness' of which the Savior of man spoke in warning to those who are the enemies of themselves, of their race, and of their God."

This fearful discharge of rhetorical fireworks at the President fitly voiced the general sentiment of the Republicans. Party madness was in the air, and quite naturally gave birth to the " hole in the sky " in the agony of its effort to find expression. No extravagance of speech or explosion of wrath was deemed out of order during this strange dispensation in our politics.

The trial proceeded with unabated interest, and on the afternoon of the eleventh of May the excitement reached its highest point. Reports came from the Senate, then in secret session, that Grimes,

Fessenden and Henderson were certainly for acquittal; and that other senators were to follow them. An indescribable gloom now prevailed among the friends of impeachment, which increased during the afternoon, and at night when the Senate was again in session. At the adjournment there was some hope of conviction, but it was generally considered very doubtful. On meeting my old anti-slavery friend, Dr. Brisbane, he told me he felt as if he were sitting up with a sick friend who was expected to die. His face was the picture of despair. To such men it seemed that all the trials of the war were merged in this grand issue, and that it involved the existence of Free Government on this continent. The final vote was postponed till the sixteenth, owing to Senator Howard's illness, and on the morning of that day the friends of impeachment felt more confident. The vote was first taken on the eleventh article. The galleries were packed, and an indescribable anxiety was written on every face. Some of the members of the House near me grew pale and sick under the burden of suspense. Such stillness prevailed that the breathing in the galleries could be heard at the announcement of each senator's vote. This was quite noticeable when any of the doubtful senators voted, the people holding their breath as the words " guilty" or " not guilty " were pronounced, and then giving it simultaneous vent. Every heart throbbed more anxiously as the name of Senator Fowler was reached, and the Chief Justice propounded to him the prescribed question : " How say you, is the respondent, Andrew Johnson, President of the United States, guilty or not guilty of a high misdemeanor, as charged in this article of impeachment ?" The senator, in evident excitement, inadvertently answered " guilty," and thus lent a momentary relief to the friends of impeachment; but this was immediately dissipated by correcting his vote on the statement of the Chief Justice that he did not understand the senator's response to the question. Nearly all hope of conviction fled when Senator Ross, of Kansas, voted " not guilty," and a long breathing of disappointment and despair followed the like vote of Van Winkle, which settled the case in favor of the President.

It is impossible now to realize how perfectly overmastering was the excitement of these days. The exercise of calm judgment was simply out of the question. As I have already stated, passion ruled the hour, and constantly strengthened the tendency to one-sidedness and exaggeration. The attempt to impeach the President was undoubtedly inspired, mainly, by patriotic motives ; but the spirit of intolerance among Republicans toward those who differed with them in opinion set all moderation and common sense at defiance. Patriotism and party animosity were so inextricably mingled and confounded that the real merits of the controversy

could only be seen after the heat and turmoil of the
strife had passed away.   Time has made this manifest.   Andrew Johnson was not the Devil-incarnate
he was then painted, nor did he monopolize, entirely, the " wrong-headedness " of the times.   No
one will now dispute that the popular estimate of
his character did him very great injustice.   It is
equally certain that great injustice was done to
Trumbull, Fessenden, Grimes and other senators
who voted to acquit the President, and gave proof
of their honesty and independence by facing the
wrath and scorn of the party with which they had
so long been identified.   The idea of making the
question of impeachment a matter of party discipline was utterly indefensible and preposterous.
" Those senators," as Horace Greeley declared,
" were sublimely in the right who maintained their
independent judgment—whether it was correct or
erroneous, in a matter of this kind, and who indignantly refused all attempts to swerve them from
their duty as they had undertaken to perform it by
solemn oaths."   The Chief Justice was also cruelly
and inexcusably wronged by imputing corrupt motives to his official action.   His integrity and courage
had been amply demonstrated through many long
years of thorough and severe trial ; and yet many
of his Republican friends, both in the Senate and
House, who had known him throughout his political career, denounced him as an apostate and a
traitor, and even denied him all social recognition.

Senator Howe, of Wisconsin, was especially abusive, and made himself perfectly ridiculous by the extravagance and malignity of his assaults. The judicial spirit was everywhere wanting, and the elevation of Senator Wade to the Presidency in the midst of so much passion and tumult, and with the peculiar political surroundings which the event foreshadowed, would have been, to say the least, a very questionable experiment for the country.

The excitement attending the trial of the President soon subsided, but the Republicans continued anxious about the state of the country. The work of reconstruction was only fairly begun, and its completion was involved in the approaching presidential election. Chase and Seward had lost their standing in the party, and there was no longer any civilian in its ranks whose popularity was especially commanding or at all over-shadowing. Under these circumstances it was quite natural to turn to the army, and to canvass the claims of Gen. Grant. The idea of his nomination was exceedingly distasteful to me. I personally knew him to be intemperate. In politics he was a Democrat. He did not profess to be a Republican, and the only vote he had ever given was cast for James Buchanan in 1856, when the Republican party made its first grand struggle to rescue the Government from the clutches of slavery. Moreover, he had had no training whatever in civil administration, and no one thought of him as a statesman. But the plea of his

availability as a military chieftain was urged with
great effect, and was made irresistible by the apprehension that if not nominated by the Republicans
the Democrats would appropriate him, and make
him a formidable instrument of mischief. His nomination, however, was only secured by cautious and
timely diplomacy, and potent appeals to his sordid-
ness, in the shape of assurances that he should have
the office for a second term. But as the nominee
of his party, fairly committed to its principles and
measures touching the unsettled questions of reconstruction and suffrage, I saw no other practicable alternative than to give him my support. I
was still further reconciled to this by the action of
the Democrats in the nomination of Seymour and
Blair, and the avowal of the latter in his famous
" Broadhead letter," that " we must have a President who will execute the will of the people by
trampling in the dust the usurpations of Congress
known as the Reconstruction Acts."   .

In my new Congressional district I was unanimously re-nominated by the Republicans, and entered at once upon the canvass, though scarcely
well enough to leave my bed. The issue was doubtful, and my old-time enemies put forth their whole
power against me at the election. They were determined, this time, to win, and to make sure of
this they embarked in a desperate and shameless
scheme of ballot-stuffing in the city of Richmond,
which was afterward fully exposed; but in spite of

this enterprise of " Ku Klux Republicans," I was elected by a small majority. The result, however, foreshadowed the close of my congressional labors, which followed two years later, just as the XV Constitutional Amendment had made voters of the colored men of the State; but it was only made possible by my failing health, which had unfitted me for active leadership. In my old district I had made myself absolutely invincible. For twenty-one years in succession, that is to say, from the year 1848 to the year 1868, both inclusive, I canvassed that district by townships and neighborhoods annually on the stump. In the beginning, public opinion was overwhelmingly and fiercely against me, but I resolved, at whatever cost, to reconstruct it in conformity with my own earnest convictions. I literally wore myself out in the work, and am perfectly amazed when I recall the amount of it I performed, and the complete abandon of myself to the task. From the beginning to the end of this struggle the politicians of the district were against me, and they were numerous and formidable, and in every contest were reinforced by the politicians of the State. Although the ranks of my supporters were constantly recruited and no man ever had more devoted friends, I was obliged, during all these years, to stand alone as the champion of my cause in debate. I believe no Congressional district in the Union was ever the theatre of so much hard toil by a single man; but although it in-

21

volved the serious abridgement of health and life, the ruinous neglect of my private affairs, and the sacrifice of many precious friendships, I was not without my reward. I succeeded in my work. Step by step I saw my constituents march up to my position, and the district at last completely disenthralled by the ceaseless and faithful administration of anti-slavery truth. The tables were completely turned. Almost everybody was an Abolitionist, and nobody any longer made a business of swearing that he was not. In canvassing my district it became the regular order of business for a caravan of candidates for minor offices, who were sportively called the "side show," to follow me from point to point, all vieing with each other as to which had served longest and most faithfully as my friends. They had always been opposed to slavery, and men who had taken the lead in mobbing Abolitionists in earlier days and gained a livelihood by slave-catching, were now active and zealous leaders in the Republican party. It was a marvelous change. Slavery itself, greatly to the surprise and delight of its enemies, had perished; but it was, after all, only one form of a world-wide evil. The abolition of the chattel slavery of the Southern negro was simply the introduction and prelude to the emancipation of all races from all forms of servitude, and my Congressional record had been a practical illustration of my faith in this truth. The rights of man are sacred, whether trampled down by Southern slave-drivers, the monopolists of the soil, the grinding power of corporate wealth, the legalized robbery of a protective tariff, or the power of concentrated capital in alliance with labor-saving machinery.

During the winter preceding the inauguration of the President I was besieged by place-hunters more than ever before. They thronged about me constantly, while I generally wrote from twenty to thirty letters per day in response to inquiries about appointments from my district. The squabbles over post-office appointments were by far the most vexatious and unmanageable. They were singularly fierce, and I found it wholly impossible to avoid making enemies of men who had supported me with zeal. I was tormented for months about the post-office of a single small town in Franklin county, where the rival parties pounced upon each other like cannibals, and divided the whole community into two hostile camps. I was obliged to give my days and nights to this wretched business, and often received only curses for the sincerest endeavors to do what I believed was right. This experience became absolutely sickening, and could not be otherwise than seriously damaging to me politically. Such matters were wholly foreign to the business of legislation, and I wrote a very earnest letter to Mr. Jenckes, of Rhode Island, heartily commending his measure proposed in the preceding Congress for the reform of our Civil

Service, and for which, as the real pioneer of this movement, he deserves a monument.

It was on the eighth of December, 1868, that I submitted a proposed amendment to the Constitution, declaring that "the right of suffrage in the United States shall be based upon citizenship, and shall be regulated by Congress"; and that "all citizens of the United States, whether native or naturalized, shall enjoy this right equally, without any distinction or discrimination whatever founded on race, color, or sex. This was prior to the ratification of the XV Amendment, and I so numbered the proposition; but on further reflection I preferred an amendment in the exact form of the fifteenth, and early in the next Congress I submitted it, being the first proposition offered for a sixteenth amendment to the Constitution. My opinions about woman suffrage, however, date much farther back. The subject was first brought to my attention in a brief chapter on the "political non-existence of woman," in Miss Martineau's book on " Society in America," which I read in 1847. She there pithily states the substance of all that has since been said respecting the logic of woman's right to the ballot, and finding myself unable to answer it, I accepted it. On recently referring to this chapter I find myself more impressed by its force than when I first read it. " The most principled Democratic writers on Government," she said, " have on this subject sunk into fallacies as disgraceful a any advocate of despotism has adduced. In fact, they have thus sunk, from being, for the moment, advocates of despotism. Jefferson in America, and James Mill at home, subside, for the occasion, to the level of the Emperor of Russia's catechism for the young Poles." This she makes unanswerably clear; but my interest in the slavery question was awakened about the same time. I regarded it as the *previous* question, and as less abstract and far more immediately important and absorbing than that of suffrage for woman. For the sake of the negro I accepted Mr. Lincoln's philosophy of " one war at a time," though always ready to show my hand; but when this was fairly out of the way, I was prepared to enlist actively in the next grand movement in behalf of the sacredness and equality of human rights.

CHAPTER XV.

GRANT AND GREELEY.

THE inaugural speech of Gen. Grant was a feeble
performance, and very unsatisfactory to his friends.
When he announced his Cabinet, disappointment
was universal among Republicans, and was greatly
increased when he asked Congress to relieve A. T.
Stewart, his nominee for Secretary of the Treasury, from the disability wisely imposed by the Act
of Congress of 1789, forbidding the appointment
to that position of any one engaged " in carrying
on the business or trade of commerce." Senator
Sherman·at once introduced a bill˙to repeal this
enactment, but Mr. Sumner vigorously opposed
the measure, and the President soon afterward sent
a message to the Senate asking leave to withdraw
his request as to Mr. Stewart. It was doubtless
the prompt and decided stand taken by Mr. Sumner in this matter which laid the foundation for the

President's personal hostility to him, which so remarkably developed itself during the following
years. The seeds of a party feud were thus planted, and as the Administration continued to show
its hand, bore witness to a vigorous growth.

In June of this year I made a trip to California
in search of health, which I had lost through over-
work, and was now paying the penalty in a very
distressing form of insomnia. I took one of the
first through trains to the Pacific, and on reaching
the State, I found sight-seeing and travel so irresistible a temptation, that I lost the rest and quiet
I so absolutely needed. I was constantly on the
wing ; and I encountered at every point, the " settler," who was anxious to talk over the land squabbles of the State, with which I had had much to do
in Congress, but now needed for a season to forget. I found that the half had not been told me
respecting the ravages of land-grabbing under the
Swamp Land Act of 1850, and the mal-administration of Mexican and Spanish grants. I was full of
the subject, and was obliged, also, to give particular
attention to the pre-emption of J. M. Hutchings,
in the Yosemite Valley, for the protection of which
I had reported a bill which was then pending ; and
I came near losing my life in the valley through
the fatigue I suffered in reaching it. After a stay
of over two months in California, and a trip by
steamer to Oregon and Washington Territory, I
returned home early in September, but in no better

health than when I left; and a like experience attended a journey to Minnesota soon afterward, where I was captured by leading railroad men who belabored me over the land-grant to the St. Croix and Bayfield railroad, the revival of which I had aided in defeating at the previous session of Congress.

I returned to Washington in December, but physically unfit for labor, spending most of the session in New York under the care of a physician. I deeply regretted this, for the railway lobby was in Washington in full force, as it was during the closing session of the Forty-first Congress, when I was equally unfit for business. I was not, however, without consolation. Under the popular reaction against the Land-grant system which I had done my part to create, the huge pile of land bills on the Speaker's table failed, save the Texas Pacific project, which was carried by the most questionable methods, and against such a general protest as clearly indicated the end of this policy. A vote of nearly two to one was carried in the House in favor of a bill reported by the Land Committee defining swamp and overflowed lands, and guarding against the enormous swindles that had disgraced the Land Department and afflicted honest settlers. A like vote was secured in favor of the bill to prevent the further disposition of the public lands save under the pre-emption and homestead laws, for which I had labored for years

Many thousands of acres had been saved from the clutches of monopolists by attaching to several important grants the condition that the lands should be sold only to actual settlers, in quantities not exceeding a quarter section, and for not more than two dollars and fifty cents per acre. A very important reform, already referred to, had been made in our Indian treaty policy, by which lands relinquished by any tribe would henceforth fall under the operation of our land laws, instead of being sold in a body to some corporation or individual monopolist. The Southern Homestead law had dedicated to actual settlement millions of acres of the public domain in the land States of the South, while the Homestead Act of 1862 was splendidly vindicating the wisdom of its policy. Congress had declared forfeited and open to settlement a large grant of lands in Louisiana for non-compliance with the conditions on which it was made, and the public domain had been saved from frightful spoliation by the fortunate defeat of a scheme of land bounties that would completely have overturned the policy of the pre-emption and homestead laws, while practically mocking the claims of the soldiers. The opportunity, now and then, to strangle a legislative monster like this, or to further the passage of beneficent and far-reaching measures, is one of the real compensations of public life.

The final ratification of the Fifteenth Constitu-

tional Amendment, which was declared in force on
the thirtieth of March, 1870, perfectly consummated
the mission of the Republican party, and left its
members untrammeled in dealing with new questions.   In fact, the Republican movement in the
beginning was a political combination, rather than
a party.   Its action was inspired less by a creed
than an object, and that object was to dedicate our
National Territories to freedom, and denationalize
slavery.   Aside from this object, the members of
the combination were hopelessly divided.   The organization was created to deal with this single question, and would not have existed without it.   It was
now regarded by many as a spent political force,
although it had received a momentum which threatened to outlast its mission ; and if it did not keep
the promise made in its platform of 1868, to reform
the corruptions of the preceding Administration,
and at the same time manfully wrestle with the
new problems of the time, it was morally certain to
degenerate into a faction, led by base men, and
held together by artful appeals to the memories of
the past   Our tariff legislation called for a thorough revision.   Our Civil Service was becoming a
system of political prostitution.   Roguery and
plunder, born of the multiplied temptations which
the war furnished, had stealthily crept into the
management of public affairs, and claimed immu--
nity from the right of search.   What the country
needed was not a stricter enforcement of party dis-

cipline, not military methods and the fostering of
sectional hate, but oblivion of the past, and an
earnest, intelligent, and catholic endeavor to grap-
ple with questions of practical administration.

But this, in the very nature of the case, was not
to be expected. The men who agreed to stand
together in 1856, on a question which was now
out of the way, and had postponed their differences
on current party questions for that purpose, were
comparatively unfitted for the task of civil administration in a time of peace. They had had no
preparatory training, and the engrossing struggle
through which they had passed had, in fact, dis-
qualified them for the work. While the issues of
the war were retreating into the past the mercenary
element of Republicanism had gradually secured
the ascendancy, and completely appropriated the
President. The mischiefs of war had crept into
the conduct of civil affairs, and a thorough school-
ing of the party in the use of power had famil-
iarized it with military ideas and habits, and
committed it to loose and indefensible opinions
respecting the powers of the General Government.
The management of the Civil Service was an utter
mockery of political decency, while the animosities
engendered by the war were nursed and coddled
as the appointed means of uniting the party and
covering up its misdeeds. The demand for reform,
as often as made, was instantly rebuked, and the
men who uttered it branded as enemies of the

party and sympathizers with treason. It is needless to go into details ; but such was the drift of
general demoralization that the chief founders and
pre-eminent representatives of the party, Chase,
Seward, Sumner and Greeley were obliged to
desert it more than a year before the end of Gen.
Grant's first administration, as the only means of
maintaining their honor and self-respect. My
Congressional term expired a little after Grant
and Babcock had inaugurated the San Domingo
project, and Sumner had been degraded from the
Chairmanship of the Committee on Foreign Affairs
to make room for Simon Cameron. The "irrepressible conflict " had just begun to develop itself between the element of honesty and reform in the
party, and the corrupt leadership which sought to
make merchandise of its good name, and hide its
sins under the mantle of its past achievements.

After the adjournment of the Forty-first Congress in March, 1871, I visited New York, where
I called on Greeley. We took a drive together,
and spent the evening at the house of a mutual
friend, where we had a free political talk. He denounced the Administration and the San Domingo
project in a style which commanded my decided
approval, for my original dislike of Grant had been
ripening into disgust and contempt, and, like
Greeley, I had fully made up my mind that under
no circumstance could I ever again give him my
support. After my return home I wrote several

articles for the Press in favor of a "new departure" in the principles of the party. Mr. Vallandingham had just given currency to this phrase by
employing it to designate his proposed policy of
Democratic acquiescence in the XIV and XV
Constitutional Amendments, which was seconded
by the "Missouri Republican," and accepted by
the party the following year. The "new departure" I commended to my own party was equally
thorough, proposing the radical reform of its Tariff
and Land Policy, and its emancipation from the
rule of great corporations and monopolies; a thorough reform of its Civil Service, beginning with a
declaration in favor of the "one-term principle,"
and condemning the action of the President in
employing the whole power and patronage of his
high office in securing his re-election for a second
term by hurling from office honest, capable and
faithful men, simply to make places for scalawags
and thieves; and the unqualified repudiation of
his conduct in heaping honors and emoluments
upon his poor kin, while accepting presents of fine
houses and other tempting gifts from unworthy
men, who were paid off in fat places. I did not
favor the disbanding of the party, or ask that it
should make war on Gen. Grant, but earnestly protested against the policy that sought to Tammany-
ize the organization through his re-nomination.

Returning to Washington on the meeting of
Congress in December, I conferred with Trumbull,

Schurz and Sumner, respecting the situation, and the duty of Republicans in facing the party crisis which was evidently approaching. During the session, I listened to the great debate in the Senate on Sumner's resolution of inquiry as to the sale of arms to the French, and was delighted with the replies of Schurz and Sumner to Conkling and Morton. My dislike of the President steadily increased, and his disgraceful conduct towards Sumner and alliance with Morton, Conkling, Cameron, and their associates rendered it morally impossible for me any longer to fight under his banner. The situation became painfully embarrassing, since every indication seemed to point to his re-nomination as a foregone conclusion. But I clung to the hope that events would in some way order it otherwise. In February, I was strongly urged to become a candidate for Congressman at large under the new Congressional apportionment; and although failing health unfitted me for active politics, to which I had no wish to return, I really wanted the compliment of the nomination. The long-continued and wanton opposition which had been waged against me in my own party led me to covet it, and in the hope that General Grant's nomination might yet be averted I allowed my friends to urge my claims, and to believe I would accept the honor if tendered, which I meant to do should this hope be realized. I saw that I could secure it. My

standing in my own party was better than ever
before. The " Indianapolis Journal," for the first
time, espoused my cause, along with other leading
Republican papers in different sections of the State.
The impolicy and injustice of the warfare which had
long been carried on against me in Indiana were so
generally felt by all fair-minded Republicans that
Senator Morton himself, though personally quite
as hostile as ever, was constrained to call off his
forces, and favor a policy of conciliation. It was
evident that my nomination was assured if I remained in the field ; but as time wore on I saw that
the re-nomination of General Grant had become
absolutely inevitable ; and as I could not support
him I could not honorably accept a position which
would commit me in his favor. The convention
was held on the 22d of February, and on the
day before I sent a telegram peremptorily refusing to stand as a candidate ; and I soon afterward
formally committed myself to the Liberal Republican movement. I could not aid in the re-election
of Grant without sinning against decency and my
own self-respect. I deplored the fact, but there
was no other alternative. If it had been morally
possible, I would have supported him gladly. I
had no personal grievances to complain of, and
most sincerely regretted the necessity which compelled my withdrawal from political associations
in which I had labored many long years, and
through seasons of great national danger. If I

had consulted my own selfish ambition I would
have chosen a different course, since I knew by
painful experience the cost of party desertion, while
the fact was well known that the prizes of politics
were within my reach, if I had sought them through
the machinery of the Republican organization and
the support of General Grant. Had the party,
having accomplished the work which called it
into being, applied itself to the living questions
of the times, and resolutely set its face against
political corruption and plunder, and had it freely
tolerated honest differences of opinion in its own
ranks, treating the question of Grant's re-nomination as an open one, instead of making it a test of
Republicanism and a cause for political excom-
munication, I could have avoided a separation, at
least at that time. I made it with many keen
pangs of regret, for the history of the party had
been honorable and glorious, and I had shared in its
achievements. My revolt against its discipline forcibly reminded me of the year 1848, and was by far
the severest political trial of my life. My new position not only placed me in very strange relations to
the Democrats, whose misdeeds I had so earnestly
denounced for years; but I could not fail to see
that the great body of my old friends would now
become my unrelenting foes. Their party intolerance would know no bounds, and I was not un-
mindful of its power; but there was no way of
escape, and with a sad heart, but an unflinching

purpose, I resolved to face the consequences of my decision. My chief regret was that impaired health deprived me of the strength and endurance I would now sorely need in repelling wanton and very provoking assaults.

I attended the Liberal Republican Convention at Cincinnati on the first of May, where I was delighted to meet troops of the old Free Soilers of 1848 and 1852. It was a mass convention of Republicans, suddenly called together without the power of money or the help of party machinery, and prompted by a burning desire to rebuke the scandals of Gen. Grant's administration, and rescue both the party and the country from political corruption and misrule. It was a spontaneous and independent movement, and its success necessarily depended upon the wisdom of its action and not the force of party obligation. There were doubtless political schemers and mercenaries in attendance, but the rank and file were unquestionably conscientious and patriotic, and profoundly in earnest. I never saw a finer looking body assembled. It was a more formidable popular demonstration than the famous Convention at Buffalo, in 1848, and gave promise of more immediate and decisive results. There was a very widespread feeling that the Cincinnati ticket would win, and the friends of Gen. Grant could not disguise their apprehension. The thought seemed to inspire every one that a way was now fortunately opened

22

for hastening the end of sectional strife and purifying the administration of public affairs. The capital speech of Stanley Matthews, on accepting the temporary chairmanship of the Convention, was but the echo of the feeling of the Convention, and its confident prophecy of victory. "Parties," said he, "can not live on their reputations. It was remarked, I believe, by Sir Walter Raleigh, in· reference to the strife of ancestry, that those who boasted most of their progenitors were like the plant he had discovered in America, the best part was under ground." He declared that "the time has come when it is the voice of an exceedingly large and influential portion of the American people that they will no longer be dogs to wear the collar of a party." All that now seemed wanting was wise leadership, and a fair expression of the real wish and purpose of the Convention.

The principal candidates were Charles Francis Adams, Horace Greeley, Lyman Trumbull, David Davis, and B. Gratz Brown. Mr. Chase still had a lingering form of the Presidential fever, and his particular friends were lying in wait for a timely opportunity to bring him forward; but his claims were not seriously considered. The friends of Judge Davis did him much damage by furnishing transportation and supplies for large Western delegations, who very noisily pressed his claims in the Convention. With prudent leadership his chances for the nomination would have been good, and he

would have been a very formidable candidate; but
he was "smothered by his friends." The really
formidable candidates were Adams and Greeley,
and during the first and second days the chances
were decidedly in favor of the former. On the
evening of the second day Mr. Brown and Gen.
Blair arrived in the city, pretending that they had
come for the purpose of arranging a trouble in
the Missouri delegation; but their real purpose
was to throw the strength of Brown, who was
found to have no chance for the first place, in
favor of Greeley, who had said some very flattering words of Brown some time before in a letter
published in a Missouri newspaper. This new
movement further included the nomination of
Brown for the second place on the ticket, and was
largely aimed at Carl Schurz, who was an Adams
man, and had refused, though personally very
friendly to Brown, to back his claims for the Presidential nomination. It seemed to be a lucky hit
for Greeley, who secured the nomination; but the
real cause of Mr. Adams' defeat, after all, was the
folly of Trumbull's friends, who preferred Adams
to Greeley, in holding on to their man in the vain
hope of his nomination. They could have nominated Adams on the fourth or fifth ballot, if they
had given him their votes, as they saw when it was
too late. Greeley regretted Brown's nomination,
and afterward expressed his preference for another
gentleman from the West; and he had, of course,

nothing to do with the movement which placed him on the ticket.

I was wofully disappointed in the work of the Convention, having little faith in the success of Greeley, and being entirely confident that Adams could be elected if nominated. I still think he would have been, and that the work of reform would thus have been thoroughly inaugurated, and the whole current of American politics radically changed. The time was ripe for it. His defeat was a wet blanket upon many of the leading spirits of the Convention and their followers. The disappointment of some of these was unspeakably bitter and agonizing. Stanley Matthews, illustrating his proverbial instability in politics, and forgetting his brave resolve no longer "to wear the collar of a party," abruptly deserted to the enemy. The " New York Nation " also suddenly changed front, giving its feeble support to General Grant, and its malignant hostility to Greeley. The leading Free Traders in the Convention who had enlisted zealously for Adams became indifferent or hostile. Many of the best informed of the Liberal leaders felt. that a magnificent opportunity to launch the work of reform and crown it with success had been madly thrown away. With the zealous friends of Mr. Adams it was a season of infinite vexation; but for me there was no backward step. The newborn movement had blundered, but Republicanism under the lead of Grant remained as odious as

ever. It was still the duty of its enemies to oppose it, and no other method of doing this was
left them than through the organization just formed.
That a movement so suddenly extemporized should
make mistakes was by no means surprising, while
there was a fairly implied obligation on the part of
those who had joined in its organization to abide
by its action, if not wantonly recreant to the principles that had inspired it. The hearts of the liberal masses were for Greeley, and if he could not
be elected, which was by no means certain, his
supporters could at least make their organized protest against the mal-administration of the party in
power.

I attended the Democratic State Convention of
Indiana on the twelfth of June, which was one of
the largest and most enthusiastic ever held in the
State. The masses seemed to have completely
broken away from their old moorings, and to be
rejoicing in their escape, while their leaders, many
of them reluctantly, accepted the situation. Both
were surprisingly friendly to me, and their purpose
was to nominate me as one of the candidates for
Congressman-at-large, which they would have done
by acclamation if I had consented. I was much
cheered by such tokens of union and fraternity in
facing the common enemy. The State campaign
was finely opened at Indianapolis on the eleventh
of July, where I presented the issues of the canvass from the Liberal standpoint; and I continued

almost constantly on the stump till the State election in October, having splendid audiences, and
gathering strength and inspiration from the prevailing enthusiasm of the canvass.   The meetings
toward the close were real ovations, strikingly re-
minding me of the campaign of 1856.   Up to the
time of the North Carolina election I had strong
hopes of victory; but owing to the alarm which had
seized the Grant men on account of Greeley's unexpected popularity, and the lavish expenditure
of their money which followed, the tide was turned,
and was never afterward checked in its course.
They became unspeakably bitter and venomous,
and I never before encountered such torrents of
abuse and defamation, outstripping, as it seemed to
me, even the rabidness which confronted the Abolitionists in their early experience.   At one of my
appointments a number of colored men came armed
with revolvers, and breathing the spirit of war
which Senator Morton was doing his utmost to
kindle.   He had been telling the people everywhere that Greeley and his followers were Rebels,
seeking to undo all the work of the war, to re-en-
slave the negro, and saddle upon the country the
rebel debt; and these colored men, heeding his
logic, thought that killing Rebels now was as
proper a business as during the war, and would
probably have begun their work of murder
if they had not been restrained by the more prudent counsel of their white brethren.   Even in one

of the old towns in Eastern Indiana which had been
long known as the headquarters of Abolitionism,
a large supply of eggs was provided for my enter-
tainment when I went there to speak for Greeley;
and they were not thrown at me simply because
the fear of a reaction against the party would be
the result. The Democrats in this canvass were
rather handsomely treated; but the fierceness and
fury of the Grant men toward the Liberal Republicans were unrelieved by a single element of honor
or fair play.

This was pre-eminently true in Indiana, and especially so as to myself. The leaders of Grant,
borrowing the spirit of the campaign, set all the
canons of decency at defiance. "Sore head,"
"Renegade," "Apostate," "Rebel," and "dead-
beat," were the compliments constantly lavished.
Garbled extracts from my old war speeches were
plentifully scattered over the State, as if we had
been still in the midst of the bloody conflict, and I
had suddenly betrayed the country to its enemies.
Garbled and forged letters were peddled and parad-
ed over the State by windy political blatherskites,
who were hired to propagate the calumnies of
their employers. In fact, my previous political
experience supplied no precedent for this warfare
of my former Republican friends. But I was not
unprepared for it, and fully availed myself of the
right of self-defense and counter attack. I would
not make myself a blackguard, but I met my as-

sailants in every encounter with the weapons of
argument and invective, and stretched them on the
rack of my ridicule; while their prolonged howl
bore witness to the effectiveness of my work.   My
whole heart was in it.   The fervor and enthusiasm
of earlier years came back to me, and a kindred
courage and faith armed me with the strength
which the work of the canvass demanded.

The novelty of the canvass was indeed remarkable in all respects.   The Liberal Republicans had
not changed any of their political opinions, nor
deserted any principle they had ever espoused,
touching the questions of slavery and the war;
and yet they were now in the fiercest antagonism
with the men who had been politically associated
with them ever since the organization of the party,
and who had trusted and honored them through
all the struggles of the past.   They were branded
as "Apostates" from their anti-slavery faith; but
slavery had perished forever, and every man of
them would have been found fighting it as before,
if it had been practicable to call it back to life;
while many of their assailants had distinguished
themselves by mobbing Abolitionism in the day
of its weakness.   How could men apostatize from
a cause which they had served with unflinching
fidelity until it was completely triumphant?   And
how was it possible to fall from political grace by
withdrawing from the fellowship of the knaves and
traders that formed the body-guard of the Presi-

dent, and were using the Republican party as the instrument of wholesale schemes of jobbery and pelf? To charge the Liberal Republicans with apostasy because they had the moral courage to disown and denounce these men was to invent a definition of the term which would have made all the great apostates of history " honorable men."

They were called " Rebels ";' but the war had been over seven years and a half, and if the clock of our politics could have been set back and the bloody conflict re-instated, every Liberal would have been shouting, as before, for its vigorous prosecution. No man doubted this who was capable of taking care of himself without the help of a guardian.

It was charged that " they changed sides " in politics; but the sides themselves had been changed by events, and the substitution of new issues for the old, and nobody could deny this who was not besotted by party devil-worship or the density of his political ignorance.

They were called " sore-heads " and " disappointed place-hunters ;" but the Liberal Leaders, in rebelling against their party in the noon-day of its power, and when its honors were within their grasp, were obliged to "put away ambition " and taste political death, and thus courageously illustrate the truth that "the duties of life are more than life." The charge was as glaringly stupid as it was flagrantly false.

But the novelty of this canvass was equally manifest in the political fellowships it necessitated. While facing the savage warfare of their former friends Liberal Republicans were suddenly brought into the most friendly and intimate relations with the men whose recreancy to humanity they had unsparingly denounced for years. They were now working with these men because the subjects on which they had been divided were withdrawn, and the country had entered upon a new dispensation. The mollifying influence of peace, aided, no doubt, by the organized roguery which in the name of Republicanism held the Nation by the throat, unveiled to Liberals a new political horizon, and they gladly exchanged the key-note of hate and war for that of fraternity and reunion. They saw that the spirit of wrath which had so moved the Northern States during the conflict was no longer in order. The more they pondered the policy of amnesty and followed up the work of the canvass the more thoroughly they became reconstructed in heart. They discovered that the men whom they had been denouncing with such hot indignation for so many years were, after all, very much like other people. Personally and socially they seemed quite as kindly and as estimable as the men on the other side, while very many of them had undoubtedly espoused the cause of slavery under a mistaken view of their constitutional obligations, and as a phase of patriotism, while sincerely condemning it on principle.

Besides, Democrats had done a very large and in-
dispensable work in the war for the Union, and they
now stood upon common ground with the Republicans touching the questions on which they had
differed. On these questions the party platforms
were identical. If their position was accepted as a
necessity and not from choice, they were only a
little behind the Republicans, who, as a party, only
espoused the cause of the negro under the whip
and spur of military necessity, and not the prompt-
ings of humanity. In the light of such considerations it was not strange that the Greeley men gladly
accepted their deliverance from the glamour which
was blinding the eyes of their old associates to the
policy of reconciliation and peace, and blocking up
the pathway of greatly needed reforms.

Soon after the State election I resumed my
work on the stump, which included a series of
appointments in Kansas, where I addressed by far
the most enthusiastic meetings of the campaign.
My welcome to the State was made singularly
cordial by the part I had played in Congress in
opposing enormous schemes of land monopoly
and plunder, which had been concocted by some
of her own public servants in the interest of railway corporations and Indian rings. On my return
to Indiana the signs of defeat in November became
alarming, and they were justified by the result.
It was overwhelming and stunning. Democrats
and Liberals were completely dismayed and be-

wildered. The cause of Mr. Greeley's defeat,
speaking generally, was - the perfectly unscrupulous and desperate hostility of the party for which
he had done more than any other man, living
or dead; but the disaster resulted, more immediately, from the stupid and criminal defection of
the Bourbon element in the Democratic party,
which could not be rallied under the banner of
an old anti-slavery chief. Thousands of this class,
who sincerely hated Abolitionism, and loved negro
slavery more than they loved their country, voted
directly for Grant, while still greater numbers declined to vote at all. Mr. Greeley's own explanation of the result, which he gave to a friend soon
after the election, was as follows: "I was an
Abolitionist for years, when it was as much as one's
life was worth even here in New York, to be an
Abolitionist; and the negroes have all voted against
me. Whatever of talents and energy I have possessed I have freely contributed all my life long
to Protection; to the cause of our manufactures.
And the manufacturers have expended millions to
defeat me. I even made myself ridiculous in the
opinion of many whose good wishes I desired by
showing fair play and giving a fair field in the
'Tribune' to Woman's Rights; and the women have
all gone against me !"

Greeley, however, received nearly three million
votes, being considerably more than Governor Seymour had received four years before; but General

Grant, who had been unanimously nominated by his party, was elected by two hundred and eighty-six electoral votes, and a popular majority of nearly three quarters of a million, carrying thirty-one of the thirty-seven States. To the sincere friends of political reform the situation seemed hopeless. The President was re-crowned our King, and political corruption had now received so emphatic a premium that honesty was tempted to give up the struggle in despair. His champions were already talking about a "third term," while the Republican party had become the representative and champion of great corporations, and the instrument of organized political corruption and theft.

And yet this fight of Liberals and Democrats was not in vain. They planted the seed which ripened into a great popular victory four years later, while the policy of reconciliation for which they battled against overwhelming odds was hastened by their labors, and has been finally accepted by the country. They were still further and more completely vindicated by the misdeeds of the party they had sought to defeat. The spectacle of our public affairs became so revolting that before the middle of General Grant's second term all the great Republican States in the North were lost to the party, while leading Republicans began to agitate the question of remanding the States of the South to territorial rule, on account of their disordered condition. At the end of this term the Republican majority in the Senate had dwindled from fifty-four to seventeen, while in the House the majority of one hundred and four had been wiped out to give place to a Democratic majority of seventy-seven. No vindication of the maligned Liberals of 1872 could have been more complete, while it summoned to the bar of history the party whose action had thus brought shame upon the Nation and a stain upon Republican institutions.

After the presidential election I went to Washington, where I met Chief Justice Chase in the Supreme Court and accepted an invitation to dine with him. He looked so wasted and prematurely old that I scarcely knew him. He was very genial, however, and our long political talk was exceedingly enjoyable. It seemed to afford him much satisfaction to show me a recently reported dissenting opinion of his in which he re-asserted his favorite principle of State rights. I only met him once afterward, and this was at the inauguration of General Grant. I called on Mr. Sumner the same evening, and found him in a wretched state of health, which was aggravated by the free use of poisonous drugs. He seemed very much depressed, politically. He had lost caste with the great party that had so long idolized him, and which he had done so much to create and inspire. He had been deserted by the colored race, to whose service he had unselfishly dedicated his life. He had been de-

graded from his honored place at the head of the
Senate Committee on Foreign Relations, and for
no other reason than the faithful and conscientious
performance of his public duty. He had been
rebuked by the Legislature of his own State.
His case strikingly suggested that of John Quincy
Adams in 1807, when the anathemas of Massachusetts were showered upon him for leaving the Federal party when it had accomplished its mission
and survived its character, and joining the supporters of Jefferson. I sympathized with him profoundly; but his case was not so infinitely sad as
that of poor Greeley, over whose death, however,
the whole Nation seemed to be in mourning. He
had greatly overtaxed himself in his masterly and
brilliant campaign on the stump, in which he displayed unrivaled intellectual resources and versa-
tility. He had exhausted himself in watching by
the bedside of his dying wife. He had been assailed
as the enemy of his country by the party which he
had done more than any man in the Nation to
organize. He had been hunted to his grave by
political assassins whose calumnies broke his heart.
He was scarcely less a martyr than Lincoln, or less
honored after his death, and his graceless defamers
now seemed to think they could atone for their
crime by singing his praises. It is easy to speak
well of the dead. It is very easy, even for base and
recreant characters, to laud a man's virtues after he
has gone to his grave and can no longer stand in

their path.   It is far easier to praise the dead than do justice to the living; and it was not strange, therefore, that eminent clergymen and doctors of divinity who had silently witnessed the peltings of Mr. Greeley by demagogues and mercenaries during the canvass now poured out their eloquence at his grave.   What he had sorely needed and was religiously entitled to was the sympathy and succor of good men while he lived, and especially in his heroic struggle for political reconciliation and reform.   The circumstances of his death made it peculiarly touching and sacramental, and I was inexpressibly glad that I had fought his battle so unflinchingly, and defended him everywhere against his conscienceless assailants.

CHAPTER XVI.

CONCLUDING NOTES.

Party changes caused by the slavery issue—Notable men in Congress during the war—Sketches of prominent men in the Senate and House—Scenes and incidents—Butler and Bingham—Cox and Butler—Judge Kelley and Van Wyck—Lovejoy and Wickliffe—Washburne and Donnelly—Oakes Ames—Abolitionism in Washington early in the war—Life at the capital—The new dispensation and its problems.

IN the early part of the period covered by the preceding chapters our political parties were divided on mere questions of policy and methods of administration. Trade, Currency, Internal Improvements, and the Public Lands were the absorbing issues, while both parties took their stand against the humanitarian movement which subsequently put those issues completely in abeyance, and compelled the country to face a question involving not merely the policy of governing, but the existence of the Government itself. When the slavery question finally forced its way into recognition it naturally brought to the front a new class of public men, and their numbers, as I have shown, steadily increased in each Congress from the year 1845 till the outbreak of the Rebellion in 1861. The Con-

23 (353)

gress which came into power with Mr. Lincoln
did not fully represent the anti-slavery spirit of the
Northern States, but it was a decided improve-
ment upon its predecessors. In the Senate were
such men as Collamer, Fessenden, Doolittle,
Baker, Browning, Anthony, Grimes, Hale, Harlan,
Sherman, Trumbull, Sumner, Wade, Henry Wil-
son, Chandler, Lane of Indiana, Harris of New
York, Andrew Johnson, B. Gratz Brown and
Howard. In the House were Conkling, Bingham-
Colfax, Dawes, Grow, Hickman, Kelley, Potter,
Lovejoy, Pike of Maine, Ashley, Rollins of Mis-
souri, Shellabarger, Thaddeus Stevens, Elihu B.
Washburn, Isaac N. Arnold and James F. Wilson.

During the Rebellion and the years immediately
following, Ferry of Connecticut, Cresswell, Ed-
monds, Conkling, Morgan, Morton, Yates, Carpenter, Hamlin, Henderson, Morrill of Maine,
and Schurz, were added to the prominent men of
the Senate, and Boutwell, Blair, Henry Winter
Davis, Deming, Jenckes, Garfield, Schenck, Banks,
Orth, Raymond, Butler, Hoar, McCrary, to the
list in the House. During this period the Democrats had in the Senate such men as Bayard, Garret
Davis, Hicks, Saulsbury, Buckalew, Hendricks,
Bright, Reverdy Johnson, Thurman, and F. P.
Blair; and in the House, S. S. Cox, Crittenden,
Holman, Kerr, Pendleton, Richardson, Vallandingham, Niblack, Voorhees, Brooks, Randall,
and Woodward. The men who controlled Con-

gress during these years of trial were not the intellectual equals of the famous leaders who figured in the great crisis of 1850, but they were a different and generally a better type. They were summoned to the public service to deal with tremendous problems, and lifted up and ennobled by the great cause they were commissioned to serve. It did more for them than it was possible for them to do for it. It took hold on the very foundations of the Government, and electrified all the springs of our national life; and although great mistakes were made, and the fervor of this period was followed by a sickening dispensation of demoralized politics, it was a great privilege to be permitted to share in the grand battle for the Nation's life, and the work of radical re-adjustment which followed.

I have already referred to several of the conspicuous characters whose names I have grouped. Such men as Collamer, Fessenden, Browning and Trumbull, were among the famous lawyers and conservatives on the Republican side of the Senate. They were conscientious and unflinching partisans, but were studiously anxious to save the Union. according to the Constitution, and deprecated all extreme and doubtful measures. Opposed to them stood Sumner, Wade, Chandler, and their radical associates, who believed in saving the Union at all hazards, and that not even the Constitution should be allowed to stay the arm of the Government in blasting the power of the Rebels. It was perhaps

fortunate for the country that these divisions existed, and held each other in check. Mr. Collamer
was the impersonation of logical force and the
beau ideal of a lawyer and judge. There was a
sort of majesty in the figure and brow of Fessenden when addressing the Senate, and his sarcasm
was as keen as it was inimitable; but his nature
was kindly, and his integrity perfect. Trumbull
was a less commanding figure, but he greatly honored his position as chairman of the Judiciary
Committee of the Senate, and his memory will be
held in perpetual remembrance as the author of the
Civil Rights Bill and of the XIII Amendment to
the Constitution. Sumner, I think, was the purest
man in the Senate, if not the ablest. He was pre-
eminently the hero of duty, and the servant of
what he believed to be the truth. No man could
have made a more absolute surrender of himself to
his country in the great conflict which threatened
its life. His weary and jaded look always excited
my sympathy, for he seemed to be sacrificing all
the joys of life, and life itself, in his zeal for the
public service. I knew Wade more intimately
than any man in the Senate, through my associa-
tion with him as a member of the same Committee
for successive years, and was always interested in
his personal traits and peculiarities. He was "a
man of uncommon downrightness." There was
even a sort of fascination about his profanity. It
had in it a spontaniety and heartiness which made

it almost seem the echo of a virtue. It was unlike
the profane words of Thaddeus Stevens, which
were frequently carried on the shafts of his wit and
lost in the laughter it provoked. Edmunds, now
so famous as a lawyer, and leader in the Senate,
and so well known by his reputed resemblance to
St. Jerome, was simply respectable on his first appearance; but his ability, industry, and constant
devotion to his duties soon gave him rank among
the prominent men in that body. Grimes of Iowa
was one of the really strong men of this period,
while Harlan, his colleague, possessed a vigor
and grasp of mind which I think the public never
fully accorded him. Lane of Indiana was full of
patriotic ardor, and like Baker of Oregon, had the
rare gift of eloquent impromptu speech. Henry
Wilson earned the gratitude of his country by his
unswerving loyalty to freedom, and his great labors
and invaluable services as chairman of the Military
Committee. Howard ranked among the first lawyers and most faithful men in the body, and no
man had a clearer grasp of the issues of the war.
Henderson was a strong man, whose integrity and
political independence were afterward abundantly
proved. Doolittle was a man of vigor, and made
a good record as a Republican, but he naturally
belonged to the other side of the Senate, and finally
found his way to it through the quarrel with
Johnson.

Garret Davis was always an interesting figure.

His volubility of talk bordered on the miraculous; and whenever he began to swathe the Senate in his interminable rhetoric it awakened the laughter or the despair of everybody on the floor or in the galleries. Bayard and Thurman were recognized as the strong men on their side of the Senate in the Forty-first Congress. Buckalew was one of the really sterling men of his party, but he was a modest man, and only appreciated by those who knew him intimately. As a leading Democrat, Hendricks stood well in the Senate. He was so cautious and diplomatic in temper and so genial and conciliatory in his manner that he glided smoothly through the rugged conflict of opinions in which his side of the chamber was unavoidably involved. B. Gratz Brown was known as an intense radical, but he made little mark in this crisis. He wrote out elaborate and scholarly essays which he read to the Senate, but they received slight attention from members, and seemed to bear little fruit. Carpenter, Schurz and Morton took their seats after the war, and were not long in finding honorable recognition. Carpenter was as brilliant and versatile in intellect as he was naturally eloquent in speech and wayward in morals. Carl Schurz displayed ability in the famous debate with Morton and Conkling on the sale of arms to the French, and his political independence in 1872 gave him great prominence as a Liberal Republican leader; but that virtue has been less conspicuously illustrated in later years. Morton became famous soon after he entered the Senate. The " logic of events " had revolutionized the opinions so vigorously espoused by him only a few months before, and his great speech on reconstruction, in which he avowed and defended his change of base, brought him into great prominence, and multiplied his friends in every section of the country.

In the House, Roscoe Conkling was recognized as a man of considerable talent and great self-esteem. I have elsewhere referred to his passage at arms with Blaine. He never linked his name with any important principle or policy, and was singularly wanting in the qualities of a party leader. No one questioned his personal integrity, but in later years he was prompt and zealous in the defense of the worst abuses which found shelter in his party. Mr. Sherman was shrewd, wiry and diplomatic, but gave little promise of the career he has since achieved through ambition, industry and favoring conditions. Shellabarger was one of the ablest men in the House, and was so rated. He was always faithful and vigilant, and I have before given an instance of this in his timely action on the question of reconstruction. Mr. Blaine, during the first years of his service, showed little activity. He spoke but seldom and briefly, but always with vigor and effect. He steadily grew into favor with his party in the House as a man of force, but without seeming to strive for it. I think his abilities were never fully appreciated till he became speaker. His personal magnetism was as remarkable as his readiness to serve a friend was unfailing; but, like Mr. Conkling, he never identified himself with any great legislative measure.

Henry Winter Davis was the most formidable debater in the House. He was full of resources, while the rapidity of his utterance and the impetuosity of his speech bore down every thing before it. The fire and force of his personality seemed to make him irresistible, and can only be likened to the power displayed by Mr. Blaine in the House in his later and palmier years. When Gen. Garfield entered the Thirty-eighth Congress there was a winning modesty in his demeanor. I was interested in his first effort on the floor, which was brief, and marked by evident diffidence. He was not long, however, in recovering his self-possession, and soon engaged actively in general debate. His oratory, at first, was the reverse of winning, owing to the peculiar intonation of his voice, but gradually improved, while his hunger for knowledge, unflagging industry, and ambition for distinction, gradually revealed themselves as very clearly defined traits. During the first years of his service the singular grasp of his mind was not appreciated, but it was easy to see that he was growing, and that a man of his political ambition and great industry could not be satisfied with any position of political mediocrity. His situation as a Representative of the Nineteenth Ohio District was exceedingly favorable to his aspirations, as it was the custom of that district to continue a man in its service when once installed, and its overwhelming majority relieved him of all concern about the result. He could thus give his whole time and thought to the study of politics, and the mastery of those historical and literary pursuits which he afterward made so available in the finish and embellishment of his speeches.

As a parliamentary leader, Mr. Stevens, of course, was always the central figure in the House. No possible emergency could disconcert him. Whether the attack came from friend or foe, or in whatever form, he was ready, on the instant, to repel it and turn the tables completely upon his assailant. He exercised the most absolute freedom of speech, making his thrusts with the same coolness at " unrighteous copperheads and self-righteous Republicans." In referring to the moderate and deprecatory views of Colfax and Olin, in January, 1863, he said he had always been fifteen years in advance of his party, but never so far ahead that its members did not overtake him. His keenest thrusts were frequently made in such a tone and manner as to disarm them of their sting, and create universal merriment. When Whaley of West Virginia begged him, importunately, to yield the floor a moment for a brief statement, while Mr. Stevens was much engrossed with an important discussion, he finally

gave way, saying, " Mr. Speaker, I yield to the gentleman from West Virginia for a few feeble remarks."   When he lost his temper and waged war
in earnest his invective was absolutely remorseless,
as in the example I have given of it in a previous
chapter.

I have before referred to the oratory of Bingham.
He was a reader of books and a master of English.   He loved poetry, and was one of the most
genial and companionable of men, but he was
irritable and crispy in temper, and a formidable cus-
tomer in debate.   He had several angry bouts
with Butler, in one of which he spoke sneeringly
of the "hero of Fort Fisher," to which Butler replied that the gentleman from Ohio had shown *his*
prowess in the hanging of Mrs. Surratt, an innocent woman, upon the scaffold.   Bingham re-
torted that such a charge was "only fit to come
from a man who lives in a bottle, and is fed with a
spoon."   He was often dogmatic and lacking in
coolness and balance, but in later years he showed
uncommon tact in extricating himself from the
odium threatened by his connection with the
Credit Mobilier scheme.

One of the really strong men in the House was
John Hickman, of Pennsylvania, who had been a
prominent figure in Congress during Buchanan's
administration.   He was a man of brains, courage,
and worth.   Potter was a true and brave man,
whose acceptance of a challenge from Roger A.

Pryor, and choice of butcher knives as the weapons
of warfare, had made him very popular at the
North. Rollins of Missouri was an eloquent
man, of superior ability and attainments, and large
political experience. Pike of Maine was one of
the first men in the House, but too honest and independent to sacrifice his convictions for the sake
of success. Deming of Connecticut was a man
of real calibre, and on rare occasions electrified the
House by his speeches, but he lacked industry.
One of the finest debaters in the House was Henry
J. Raymond. He displayed very decided power
in the debate on Reconstruction, and very effect-
ively exposed the weakness of the Republicans in
practically dealing with the Rebel States as if they
were at once in and out of the Union. Among the
most striking figures in the House were Butler and
Cox, whose contests were greatly relished. They
were well matched, and alternately carried off the
prize of victory. Butler, in the first onset, achieved a
decided triumph in his reply to a very personal assault by Cox. " As to the vituperation of the member from New York," said he, " he will hear my
answer to him by every boy that whistles it on the
street, and every hand-organ, ' Shoo, fly, don't bod-
der me ' ! " Cox, for the time, was extinguished, but
patiently watched his opportunity till he found his
revenge, which Butler afterward frankly acknowledged. For a time there was bad blood between
them, but they finally became friends, and I think
so continued.

General Banks was always a notable personality. His erect figure, military eye, and splendid voice secured for him the admiring attention of the galleries whenever he addressed the House. Ashley of Ohio who took the lead in the impeachment movement, in which he was so zealous that he became known as "Impeachment Ashley," was another picturesque figure. His fine *physique*, frolicsome face, and luxuriant suit of curly brown hair singled him out among the bald heads of the body as one of its most attractive members. Boutwell impressed the House as a man of solid qualities, and a formidable debater. He acquitted himself admirably in his defense of Butler against a savage attack by Brooks. Blair was a man of ability, independence, and courage, of which his record in the House gave ample proof. Wilson of Iowa was a young man when he entered Congress, but soon gave proof of his ability, and took rank as one of the best lawyers on the Judiciary Committee. Judge Kelley, since known as the " Father of the House," and one of the fathers of the Greenback movement, first attracted attention by the wonderful volume and power of his voice. It filled the entire Hall, and subdued all rival sounds ; but to the surprise of everybody, he met with more than his match when he was followed, one day, by Van Wyck, of New York, who triumphantly carried off the palm. Kelley's voice was little more than a zephyr, in comparison with the ·roar and thunder that followed it and called forth shouts of laughter, while Kelley quietly occupied his seat as if in dumb amazement at what had happened.

James Brooks was always a conspicuous figure on the Democratic side of the House. I first knew him in the log cabin days of 1840, and afterward served with him in the Congress of 1849. He was a man of ability, a genuine hater of the negro, and a bitter partisan ; but I never saw any reason to doubt his personal integrity, and I think the affair which threw so dark a cloud over his reputation in later years was a surprise to all who knew him. Michael C. Kerr was one of the very first men in the House, and a man of rare purity and worth. Randall, like Garfield, was a growing man during the war, and through his ambition, natural abilities, and Congressional training, he became one of the chief magnates of his party. Pendleton was counted an able man, and made his mark as a Bourbon Democrat and the champion of hard money; but he subsequently spoiled his financial record by his scheme for flooding the country with greenbacks. Vallandingham was conspicuous for his intellectual vigor, passionate earnestness, and hatred of Abolitionism. He had the courage of his opinions. The Republicans hated him consumedly. He was a member of the House Committee on Public Lands, which reported the Homestead Bill, and I remember that no Republican member, except the chairman, showed the slightest disposition to recognize him. After the war was ended, however, and the work of reconstruction was accomplished, his temper and qualities seemed to have spent much of their force. He was among the very first to plead for acquiescence and the policy of reconciliation; and if his life had been spared I believe his catholic spirit and active leadership in the " New Departure " would have re-instated him in the sincere regard of men of all parties. Lovejoy was the most impassioned orator in the House. His speeches were remarkable for their pungency and wit, and when the question of slavery was under discussion his soul took fire. He hated slavery with the animosity of a regular Puritan, and when he talked about it everybody listened. Wickliffe of Kentucky was one of the most offensive representatives of the Border State policy, and whenever he spoke Lovejoy was sure to follow. As often as Wickliffe got the floor it was noticed that Lovejoy's brow was immediately darkened in token of the impending strife, while his friends and enemies prepared themselves for the scene. Wickliffe was a large, fierce-looking man, with a shrill voice, and quite as belligerent as Lovejoy; and their contests were frequent, and always enjoyed by the House, and for some time became a regular feature of its business.

Elihu B. Washburn was conspicuous as the

champion of economy. He rivaled Holman as
the "watch-dog of the treasury" and the enemy
of land-grants. He was a man of force, and
rendered valuable service to the country, but he
assumed such airs of superior virtue, and frequently lectured the House in so magisterial a tone
as to make himself a little unpopular with members. This was strikingly illustrated in 1868, in his
controversy with Donnelly of Minnesota against
whom he had made some dishonorable charges
through a Minnesota newspaper. Donnelly was
an Irishman, a wit, and an exceedingly versatile
genius, and when it became known that he was to
defend himself in the House against Washburn's
charges, and make a counter attack, every member
was in his seat, although the weather was intensely
hot and no legislative business was to be trans-
acted. Donnelly had fully prepared himself, and
such a castigation as he administered, has rarely,
if ever, been witnessed in a legislative body. He
kept up a ceaseless and overwhelming fire of
wit, irony, and ridicule, for nearly two hours, during
which the members frequently laughed and sometimes applauded, while Washburn sat pale and mute
under the infliction. The tables were turned upon
him, although portions of Donnelly's tirade were
unparliamentary, and indefensible on the score of
coarseness and bad taste. No member, however,
raised any point of order; but the friends of Mr.
Washburn afterward surrounded Donnelly, and

by artful appeals to his good nature prevailed
upon him to suppress a portion of the speech, and
to proffer statements which tended to destroy its
effect and to restore to Washburn the ground he
had lost. The House had its fun, while Washburn deigned no reply except to re-affirm his
charges, and Donnelly's friends were vexed at his
needless surrender of his vantage-ground. It was
an odd and unexpected *denouement* of a very remarkable exhibition.

Oakes Ames was one of the members of the
House with whom I was best acquainted. I thought
I knew him well, and I never had the slightest
reason to suspect his public or private integrity.
Personally and socially he was one of the kindliest
men I ever knew, and I was greatly surprised when
I learned of his connection with the Credit Mobilier
project. It first found its way into politics through
a speech of Horace Greeley near the close of the
canvass of 1872, but it had been fully exposed by
Washburn of Wisconsin in a speech in Congress
in the year 1868. The history of its connection
with American politics and politicians forms an exceedingly interesting and curious chapter. The
fate of the men involved in it seems like a perfect
travesty of justice and fair play. Some of them
have gone down under the waves of popular condemnation. Others, occupying substantially the
same position, according to the evidence, have made
their escape and even been honored and trusted by

the public, while still others are quietly whiling away their lives under the shadow of suspicion. The case affords a strange commentary upon the principle of historic justice.

One of the most remarkable facts connected with the first years of the war was the descent of the Abolitionists upon Washington. They secured the hall of the Smithsonian Institute for their meetings, which they held weekly, and at which the Rev. John Pierpont presided. It was with much difficulty that the hall was procured, and one of the conditions of granting it was that it should be distinctly understood and announced that the Smithsonian Institute was to be in no way responsible for anything that might be said by the speakers. This was very emphatically insisted on by Professor Henry, and was duly announced at the first meeting. At the following, and each succeeding lecture, Mr. Pierpont regularly made the same announcement. These gatherings were largely attended and very enthusiastic; and as the antislavery tide constantly grew stronger, the weekly announcement that "the Smithsonian Institute desires it to be distinctly understood that it is not to be held responsible for the utterances of the speakers," awakened the sense of the ludicrous, and called forth rounds of applause and explosions of laughter by the audience, in front of which Professor Henry was seated. Each meeting thus began with a frolic of good humor, which Mr.

24

Pierpont evidently enjoyed, for he made his announcement with a gravity which naturally provoked the mirth which followed. These meetings were addressed by Wendell Phillips, Gerrit Smith, Ralph Waldo Emerson, Dr. Brownson, and other notable men, and were enjoyed as a sort of jubilee by the men and women who attended them.

The services in the Hall of Representatives each Sabbath formed the fitting counterpart of these proceedings The crowds in attendance filled every part of the floor and galleries, and were full of enthusiasm. The most terrific arraignment of slavery I ever listened to was by Rev. Dr. George B. Cheever, in the course of these services. He was a man of great ability, unquenchable zeal, fervid eloquence, and an Old Testament Christian who was sometimes called the Prophet Isaiah of the anti-slavery cause. He carried his religion courageously into politics, and while arraigning slavery as the grand rebel, he also severely criticised the management of the war and the Border State policy of the President. The most pronounced anti-slavery sermons were also preached in the Capital by Dr. Boynton, Mr. Channing and others, while the Hutchinson family occasionally entertained the public with their anti-slavery songs. All this must have been sufficiently shocking to the slave-holding politics and theology of the city, whose slumbers were thus rudely disturbed.

There was a peculiar fascination about life in

Washington during the war. The city itself was unattractive. Its ragged appearance, wretched streets, and sanitary condition were the reproach of its citizens, who could have had no dream of the Washington of to-day ; but it was a great military as well as political center. Our troops were pouring in from every loyal State, and the drum-beat was heard night and day, while the political and social element hitherto in the ascendant, was completely submerged by the great flood from the North. The city was surrounded, and in part occupied by hospitals, and for a time many of the principal churches were surrendered to the use of our sick and wounded soldiers, whose numbers were fearfully swelled after each great battle. The imminent peril to which the Capital was repeatedly exposed, and the constantly changing fortunes of the war, added greatly to the interest of the crisis, and marked the alternations of hope and fear among the friends and enemies of the Union. But notwithstanding the seriousness of the times, there was a goodly measure of real social life. Human nature demanded some relaxation from the dreadful strain and burden of the great conflict, and this was partially found in the levees of the President and Cabinet ministers, and the receptions of the Speaker, which were largely attended and greatly enjoyed ; and this enjoyment was doubtless much enhanced by the peculiar bond of union and feeling of brotherhood which the state of the country

awakened among its friends. The most pleasant
of these occasions, however, were the weekly receptions of the Speaker. Those of Speaker Grow
were somewhat marred, and sometimes interrupted,
by his failing health, but the receptions of Mr.
Colfax were singularly delightful. He discharged
the duties of his great office with marked ability
and fairness, and was personally very popular ; and
there always gathered about him on these occasions
an assemblage of charming and congenial people,
whose genuine cordiality was a rebuke to the insincerity so often witnessed in social life.

But I need not further pursue these personal details, nor linger over the by-gones of a grand epoch.
We have entered upon a new dispensation. The
withdrawal of the slavery question from the strife of
parties has changed the face of our politics as completely as did its introduction. The transition
from an abnormal and revolutionary period to the
regular and orderly administration of affairs, has
been as remarkable as the intervention of the great
question which eclipsed every other till it compelled its own solution. Although this transition
has given birth to an era of "slack-water politics,"
it has gradually brought the country face to face
with new problems, some of which are quite as
vital to the existence and welfare of the Republic
as those which have taxed the statesmanship of the
past. The tyranny of industrial domination, which
borrows its life from the alliance of concentrated

capital with labor-saving machinery, must be overthrown. Commercial feudalism, wielding its power through the machinery of great corporations which are practically endowed with life offices and the right of hereditary succession and control the makers and expounders of our laws, must be subordinated to the will of the people. The system of agricultural serfdom called Land Monopoly, which is now putting on new forms of danger in the rapid multiplication of great estates and the purchase of vast bodies of lands by foreign capitalists, must be resisted as a still more formidable foe of democratic Government. The legalized robbery now carried on in the name of Protection to American labor must be overthrown. The system of spoils and plunder must also be destroyed, in order that freedom itself may be rescued from the perilous activities quickened into life by its own spirit, and the conduct of public affairs inspired by the great moralities which dignify private life.

These are the problems which appeal to the present generation, and especially to the honorable ambition of young men now entering upon public life. Their solution is certain, because they are directly in the path of progress, and progress is a law ; but whether it shall be heralded by the kindly agencies of peace or the harsh power of war, must depend upon the wise and timely use of opportunities. The result is certain, since justice can not finally be defeated ; but the circumstances of

the struggle and the cost of its triumph are committed to the people, who can scarcely fail to find
both instruction and warning in the story of the
anti-slavery conflict.

INDEX.